CONNECTED COMM
Creating a new knowledge

CU00969066

VALUING INTERDISCIPLINARY COLLABORATIVE RESEARCH

Beyond impact

Edited by Keri Facer and Kate Pahl

First published in Great Britain in 2017 by

Policy Press
University of Bristol
1-9 Old Park Hill
Bristol
BS2 8BB
UK
t: +44 (0)117 954 5940
pp-info@bristol.ac.uk
www.policypress.co.uk

North America office:
Policy Press
c/o The University of Chicago Press
1427 East 60th Street
Chicago, IL 60637, USA
t: +1 773 702 7700
f: +1 773-702-9756
sales@press.uchicago.edu
www.press.uchicago.edu

British Library Cataloguing in Publication Data
A catalogue record for this book is available from the British Library

Library of Congress Cataloging-in-Publication Data
A catalog record for this book has been requested

ISBN 978-1-4473-3162-9 paperback
ISBN 978-1-4473-3160-5 hardcover
ISBN 978-1-4473-3163-6 ePub
ISBN 978-1-4473-3164-3 Mobi
ISBN 978-1-4473-3161-2 ePdf

Cover design by Hayes Design
Printed and bound in Great Britain by Clays Ltd, St Ives plc
Policy Press uses environmentally responsible print partners

MIX
Paper from
responsible sources
FSC
www.fsc.org
FSC® C013604

Contents

List of figures, images and tables

Figures

Images

Tables

Notes on contributors

Katerina Alexiou is a Lecturer in Design at the Open University, where she has served as RCUK Academic Fellow in the Design Group. Katerina has been a Co-Investigator on six AHRC-funded research projects, including the recent 'Starting from Values: Evaluating Intangible Legacies', and was Principal Investigator for the *Valuing Community-Led Design* project funded under the Connected Communities: Community, Culture and Design programme.

Kim Aumann has worked as a community worker and manager of third sector organisations. Previously co-founder and Director of the award-winning charity Amaze, Kim continues to work with parents of disabled children providing a consultancy and training service for the organisation. She has a wealth of experience of research partnerships with academics and supports the UK Community Partner Network.

Martin Bashforth is a radical family historian and formerly assistant archivist at the National Railway Museum. He was previously based in York and now in Norwich, and was part of the 'How should heritage decision be made?' research team.

Mike Benson is Director of the National Coal Mining Museum and was previously Director of Bede's World and Ryedale Folk Museum and was part of the 'How should heritage decision be made?' research team.

Tim Boon is Head of Research and Public History, Science Museum and was part of the 'How should heritage decision be made?' research team. He is a curator and historian of the public culture of science, on which he has published extensively, including the book *Films of Fact* (2008).

Lianne Brigham and Richard Brigham are founders and administrators for the York Past and Present facebook group. The group has grown in popularity since beginning in the winter of 2013 and currently has 12,000 members. York Past and Present run a number of projects which involve their members in York's history and heritage. A recent project has been in collaboration with York's Mansion House where members have photographed and packed the collections prior to a major development and redisplay. Lianne and Richard were part of the 'How should heritage decision be made?' research team.

Julian Brigstocke is Lecturer in Human Geography at the University of Cardiff, formerly at the University of Plymouth. Julian is a co-founder and key member of the Authority Research Network, and has been a Co-Investigator for the recent AHRC project 'Starting from Values: Evaluating Intangible Legacies'. He is the author of *The Life of the City: Space, Humour, and the Authority of Experience in Late Nineteenth Century Paris*, recently published by Ashgate.

Karen Brookfield is Deputy Director (Strategy) at the Heritage Lottery Fund, where she leads a team of professionals developing HLF's strategy, grant-giving practice, special initiatives, research and advocacy. Karen was part of the 'How should heritage decisions be made?' research team.

Julie Brown is Lecturer in Creative Enterprise at Southampton Solent University. She has researched and published on the role of creativity in urban and rural place-making and economic development; sites and spaces of contemporary cultural production, processes and practices; critical frameworks for understanding contemporary creative and cultural work and labour; and cultural and creative-sector policy development.

Laura Brown completed her PhD in psychology at University College London in 2006. Since then, she has worked in a variety of research and teaching roles at the University of Edinburgh, the University of St Andrews, Newcastle University and Manchester Metropolitan University. She has been working in her current role as a lecturer in the School of Psychological Sciences at the University of Manchester since 2013. Her research interests focus on characterising and improving cognition, health and well-being in older people, with a particular interest in developing new methods of assessment and evaluation.

Peter Brown was Director of York Civic Trust until he retired at the end of July 2015. Peter was awarded an MBE for 'helping to preserve the heritage of York' in the Queen's New Year Honours list, 2011. Peter is currently working on *York 1660–1860*, to be published by Phillip Wilson (forthcoming, 2017) and was part of the 'How should heritage decision be made?' research team.

Gemma Burford is an interdisciplinary researcher and artist with specific interests in design, project evaluation, education, wellness and visual arts, based in the Values and Sustainability Research Group at the University of Brighton. She is Co-Director of the Global Initiative for

Traditional Systems (GIFTS) of Health and a co-editor of the *WHO Global Atlas of Traditional, Complementary and Alternative Medicine*.

Danny Callaghan is an independent consultant (Public Art, History and Engagement) and has worked on projects such as *The Potteries Tile Trail* (HLF All Our Stories), Ceramic City Stories and Pararchive, and was part of the 'How should heritage decision be made?' research team.

Jean-Phillipe Calvin is a composer and researcher and was part of the Science Museum's co-collecting electronic music strand of the 'How should heritage decision be made?' project.

Steve Connelly is Senior Lecturer at the Department of Urban Studies & Planning, University of Sheffield. His research interests are in the politics of policy making, and in particular of stakeholder involvement in governance. Within this he principally explores the legitimacy of different forms of representation and knowledge.

Richard Courtney is based in the School of Management, University of Leicester and was part of the 'How should heritage decision be made?' research team.

Kathy Cremin is currently Executive Officer at Berwickshire Association of Voluntary Services and was previously Director of Hive. She was part of the 'How should heritage decision be made?' research team.

Elizabeth Curtis is Lecturer in Primary Education at the University of Aberdeen. She has a background in both archaeology and primary school teaching and specialises in teaching and researching how people make sense of time and place. Her current research focuses on participation in community history and heritage projects.

Oliver Davis is Lecturer in Archaeology at the University of Cardiff. He is also Co-director of Caerau and Ely Rediscovering (CAER) Heritage Project, funded through the AHRC Connected Communities programme, and was Co-Investigator on the AHRC Connected Communities Legacy Project 'Heritage Legacies'.

Andy Dearden is Professor of Interactive Systems Design at Sheffield Hallam University. His research deals with participatory methods for designing and using interactive computer and communications systems to support social and economic development for people and communities. He has extensive experience working with private, public and third-sector organisations in the UK, India and Africa, with a particular focus on enabling people and groups who may have limited resources, or limited experience with technology, to shape systems for themselves.

Sophie Duncan is Deputy Director of the National Co-ordinating Centre for Public Engagement, which supports universities to engage with the public. She is joint editor of the open access journal, *Research for All*. She is committed to cultivating both high-quality engagement, and institutional cultures that support it. Previously she led engagement campaigns.

Catherine Durose is Senior Lecturer in the Institute of Local Government Studies at the University of Birmingham. Her research explores relationships between the state, communities and citizens, focusing on the politics and practice of community participation and co-production. She has a passionate interest in research supporting progressive social change.

Hugh Escott is a Lecturer in English at Sheffield Hallam University. His research interests include representations of non-standard language in mass media, the relationship between orality and literacy, and the institutional legitimation of aesthetics and practices. He currently works on projects co-producing research with young people on the influence that standard language culture, mainstream literacy and literary culture have on their everyday lives.

Keri Facer is Professor of Educational and Social Futures at the University of Bristol and AHRC Leadership Fellow for the Connected Communities Programme. Her research centres on how individuals, communities and societies learn to adapt to and challenge economic, environmental and technological change.

Colin Foskett is Business and Partnerships Executive at the Blackwood Foundation, where he is responsible for leading the Foundation, determining strategy and business planning. He has led the development of the social media platform bespoken to worldwide reach and won several awards for this work, including the Herald Digital Business Award and SSSC Innovation Award.

Paul Furness is a writer and historian based in York and Leeds and was part of the 'How should heritage decision be made?' research team. Paul is author of *York: A Walk on the Wild Side* (2014).

Justine Gaubert is Founder and CEO of Silent Cities Ltd, a social enterprise which runs co-designed digital programmes and provides creative volunteering opportunities for those without a voice in mainstream media. She has been Social Entrepreneur in Residence at the University of Sheffield and previously worked for many years in the creative industries as a communications and training consultant.

Helen Graham teaches Museum and Heritage Studies at the University of Leeds. Her research and teaching interests directly flow from working in learning and access teams in museums and coordinating community heritage projects concerned with the co-production of knowledge, archives and exhibits.

Paula Graham is a consultant and qualitative researcher specialising in HCI, co-design and networked collaboration. Paula is the AHRC/ CreativeWorks Creative Entrepreneur in Residence at Queen Mary University of London, and the founder and director of Fossbox. She is also a co-organiser of Flossie, an annual conference with the theme of diversity in technology and open-source software.

Alex Hale was formerly an archaeologist at RCAHMS, he is now an archaeologist at Historic Environment Scotland. He has been PI and Co-I on 4 AHRC Connected Communities research projects and is currently managing a project that considers historical and contemporary graffiti across Scotland.

Marie Harder leads the Values and Sustainability Research Group at the University of Brighton and holds a China National Thousand Talents Professorship in China. Marie has led 70+ projects with non-academic partners, a European project to develop values-based indicators, was Principal Investigator for the AHRC-funded project 'Starting from Values: Evaluating Intangible Legacies' and has 50 publications in diverse fields.

Paddy Hodgkiss, Riccall Archive Co-ordinator, was part of the 'How should heritage decision be made?' research team.

Elona Hoover is an interdisciplinary researcher with a background in human sciences and over seven years of experience working in research and collaborative projects in the practice of values and ethical dimensions in collective organising. She is currently researching relationality with the more-than-human in urban commoning projects.

Deborah James is Senior Research Consultant at the National Council for Voluntary Organisations (NCVO). She has nearly 20 years' experience as a researcher and evaluator working with voluntary and community organisations. She specialises in evaluation and evaluation capacity building, and in supporting organisations and teams to use research and evaluation for learning and improvement.

Robert Johnston is a Senior Lecturer in Landscape Archaeology at the University of Sheffield. He has research interests in landscape archaeology and Bronze Age Britain and Ireland. He has also led the University of Sheffield's 'Research for Community Heritage' project with HLF All Our Stories groups, and has been Co-Investigator on the AHRC Connected Communities Legacy Project 'Heritage Legacies'.

Mihaela Kelemen is Director of the Community Animation and Social Innovation Research-CASIC and Professor of Management Studies at Keele University. Mihaela's research is underpinned by a Pragmatist philosophy and a collaborative form of co-inquiry which taps into narrative methods, dramaturgical approaches, organisational theories and community studies, and explores what is considered 'actionable' knowledge by communities and what makes knowledge relevant, useful and practical at their end.

John Lawson is a storyteller based in Loftus and was part of the 'How should heritage decision be made?' research team.

Ann Light is Professor of Design and Creative Technology at the University of Sussex, a design researcher specialising in design for social well-being and sustainable futures, the politics of participation and the long-term social and cultural impact of digital networks in post-industrial and developing regions. She leads the Creative Technology Group at Sussex, has been multiply funded under the AHRC's Connected Communities and Designing for the 21st Century programmes and was recently an advisor to the EU on the sharing economy.

Rebecca Madgin is Senior Lecturer in Urban Development and Management at the University of Glasgow. Her research focuses on the emotional values of heritage as well as the reasons why historic buildings are conserved or demolished as part of urban regeneration initiatives. She is the author of *Heritage, Culture and Conservation: Managing the Urban Renaissance* (2009).

Paul Manners is Associate Professor in Public Engagement at UWE and founding director of the National Coordinating Centre for Public Engagement (NCCPE). The NCCPE was established in 2008 to coordinate public engagement practice and to support innovation and strategic change in universities. Paul was part of the 'How should heritage decision be made?' research team.

Rik Martin is the Operations Manager at Community Action Norfolk. Rik is Co-investigator of the 'Preserving Place' project, and was on the steering group for the AHRC/HLF 'All our Stories: Ideas Bank'. Rik has more than 25 years experience in project management in Norfolk, supporting vulnerable people and developing projects in rural communities. Prior to this he managed two community Technology Centres, taught management, photography and IT courses, wrote City & Guilds courses and is a published author of children's poetry.

Kimberley Marwood works on interdisciplinarity, engaged learning and public value in the Projects and Development Team in Academic and Learning Services at the University of Sheffield. She researches art history and heritage using participatory research methods, including action research and co-production.

Peter Matthews is Lecturer in Social Policy in the School of Applied Social Science, University of Stirling. In his research he is particularly interested in urban policy, urban inequalities and community engagement and empowerment. Research projects have focused on co-producing engagement and research with communities within marginalised neighbourhoods, and understanding the motivations and consequences of engagement by the affluent.

Sue Moffat (New Vic Theatre, Newcastle-under-Lyme, UK) is Keele University Honorary Research Fellow and Founding Director of *New Vic Borderline*. She has been awarded a British Crime Concern Award and two Global Ethics Awards for work with young Muslim women and victims of racism. Her work on historiographies of the Holocaust resulted in her becoming a Fellow of the Imperial War Museum in Holocaust Education.

Dave O'Brien is a Chancellors Fellow in Cultural and Creative Industries, based in the School of History of Art but working across several areas of study. Previously he was a senior lecturer in cultural policy at Goldsmiths College, University of London. He has worked on several Connected Communities projects, exploring early career researchers' experiences, dementia and imagination, and the creative economy. His most recent book is *Cultural Policy*, published by Routledge.

Kate Pahl works in the School of Education at the University of Sheffield. She is the author of *Materializing Literacies in Communities: The Uses of Literacy Revisited* (Bloomsbury Academic, 2014). Her work centres around questions of representation and meaning making in communities. Her research mainly involves collaborative work across the Arts and Humanities and Social Sciences in community settings.

Martin Phillips is based in the Geography Department at Leicester University. His research interests span rural, social and cultural geography, historical geography, society/environment relations, and philosophy in geography. Much of his recent work has focused on the material and symbolic constructions of rural space and the social relations and identities of class and gender. He is also working on museum geographies, retail-led gentrification, filmic geographies and adaptations to climate change.

Steve Pool trained as a sculptor and now works as a visual artist in multiple medias to help people realise ideas, often making physical objects or changing environments, and has an interest in stories and research. He has worked on many programmes and initiatives including Creative Partnerships and Public Understanding of Science and Regeneration through area-based renewal.

Andrew Power is Lecturer in Human Geography at the School of Geography and Environment at the University of Southampton. He is interested in the everyday geographies of voluntarism, and the role of space and place in shaping social relations. He has published on care and family caregiving, self-advocacy groups, self-directed care and localism.

Amanda Ravetz is Senior Research Fellow at MIRIAD, Manchester School of Art. She works in the interstices between anthropology, art and design. She is the editor with Alice Kettle and Helen Felcey of *Collaboration Through Craft* (Bloomsbury Academic, 2013). Her co-authored book *Observational Cinema: Anthropology, Film, and the Exploration of Social Life* was published by Indiana University Press in 2009.

Liz Richardson is Senior Lecturer in Politics at Manchester University. She is a board member for a number of national charities and community support organisations. Her work is dedicated to trying out ways in which academics, practitioners, and citizens can develop more democratic and participatory ways of doing politics.

David Robinson is a technical editor and musician and was part of the Science Museum's co-collecting electronic music strand of the 'How should heritage decision be made?' project.

Robert Rutherfoord is Principal Research Officer in the Department for Communities and Local Government. He is responsible for analysis on neighbourhood decentralisation and neighbourhood planning, and has a particular interest in linking up the civil service with academic research, to share insights and solve problems. Previous roles included research on regeneration, spatial analysis and small business studies.

Colin Shepherd is an independent archaeologist based in Aberdeenshire, Scotland. His interests are in landscape history and community participation in heritage research. He was Community Co-Investigator for the AHRC Connected Communities Legacy Project 'Heritage Legacies'.

Karen Smyth is Senior Lecturer in Medieval and Early Modern Literature in the School of Literature, Drama and Creative Writing at the University of East Anglia. She has over a decade of experience in co-producing heritage projects with community groups. She has published on medieval East Anglian literature, digital humanities and life writing of people and places for both academic and public audiences.

Sophia de Sousa is Chief Executive at the national charity The Glass-House Community Led Design. She is an impassioned champion of design quality for our built environment and an enabler of design practices that empower people and organisations and that help neighbourhoods thrive. Sophia is also a leader in the field of research on community-led, participatory and co-design practices.

John Stanley is a writer and electronic musician and was part of the Science Museum's co-collecting electronic music strand of the 'How should heritage decision be made?' project.

Martin Swan is a musician and educator and was part of the Science Museum's co-collecting electronic music strand of the 'How should heritage decision be made?' project.

Jenny Timothy is a building conservation and historic environmental specialist working in consultancy for Mott MacDonald and was previously Senior Building Conservation Officer, Leicester City Council. In her professional career Jenny has been directly involved in informing and making decisions which affect the historic environment and how it is managed. Jenny was part of the 'How should heritage decision be made?' research team.

Rachael Turner is Director, MadLab and *The Ghosts of St Pauls* (HLF All Our Stories) and was part of the 'How should heritage decision be made?' research team.

Dave Vanderhoven has worked with marginalised communities, including drug users and Irish Travellers, public bodies and policy makers. He focuses on the intersections between knowledge, policy and the artistry of practice, is on the boards of a local domestic violence support organisation and the *Community Development Journal*, and is a Research Associate at the University of Sheffield.

Jo Vergunst is Lecturer in Social Anthropology at the University of Aberdeen. His research interests are in relations between people and the landscape, and his main areas of fieldwork are Orkney and northern Scotland. He was Principal Investigator for the AHRC Connected Communities Legacy Project 'Heritage Legacies'.

Theodore Zamenopoulos is a Senior Lecturer in Design at The Open University. He is a professional architect with expertise in design cognition, community led design practices and complexity research. His research focuses on the conditions that foster design thinking in everyday life and empower people to develop their ideas into social innovations. He has been involved in a number of research projects around the themes of civic engagement in design and the empowerment of people through design.

Acknowledgements

Our thanks, as a collective of authors and editors, to the UK Arts and Humanities Research Council and to the Connected Communities Programme, for funding the initial university-community research collaborations reported in this book, the legacy projects which have aimed to understand them, the Community Partner Network, and Keri's Leadership Fellowship which has allowed us to meet, discuss and reflect on our work. Our thanks also to all the project teams and collaborators who have contributed to the thinking and testing out the ideas in these chapters. And finally, we want to acknowledge and thank, in particular, the brilliant Gary Grubb who has been such a driving force behind collaborative, publicly-engaged and community-based research in the UK.

Introduction

Keri Facer and Kate Pahl

What is at stake when we value collaborative research?

The boundaries between universities and publics are becoming more fluid and new research collaborations are proliferating. Indeed, there is an increasing emphasis, in particular in the UK, on the development of partnerships in the design and conduct of research. This 'participatory turn' is fuelled variously by: communities seeking evidence and validation for their practice in pursuit of organisational learning and/or further funding; the increasingly fluid careers and identities of practitioners and researchers moving in and out of the university and building new collaborations between civil society and academia as they go; the long legacy of critical theory and poststructuralist thinking, which has fuelled a generation of academics alert to the limits of their own perspectives and seeking to pluralise their accounts of reality; government and policy bodies seeking evidence of 'relevant' public research; and a generation of civil society activists and communities increasingly well placed to challenge the dominant accounts of society with which they are presented (Facer and Enright, 2016).

For these reasons participatory and collaborative research is flourishing across all fields – from medicine to the arts, from urban studies to education. What has not kept pace, however, are the theories and methods needed to understand and make good judgements about the value and quality of this research. Rather, much of the effort has been focused on making these sorts of 'engagements' happen and struggling with the complexity of these processes and practices as they are happening. Much less attention has been paid to understanding the legacy of these moments of collaboration between academics and communities or to how and whether these processes deliver on the significant claims about quality, democracy and equity that such projects are often bound up with.

As project teams and as funders of research seeking to make sense of this new landscape, therefore, we need to ask ourselves: What should we be looking for if we want to understand the contribution that this sort of research is making to the knowledge base? How can we examine the contribution of this research to the wider public good?

What theoretical resources can help us in evaluating and valuing this sort of research? And what methods, tools and approaches are available to assist with making sense of the complex and messy dynamics of these collaborative research practices?

Understanding better how to answer such questions is important for many reasons – such understanding will help us work out how better to conduct research, why different forms of research should be valued, and how we should develop our capacity for new forms of research. These are urgent questions, in particular, for the form of research – collaborative partnerships between universities and communities – that is at stake in this book. Such research is seen by some as a means of creating greater 'impact' on the social world and by others as a way of enhancing the quality of knowledge; by some as a form of democratic recalibration of knowledge production and by others as a way of generating more robust products and services. There are therefore very different measures of value against which these research collaborations might be judged.

Many different answers to these questions of value and legacy are being proposed – from the economic cost-benefit analyses of the accountants, to the bibliometrics of a burgeoning software industry, to the multi-million-pound deliberations of academic panels in which researchers judge each other's work with all the impartiality and disinterest inherent in peer review processes. Such answers are all necessarily imperfect. Research is a practice that refuses to sit in simple boxes.

To avoid a judgement of value, however, is impossible. To refuse to tell the story of a project in an age of competitive contractualism, in which the next research grant, funding award or contract is premised on previous satisfactory performance, is to self-sabotage. In an audit culture, to refuse to account for what has been done or the difference that has been made, is to be seen to fail in demonstrating the proper accountability to 'the funders/the public/the taxpayers'.

More positively, telling the story of the value of the work, the impact that it has had, is also a route to future funding, to securing more resource and recognition for the work. Above all, being able to step back and tell the story of how a project has gone and what new knowledge it has produced, what changes it led to (or not), is a form of learning that can enhance the quality of future projects. The ability to narrate the value of projects, of all research projects, therefore, is at worst a necessary evil and, at best, a highly beneficial learning process. The challenge is to create a means of reflecting on and understanding what has happened in research processes that is not instrumental and performative, complicit with the worst excesses of accountability regimes, but authentic, embedded and able to enhance our understanding of what has happened.

Collaborative research – in which universities, citizens, public bodies and community organisations come together to develop joint research and collaborative projects – however, may be particularly difficult to 'narrate'. The research outcomes may not fit easily into categories familiar to funders of either research or of social action. The legacies left by such projects may exceed what is visible in a journal paper, a citation index or a tick box on a funders' form. The traces may extend beyond the organisation and academic domain into the lived experiences of participants and the material practices of communities. Moments of experiential learning and intellectual challenge may be hard to translate into the language of the end-of-project report. The intervention of an embodied arts practice may be impossible to communicate in the formal language of a written report. How, then, can stories of the value of collaborative research between universities and communities be told?

This is the question we are exploring in this book. We are writing for those participants in collaborative research who are looking for tools to ask hard questions of themselves about what they are doing as well as needing to narrate its value to sometimes sceptical audiences. We are writing for those funders and institutional backers of research who are seeking to understand what difference this sort of research makes, to whom and how. We are writing for that growing band of academics and consultants who are being asked to evaluate and make sense of these complex projects. And we are writing for the students and community members who are just beginning the difficult and rewarding process of setting up new collaborations and for whom tools to reflect on the sorts of legacies they are wishing to leave at the end of the process may be useful.

What we hope to offer to readers of this book, therefore, is a set of resources for thinking that can be used and adapted to the specific conditions in which they are working. We will not be offering one new truth, one new method, to replace all others. Rather, we will be telling stories, sharing tools and recounting difficulties we have experienced ourselves as participants in a community of researchers seeking collectively to enhance what we are doing when we do collaborative research and to improve how we understand and value it when we talk to others.

Collaborative research, its many traditions and legacies

An important place to start in thinking about how we value collaborative research is with the very idea of what we mean by 'collaboration' in the first place. After all, this is the sort of generic term that is evidently and unhelpfully imprecise – what sorts of collaborations, between whom, for what purposes? Clearly the term can mean many things, but we are using it here specifically in relation to research collaborations between university and community partners rather than between academics. Other terms have been used for this sort of activity – from 'engaged' research to 'co-produced' research. Our preference for the simplicity of 'collaborative' research is precisely because it can act as an umbrella term for the plurality of traditions of university–community/public/ audience collaborations that constitute this practice.

Indeed, it is our strong contention that if we are to develop robust theoretical and methodological resources for valuing and evaluating collaborative research, we need to begin by developing a language to talk about the different traditions that constitute this field. These traditions, after all, bring with them fundamentally different and often-competing assumptions about their desired legacy and therefore competing ideas about how such research should be valued.

Indeed, the field of collaborative research includes everything from participatory arts practice, to public history, from community-led action research to urban design practices, from patient engagement in medicine to the consultative processes of responsible innovation. We have often seen these approaches ranked in a hierarchy, with particular value attributed to those projects and practices that involve high levels of 'public' participation at all levels of the project (for example Arnstein's ever-present 'ladder of participation', 1969). Such an approach, in our view, risks creating a new dogma that falls into the familiar trap of universalising research methods that participatory projects have so often sought to avoid.

A different way of thinking about these traditions, we propose, might be in relation to the theory of change (Weiss, 1997) they are operating with – in other words, by thinking about them in terms of the specific goals that they hold, their assumptions about what their impacts and legacies might and could be, and how these relate to the processes that they are employing. Such a position might be (mis)interpreted as seeking to render a complex process merely instrumental – to map out in linear fashion how projects techniques reach project goals. Such an interpretation, however, would ignore the principle of praxis that underpins, we would contend, all traditions of collaborative research

– namely, the core idea originating variously from Aristotle (Eikeland, 2012), from Marx, from Dewey or from Freire, that knowing and acting are intimately connected. In other words, that critical reflection on the world can and does open up opportunities to change it. It would also ignore the more recent theorising that emphasises the performative nature of research – that irrespective of intentionality, the process of changing what we know in turn changes reality (Law and Urry, 2004; Gibson-Graham, 2008).

Foregrounding these theories of change, these assumptions about the relationship between research practice and wider social change, these assumptions about how different methods might create different realities, these assumptions about what a desirable change might consist of – allows us to develop a much clearer analytic attention to the processes and consequences of collaborative research. It allows us, importantly, to move away from the assumption that the value of collaborative research is to be judged only by the degree and quality of public/community engagement at all stages and instead enables us to be more precise about exactly what sorts of legacies might be imagined by the very different forms and purposes of community/public participation in the research process. After all, for some purposes deep participation may be neither desired nor desirable for participants – this depends on what projects are trying to achieve.

We can cluster the myriad different forms of collaborative research under four broad headings according to how they conceptualise the relationship between collaborative research processes and an envisaged future change or consequence. Such clusterings are necessarily crude and risk obscuring differences within as well as overlaps between these types; such orientations are also often implicit; the purpose, however, is not to establish a new orthodoxy into which all projects must fit but to try to tease out the rationales for different forms of research and the implications that these bring for how we might want to value these projects.

Type 1: mutual learning

This approach to collaborative research includes traditions such as action research, participatory action research, communities of practice approaches and critical pedagogy. Here the theory of change is premised around the embodied learning that is achieved by the participants in the research team who are collaboratively defining and conducting research on real world experiences and practices. Here 'communities' tend to pre-exist the research and it is in relation to these communities that the value of the research is to be judged. The purpose of the research is to build practical theory; in other words, to develop the understanding, behaviour and practice of the individuals and organisations concerned as a basis for future action. These research partnerships are profoundly educational, building the capacity of communities and academics to see, understand and act on the world in different ways. Such research can produce research outputs and products that are of significance and use to others – and many do – but the theory of change that underpins the projects is dependent on the capacity of the project to empower participants to know and think differently, and to inform their future capacities for thought and action.

Type 2: crowd and open

The second approach to collaborative research can be understood as the development by researchers of a frame within which many and different contributions can be made to a common project by a large public constituted precisely by this call to action. Here the theory of change is premised on the new knowledge that can be produced when large numbers of people are mobilised to generate and work on large amounts of information around a particular topic, issue or interest – either by adding new information, contributing distinctive expertise to a part of a puzzle, or acting as fresh eyes on a large amount of data. These approaches are most visible in open source software, or citizen science activities. Many community, civic and cultural heritage projects, however, also benefit from these approaches, mobilising a mass of volunteer 'boots on the ground' to gather and share historical, social and cultural information. Such research is premised on the idea that new knowledge can be produced by working at a massive scale and by building communities that are able to voluntarily and relatively autonomously make contributions to a collective endeavour. There may be many personal benefits to participants, but the quality of the project usually stands or falls on the new insights and achievements embodied in the collective product – these insights may be generated simply through scale (it was not possible to know these things in this way without this many people's involvement); by aggregation and pattern (new insights are achieved when patterns in large datasets are identified); or by the new artefact that has been created (something has been made that could not have been made without massive collective effort).

Type 3: design and innovation

The involvement of publics/communities/users in the early stages of design processes constitutes a third type of collaborative research. Here what is at stake is the design of services, or policies, products or new technologies. It includes everything from the consultative processes concerned with responsible innovation to the user-centred design increasingly prevalent in the creation of consumer products or public health services. The 'publics' that are participants here may be pre-existing communities of users, or 'representative' publics who are pulled together for the purposes of consultation. The theory of change that underpins this research is that better, more legitimate and more publicly valuable products and services will be created by incorporating the views of relevant or representative publics through consultation and collaboration in the design process. The value of such work is therefore judged both on its process (legitimacy claims are premised upon the modes and forms and type of engagement involved) and upon its products (are they valued by the publics they are designed for?). In other words, the key question here is whether the quality of the product – a long-term science policy, a new form of medicine or a piece of assistive technology – is better in terms of meeting the needs and aspirations of the specific demographics at stake.

Type 4: Correcting the record

The fourth category of collaborative research is constituted on the basis of correcting embedded inequalities and silences in the knowledge landscape. While all of the three preceding types may produce this result as an incidental benefit – the explicit aim of this type of collaborative research is to critically engage with and correct the absences, inaccuracies and negative consequences of mainstream research that has been produced from elite or partial positions. This practice includes everything from the long-standing traditions of history from below, to feminist studies, critical race theory and southern theory, to the more recent development of more-than-human studies. Here, the collaboration between academics and diverse publics is premised on the assumption that an accurate or adequate account of reality cannot be achieved without the specific and distinctive expertise of groups previously missing from the record. The community collaborator is constituted through the definition of the lack in the contemporary knowledge landscape. The theory of change here is one that focuses on pluralising the knowledge landscape, in bringing new and overlooked facts and experiences into the domain and in so doing, opening up space for more equitable social action. Such work aims to challenge the conceptual reason on which commonsense accounts of the world are produced. The value of such work, then, is judged on the extent to which the research is able to produce distinctively new insights and to pluralise and influence the 'mainstream' knowledge base.

Recognising these four implicit theories of change that often underpin the main traditions of collaborative research helps us to begin to clarify some of the theoretical and methodological resources we might need in order to start to interrogate and narrate the value of this research. We already have many building blocks in place, but we are a long way from having the fluent access to a repertoire of resources that can be drawn on to help participants, funders and publics to understand the value of these highly diverse research practices.

This book begins to address this need by providing a set of examples of attempts to evaluate the legacy of collaborative research projects as well as a 'lexicon' of different elements of the legacies that are discernible in this sort of work. We explore the question through the concept of 'legacy' as this term – rather than 'impact' – helps to give a feel for the embodied labour, the lived experiences and both the tangible and intangible outcomes from collaborative interdisciplinary research; outcomes that include divergence, complexity and disorientation that sometimes may not look like 'success'. In so doing we propose that the question 'what does success look like for this project?' needs to be asked in a way that genuinely interrogates the assumptions of all partners in collaborative research. While universities might want to tick a box that includes 'impact' and 'public engagement', community partners might want to create sustainable resources for future funding bids, or enable a certain kind of reflective practice to take place. This book throws up these questions, through the experiences described in the chapters, but also begins to provide a language of description for those practices.

What we want to do in this book, therefore, is to begin to map out how we might approach understanding the value of these different types of collaborative research practice, in particular as they play out in the Arts, Humanities and Social Sciences research arenas. To do so, we draw on the research programme that brought together all the authors of this book: the Connected Communities Programme.

The Connected Communities programme

In 2010 the Connected Communities Programme was launched by Research Councils UK and the Arts and Humanities Research Council, with the aim of funding research projects, partnerships and networks that would create a deeper and richer understanding of 'communities' in all their historic and contemporary forms. Underpinning the programme was a commitment to encourage distinctive and risk-taking projects that would be characterised by two attributes:

- First, community-university collaboration. Connected Communities projects are explicitly encouraged to draw on the combined expertise, experience and aspirations of individuals working in both communities and in universities.
- Second, interdisciplinarity. Projects are explicitly encouraged to bring the methods and theories of the Arts and Humanities (which includes everything from philosophy, history and literature to design, cultural studies, architecture and drama) into dialogue with other forms of scholarship, research and practice.

Since 2010, the programme has funded over 300 projects, involved over 500 collaborating organisations and worked with over 700 academics from universities across the UK, on topics ranging from festivals to community food, from everyday creativity to care homes, from hyperlocal journalism to community energy. Projects are highly diverse – some lasting five years and involving many hundreds of collaborating organisations and contributors, others lasting eight months and working with a small, close-knit team. The models of collaboration also vary wildly – from radical innovations with research governance in which community and academic partners share more equally the financial and intellectual agenda, to massive crowd-sourcing activities and volunteer projects, to the deeply engaged processes of developing communities of inquiry between professionals, service users and academics. The university departments involved range from Philosophy to Healthcare to Education and Computer Science; and the community partners are equally diverse, ranging from large national NGOs and social enterprises, to volunteer-run community organisations and individual activists.

There is therefore no single type of 'Connected Communities' project, rather the programme has encouraged the creation of a new generation of academic and community researchers who are beginning to experiment with what it means to create research collaborations in many different forms across the Arts, Humanities and Social Sciences. Participants in the programme are both old hands, with deep experience of participatory and community research traditions, and newbies, moving out of their comfort zone and trying collaborative research for the first time.

In funding this sort of interdisciplinary, collaborative and often risk-taking research, the Connected Communities programme is at the heart of a much wider and long-standing debate about how new knowledge, scholarship, ideas and practices should and could be produced today. This debate includes questions about how new ideas can be nurtured: through social innovation or from scholarly research into frontiers of disciplinary knowledge? About who has the insights to really understand what is 'going on' in communities today: those people who are living and experiencing it as their day-to-day reality, or those who are able to draw on much wider historical, philosophical and geographical resources to make sense of community? About who make good custodians for the historical accounts of a diverse society: those with a passion and a personal commitment to lived traditions or those with the institutional and professional techniques to archive, analyse and maintain historical records? This programme is seeking to explore what happens when these questions are answered by saying 'both/and'– both the communities and the scholars, both the passionate personal interest and the robust, systematic modes of inquiry.

In this context, Connected Communities can be seen as a significant experiment that allows us to better understand the risks, responsibilities and new possibilities that emerge for all concerned as changing relationships are forged between universities and communities. It is part of the wider 'participatory turn' that is opening up new relationships between publics, professionals, audiences, artists, citizens and policy makers in all areas of public life (Facer and Enright, 2016).

Understanding the value of collaborative research through the Connected Communities programme

After the Connected Communities programme had been running for a few years, therefore, it became clear that new ways of valuing research were going to be needed. A quick scan of the database of research outputs, for example, showed that while the programme constituted 14% of the returns on the research council database of research outputs, it included only 4% of the total academic outputs (books, journal papers) while comprising 41% of products categorised as 'artistic and creative' and 41% of products categorised as 'tools and methods'. A different form of 'output' from this sort of research was clearly emerging.

As a consequence, in 2013, the Connected Communities programme issued a call for project teams to explore how to articulate and capture the 'legacy' of the projects taking place under the programme. Seven projects were funded through an open call for proposals; they explore the challenge of studying the legacy of collaborative research in areas ranging from new forms of policy-making to the role of artists in community-engaged research, from the sorts of debates surrounding community-based heritage decision-making to the new tools being developed by community researchers in the cultural sector.

Between 2014 and 2015, these project teams, made up of both academic and community researchers, came together four times to reflect on the lessons these projects were learning about how to conceptualise, research and analyse the legacy of collaborative research with communities in the Arts, Humanities and Social Sciences. It is these projects, with the addition of the chapter by Duncan and Aumann to introduce the establishing the important insights from their experiences of establishing the Community Partner Network (also funded by the Connected Communities Programme), as well as the collective discussions that they have generated about the theory, methods and ethics of valuing collaborative research, that form the basis for this book.

Our argument in this book is that collaborative community interdisciplinary research such as this is messy, contingent on practice, uncertain, embedded in stories and histories that could be dismissed as 'anecdotal', and located in events and practices that are themselves ephemeral and lacking disciplinary anchorage. At the same time, this research is often co-creating a form of knowledge that is useful in ways that might not be realised straight away. The codification of research into academic language is also contested and ruptured through this process. It is our contention that it is important to untangle these issues – to make sense both of the mess and uncertainty and disagreement and to robustly argue for what it evidences and produces in terms of knowledge.

Outline of the book

This book tries to create a space that opens up the intersections between different disciplines, lived practice, collaborative work and ways of knowing to ask the questions: what are the legacies of interdisciplinary collaborative work? And how might we begin to trace them in ways that are appropriate to the distinctive methods by which this research is conducted?

Section 1 'Understanding legacy in practice' presents a series of nine examples of projects that have attempted to use a range of different theoretical and methodological perspectives to understand the legacy of collaborative research. In some cases, these are stories of the attempt to understand legacy that emerges from within project teams themselves. In others, these are stories of 'outsiders' building relationships with collaborative research teams and beginning to work with them to explore how to trace legacy.

Our aim in presenting them here is to surface the highly diverse theoretical and methodological resources, intentions and purposes that might shape different approaches to valuing collaborative research in the Arts, Humanities and Social Sciences. In particular, we wish to foreground the way in which coming to understand the value of this research is often itself necessarily a process that has performative effects – the evaluation produces its own effects; and often itself requires a process of co-production – the desire to understand and evaluate legacy often requires new forms of collaborative research. In so doing, these chapters trouble the construction of 'evaluation' as a disinterested reflective process and instead position it centrally as a generative, entangled and collaborative endeavour that produces its own (unintended) consequences and trajectories. The process of attempting to 'capture' and to 'value' legacy, in other words, needs to be understood as ontologically performative, it itself brings new realities into being.

We begin with a wide view of collaborative research practice and how we might approach the challenge of understanding its value. In Chapter One Duncan and Aumann draw on their experience convening the UK's Community Partner Network (a network designed to share intelligence amongst community partners about the practice of community–university partnerships) to make the case that the value of this sort of work is evidenced in many forms: from skills, knowledge and confidence of participants, to new forms of practice, networks and resources. They argue that attention to the different forms of benefits that might be produced, along with a clear-eyed awareness of the challenges of these collaborations, can create the conditions for generating partnerships with real value.

The question of value is then taken up in two case studies of Connected Communities projects. Chapter Two explores what happens when two different modes of evaluation – one led by academics, one led by the community partners – are applied to the same set of collaborative research projects. The Evaluation for Community Research team conclude that the evaluation is both more likely to succeed and produce useful knowledge when it is driven by and deeply connected with the core values and aims of the project participants. Indeed, they argue that evaluation should be developmental, an ongoing process in which values are constantly checked in a reflective process against the dynamic development of the project. In Chapter Three, the 'Intangible Values' case study explores how different groups can be facilitated to articulate and confirm their values-in-action, and then use them as a lens with which to identify their legacies. The approach gives authority to less tangible, yet valid, legacies that are often not identified both for the main partnership in a collaborative project and also for its constituent members, showing wider impact from multiple perspectives.

In Chapter Four, the project team that convened to co-research the question 'How should heritage decisions be made' describe how they approached the challenge of understanding the legacy of their complex set of workshops, discussions and heritage interventions. Their substantive research area – the politics of heritage decision-making – shapes their approach by encouraging them to pay attention to whether the project has reshaped the relationship between everyday practices and broader contextual structures and narratives. To that end, they frame the process of understanding legacy as a process of making legacy – of enabling action, reflection, connection and situation. Such an approach to legacy is also strongly visible in the Performing Legacy project team who, in Chapter Five, describe how a collaborative research project achieves its legacy through relational processes and dialogical encounters. Seeking to make sense of the contributions of a suite of intensely co-produced projects that range from studies of volunteering to the future of a small northern town, to community recovery from earthquake, they argue that to understand legacy is, in fact, to perform it.

The Artists Legacy project, in Chapter Six explores the difference that artists make in research projects. Mobilising experiential as well as historical and qualitative research methods to review projects across the Connected Communities programme, the chapter describes how artists play a unique role in pluralising, recognising and working with difference in collaborative research. Making sense of these practices, they argue, required not merely a disinterested analysis of what had happened in these projects but a reconstruction within their own project team of the artists' practice – through drawing, through workshopping ideas, through studio methods. Again, the boundary is blurred between 'evaluating' projects and the necessity to go 'inside' them to make sense of the work they are doing.

Getting to grips with the detailed materiality and contexts of collaborative research projects is also in evidence in Chapters Seven and Eight in which context, place, space and tradition are all understood to play important roles in shaping the success of these projects. In Chapter Seven, the 'Materialising Legacy' project explores through detailed vignettes the roles played by material objects and landscapes in mediating and shaping research practices; while in Chapter Eight, the 'Translation Across Borders' team show how embedded traditions of knowledge production shape the way in which research can be 'carried' from one institution to another, and, in turn close the circle by showing how collaborative research can provide a powerful means of solving the problems of failed legacy arising from more conventional attempts to 'communicate' research. Finally, in Chapter Nine, the Cultural Mapping project draws on literary theory and cultural geography to explore how stories might be overlain onto maps, and how the different processes involved in creating miscellanies and anthologies might allow projects to narrate their eclectic emergent practices while also identifying commonalities and regularities.

Reviewing these chapters, it seems to us that this sort of collaborative research is characterised by disruptions to familiar forms of academic practice as the space, time and rules for designing and conducting projects are changed. The simple act of holding meetings in community settings, at times to suit community partners, for example, begins to de-centre most traditions of academic practice. Ways of doing things have to be constructed so that multiple voices can be heard and the 'rules' of academic meetings have to be discarded. The concept of 'expertise' becomes contingent on what is useful, right now, in the project. In these projects, for example, it is clear that many academic participants have had to let go of settled ideas of 'knowing best' and instead have had to learn across boundaries and in contexts in which their 'knowing' was not necessarily immediately useful. The process of doing this often means doing research 'without a map' (Escott et al, in press) where all concerned are uncertain of the ways of doing things and of the outcomes that might emerge. Disciplines also can get blurred, as encounters across bodies of knowledge result in encounters that unsettle and destabilise the boundaries of academic knowledge. Some kinds of knowledge can lose currency in communities where urgent issues (for example austerity, health concerns) are paramount. This can result in academics retreating into facilitation roles, and 'losing' their academic expertise, which, while well intentioned, can frustrate community partners who may often want to work with 'the university' precisely for its capacity to act as a site for credible knowledge production. Knowing together involves navigating these shared concerns and might need the construction of new roadmaps to achieve shared goals.

Another common characteristic of these chapters is their insistence that attention be paid to diverse forms of knowledge production. This includes knowledge of space, place and histories, together with specific skills such as music making, fishing, relationship building, linguistic and artistic competencies to name a few. These repertoires came from, for example, lived experience in communities and embodied understandings that academics cannot necessarily 'see' from the practices of disciplinary-led enquiry. Seeing differently often involves a decolonising process. Oral knowledge production, passed down through generations, or built over time within communities, was one form that was important in this process. Artists brought intuitive and disparate forms of knowing to cross-disciplinary projects. Other knowledge production processes identified in the chapters include specific repertoires of making and doing. Valuing diversity, both linguistically and culturally, involves an active listening to what the knowledge was that was being articulated. Often, in these projects, community partners become frustrated at academics' inability to 'hear' these forms of knowledge. Academics feel de-skilled in the face of community partners' ability to do such things and sometimes retreat as a result. Meeting in the middle requires particular skills and competencies that people have to build together. This includes the development of methodologies that involve constructing listening spaces so that different kinds of knowledge can be surfaced. As these nine chapters relate, some relationships do not last and some last over many projects and form the basis for friendships.

Experiential methodologies that value everyday perceptions and 'learning with' rather than doing things 'on' people are often privileged within these kinds of projects. These approaches to collaborative knowledge production tend to involve a lot of 'being there', witnessing everyday activities. Researchers from both universities and communities join local community meetings, walk through the streets, sit by ponds, go out on boats, walk in parks, go fishing, garden, draw together, dig together, hang out, go to folk concerts, organise festivals, hold tea parties and jamborees, participate in activist events and make zines. Skills that are not in the common toolset of 'researchers' become important, particularly for early career researchers, who find themselves in the position of going on trips, organising community partner payments, distributing fliers for events and focusing on food, drinks and supporting community partner research teams. Sensory methodologies (Pink, 2009) that acknowledge perceptual knowledge and shared experiences are useful in helping research teams notice what is going on. Methodologies from arts practice, such as practice as research, which value inquiring through a particular, formed practice, aid shared inquiry (Barrett and Bolt, 2007). Material knowing, located in embodied and tacit forms of knowledge, come to the fore in shared projects (Carter, 2004; Coessens et al, 2009). The 'everyday' as a field, becomes a key site for things to happen.

Co-analysis in these projects also tends towards processes of extended discussion, and 'data' are not defined as units of stuff but rather tend to be understood as an ongoing, unfolding of events that are then mulled over collaboratively. If interviews are conducted, or oral histories, often community and academic research teams make sense of them together, in many instances this sense-making draws on specific contextual knowledge that might not be accessible to academic teams. Co-analysis as methodology draws on techniques such as dialogic co-inquiry spaces or communities of practice (Armstrong and Banks, 2011; Hart and Wolff, 2006). Flattening knowledge hierarchies and structures is important so that insights from all the teams can be incorporated into writing. Outputs, too are often shaped by needs that lie outside universities. Academic articles might not be the priority when community organisations need to demonstrate impact and efficacy. Weaving outputs together creates a plethora of artefacts that include films, models, posters, theatre productions, workshops, art productions and participatory activities such as zine making. These all widen the scope of what could be called 'research'.

Looking at these nine chapters, then, it is clear that a key part of such modes of collaborative interdisciplinary research is the redefining of the 'work' of research. Much of this work is hard, emotional and administrative labour (Steiner, 2000) that is rarely credited by academic institutions. This 'work' can be redefined as thoughtful collaborative practice, which has core values that guide it. Rather than privileging practice that is oriented towards the solving of a particular disciplinary conundrum, this kind of research seeks to enhance and widen the ways in which knowledge is framed and constructed. It involves often telling 'untold stories' as Aumann and Duncan articulate in their chapter. The work is ontologically oriented as well as epistemologically unsettling; it makes and creates diverse realities and harnesses diverse viewpoints. This process can be uncomfortable for those academics who are often used to the experience of 'knowing best' and of working in the realm of theory. Indeed, this research often included a focus on transformation and the decolonisation of knowledge structures to create radical social change. Embedded within many of these projects, then, is a core interest in disrupting how research is constructed and knowledge is made.

In Section 2 'Understanding collaborative research practices: a lexicon', we draw on these nine chapters to explore what they tell us about the challenges inherent in attempting to value the distinctive characteristics of collaborative research and begin to develop a lexicon that might offer a language for making sense of such projects. We argue that understanding collaborative research requires language, theory and methods to help make sense of (at least) eight elements that characterise these sorts of projects. These are: *productive divergence* – the ways in which these projects work with different and sometimes disorienting ways of knowing; *materiality and place* – the ways in which collaborative research is shaped and works through objects, landscapes, cultures; *messiness and uncertainty* – the ways in which these projects are characterised by evolving and changing ways of knowing, by surprise and new possibilities; *complexity* – the entanglements between projects and contexts, between ideas, bodies and actions; *praxis* – the way in which these projects work with action as knowledge and knowledge as action, their commitment to a performative ontology that shapes the world as it studies it; *translation* – the ways in which collaborative projects seek to cross borders between situated ways of knowing, and the way that knowledge in these projects is held and carried through different modes of representation; *stories* – the function and purpose of narration as a means not only of producing knowledge within projects but as a means of creating legacy; *embodied learning* – the ways that projects are fundamentally concerned with co-constituting human relations and developing human capacities.

In Section 3 'Future directions', we return to the questions and context that we have outlined above – a world in which being able to 'account for' a project has become an increasingly important element of both community and academic life and we ask how we might develop approaches to understanding legacy that reflect the complexity of these projects while still enabling projects to 'account' for their actions and intentions. In this chapter, we propose that there is a double dynamic in collaborative research projects – towards intentionality and towards disruption, and that both are essential components of building common ground across diverse participants in a project while holding open the potential for multiple voices, forms of knowledge and expertise to be worked together. We propose that understanding this double dynamic at all stages of the research activity will better enable project participants, as well as their supporters and funders, to create ways of both understanding and creating legacy that are adequate and appropriate for these collaborative research activities.

Taken together, these examples and reflections on common themes emerging will, we hope, offer anyone seeking to tell the story of collaborative research in the Arts, Humanities and Social Sciences the beginnings of a set of tools and resources that can render more complex and more narratable the rich legacies emerging from these forms of research. This is by no means a point of ending however, a full stop to suggest that the job is done of attending to the complex question of the legacy of collaborative research. Rather, it is the beginning – as in all good collaborative research – of a dialogue through which ideas will be refined, overturned, challenged and developed. The main enemy of intelligent and rigorous approaches to understanding the legacy of complex research projects, after all, is the assumption that there is one toolkit/process/method that can capture it. This book is intended as a starting point to be complemented by the methods and processes that are appropriate for the distinct and specific set of circumstances of any given set of projects and relationships. In particular, we focus here on projects relating to work in the Arts, Humanities and Social Sciences – there is more work to be done on understanding and respecting the legacies that emerge from the non-project based relationships that academics and their partners engage in, and into the potential application or limits of what we have argued for here in engineering, sciences and medical sciences. We look forward to longer conversations and exchanges with community partners, funders, university professional services staff and academics taking this work forward in different ways.

Key resources for thinking about legacy

Getting to grips with collaborative research means getting to grips with the wide range of traditions of collaboration that this field comprises. The following provide some initial routes to explore the key assumptions and aspirations of the four types of collaborative research we have identified:

Type 1: Mutual Learning
Brydon-Miller, M., Greenwood, D. and Maguire, P. (2003). 'Why Action Research?. *Action Research* 1.1: 9–28
Burns, D. (2013) *Systemic Action Research: A Strategy for Whole System Change.* Bristol: Policy Press
Eikeland, O. (2008). *The Ways of Aristotle: Aristotelian Phronesis, Aristotelian*

Philosophy of Dialogue, and Action Research (vol. 5). Bern: Peter Lang

Fals Borda, O. and Rahman, M.A. (1991). *Action and Knowledge: Breaking the Monopoly with Participatory Action-research*. Michigan: Apex Press

Gaventa, J. (1993). 'The Powerful, the Powerless, and the Experts: Knowledge Struggles in an Information Age'. In Park, P., Brydon-Miller, M., Hall, B. and Jackson, T. (eds.), *Voices of Change: Participatory Research in the United States and* Canada. Westport, CT: Bergin and Garvey Press, 21–40

Hart, A. and Wolff, D. (2006). 'Developing Local "Communities of Practice" through Local Community-University Partnerships'. *Planning Practice and Research* 21(1) 121–38

Reason, P. and Bradbury, H. (eds). (2001). *Handbook of Action Research: Participative Inquiry and Practice*. London: Sage

Wenger, E. (1998). 'Communities of Practice. Learning as a Social System'. *Systems Thinker*, http://www.co-i-l.com/coil/knowledge-garden/cop/lss.shtml

Type 2: Open/Crowd

Benkler, Y. (2006). *The Wealth of Networks: How Social Production Transforms Markets and Freedom*. Newhaven, CT: Yale University Press

Bollier, D. and Helfrich, S. (eds) (2012). *The Wealth of the Commons: A World Beyond Markets and State*. New York: Levellers Press

Ostrom, E. (1990). *Governing the Commons: The Evolution of Institutions for Collective Action.*, Cambridge: Cambridge University Press

Ostrom, E. (1996). 'Crossing the Great Divide: Coproduction, Synergy, and Development'. *World development*, 24(6) 1073–87

Stallman, R. (2002). *Free Software, Free Society: Selected Essays of Richard M. Stallman*. Lulu.com

Type 3: Design

Alexiou, K. (2010). 'Coordination and Emergence in Design'. *CoDesign*, 6(2), 75–97

Jacobs, J. M. (2002). *Edge of Empire: Postcolonialism and the City*. London: Routledge

Kafer, A. (2013). *Feminist, Queer, Crip*. Bloomington, IN: Indiana University Press

Kretzmann, J. P., McKnight, J., and Puntenney, D. (2005). *Discovering Community Power: A Guide to Mobilizing Local Assets and Your Organization's Capacity*. Asset-Based Community Development Institute, School of Education and Social Policy, Northwestern University

Shakespeare, T. (2013). *Disability Rights and Wrongs Revisited*. London: Routledge

Stephens, L., Ryan-Collins, J. and Boyle, D. (2008). *Co-production: A Manifesto for Growing the Core Economy*. London: New Economics Foundation

Type 4: Correcting the Record

Butler, J. (1990). *Gender Trouble*, New York: Routledge

Connell, R. (2007). *Southern Theory*. Crows Nest, NSW: Allen & Unwin

De Sousa Santos, B. (ed) (2007) *Another Knowledge is Possible: Beyond Northern Epistemologies*. London: Verso Books

Fanon, F. (2008). *Black Skin, White Masks*. New York: Grove Press

Gilligan, C. (1982). *In a Different Voice*. Cambridge, MA: Harvard University Press

Haraway, D. (1991). 'Situated Knowledges'. In *Simians, Cyborgs and Women*, New York: Routledge

Irwin, A. and Wynne, B. (2003). *Misunderstanding Science?: The Public Reconstruction of Science and Technology*. Cambridge: Cambridge University Press

Jasanoff, S. (ed) (2004). *States of Knowledge: The Co-production of Science and the Social Order*. London: RoutledgeWynne, B. (1996). *A Reflexive View of the Expert-Lay Knowledge Divide. Risk, Environment and Modernity: Towards a New Ecology*. London: Sage, 44–83

References

Armstrong, A. and Banks. S. (2011). *Community-University Participatory Research Partnerships: Co-inquiry and Related Approaches*. Newcastle: Beacon NE, 2011.

Arnstein, S. (1969). 'A Ladder of Citizen Participation'. *Journal of the American Planning Association* 35(4): 216–24

Barrett, E. and Bolt, B. (2007). *Practice as Research*. Chippenham: I.B. Tauris and Co.

Coessens, K. Crispin, D. and Douglas, A. (2009). *The Artistic Turn: A Manifesto*. Ghent: The Orpheus Institute

Eikeland, O. (2012). 'Action Research – Applied Research, Intervention Research, Collaborative Research, Practitioner Research, or Praxis Research?' *International Journal of Action Research* 8(1): 9–44

Escott, H., Andrews, R., Marwood, K. and Pahl, K. (under review). 'Co-production: Processes and Practices of Research Without a Map'. *Research for All*

Facer, K. and Enright, B. (2016). *Creating Living Knowledge: The Connected Communities Programme and the Participatory Turn*. Bristol: AHRC Connected Communities Programme/University of Bristol

Gibson-Graham, J.K. (2008). 'Diverse Economies: Performative Practices for "Other Worlds"'. *Progress in Human Geography*, 1–20 DOI: 10.1177/0309132508090821

Hart, A. and Wolff, D. (2006). 'Developing Communities of Practice through Community-University Partnerships. *Planning, Practice and Research* 21(1): 121–38

Law, J. and Urry, J. (2004). 'Enacting the Social'. *Economy and Society* 33: 390–410

Pink, S. (2009) *Doing Sensory Ethnography*. London: Sage

Pink, S. (2015). *Doing Sensory Ethnography*, 2nd edition. London: Sage

Steiner. C.J. (2000). *Creative Collaboration*. Oxford: Oxford University Press

Weiss, C.H. (1997). 'Theory-based Evaluation: Past, Present, and Future'. *New Directions for Evaluation* 76: 41–55

SECTION 1
Understanding legacy in practice

ONE

Weighing value: who decides what counts?

Sophie Duncan and Kim Aumann

Introduction

This chapter is co-written by two people committed to adding the voice of community partners to the debate about the value of community–university research partnerships (CUPs). Our focus is on research partnerships and we are using the CUP acronym as shorthand. Within the UK there have been strong developments in supporting more sustained partnerships between universities and communities. The organisations we represent are at the forefront of these initiatives. Kim Aumann is a community practitioner with 12 years' experience of CUP working in the UK and abroad, and was involved in setting up the UK Community Partner Network (UKCPN), and Sophie Duncan is Deputy Director of the National Co-ordinating Centre for Public Engagement (NCCPE), which works to support universities to engage more effectively with the public, including providing international consultancy services and hosting the UKCPN.

We believe that tapping into the experience and perspectives of community partners can help us improve the benefits of CUP working (Aumann, Duncan and Hart, 2014). Our work is internationally linked, while having a UK focus. To proactively explore how to encourage, support and facilitate effective use of CUPs to benefit society, between us we have conducted focused consultations and events with community partners (and academics); met and spoken with hundreds of community partners both in the UK and internationally; participated in international networks, including Community Campus Partnerships for Health (CCPH), the Living Knowledge Network, Global University Network for Innovation, Community Based Research Canada, UNESCO Chairs for Community Based Research, and Global Alliance for Community Engaged Research; worked with research funders; and facilitated national CUP projects. It is this direct experience and our reflections on practice that we draw on here.

Our chapter is addressed to community partners and academics interested in CUP working. We are convinced that this way of working can produce more than individual partners can achieve on their own. However, we are conscious of the need to get better at articulating and evidencing the value and legacies of these ways of working if we are going to help protect the future of this form of knowledge creation and use. It is important that CUPs are an effective and appropriate use of public funding and that they do what they say they will do in a way that inspires confidence. In this chapter we offer some suggestions about ways in which their value might be evidenced and argue that developing a more reflective and effective evaluative culture within CUP working is critical to realising their value and sustaining their future.

Across the world there are great examples of CUP working (Hall, Tandon and Tremblay, 2015) and there is much to celebrate. However we think there are some challenging and important questions to consider and offer them here as the focus of our chapter:

- When exploring the value of CUPs, whose value are we talking about, and who decides what matters?
- Can the value of CUPs be evidenced and if so, how?
- When should CUPs be sustained or not?
- Is a CUP always the best way to realise the values claimed?
- Are there principles of good CUP working that are more likely to lead to relevant value?

We use the term 'community partner' throughout as a generic term to include anyone in a non-academic partner role in CUPs. While not the preferred term for some, we thought it was the best solution to finding a language that was quickly understandable.

Key resources for thinking about legacy

When we considered what might help us to understand legacy, we didn't immediately think of consulting academic journals. Instead, we gravitated towards the experience of those doing the work and looked for recorded case studies, stories and practical guidance tools. Even then it was hard to pin down, as conversations with community partners suggest that sometimes the legacy doesn't get traced, it was hidden, or people reported a myriad of connections that made it hard to contribute impact exclusively to partnership activity.

Aumann, K. and Duncan, S. (2015). Connected Communities Consultation event. 12 January

Aumann, K., Duncan, S. and Hart, A. (2014). 'What Have We Learnt? A Year On from the First UK Community Partner Summit.' *Gateways: International Journal of Community Research and Engagement.* [Online]June 19. 7:1

Centre for Social Justice and Community Action (2011). *Community-based Participatory Research: Ethical Challenges.* Centre for Social Justice and Community Action, Durham University

ESRC (2016). *Impact Toolkit – How to Maximise Impact.* http://www.esrc.ac.uk/research/impact-toolkit/developing-a-communications-and-impact-strategy/

Manners, P. and Duncan, S. (2017). *Evidencing the Impact of Engagement: An Analysis of the REF 2014 Case Studies.* Bristol: NCCPE

UKCPN (2012). *UK Community Partner Network Resources. Getting started, Potential Problems.* https://www.publicengagement.ac.uk/work-with-us/current-projects/community-partner-network/resources

Whose value are we talking about and who decides?

We have noticed that given most CUPs are supported by research funding there is a tendency to privilege the value of the partnerships as perceived by the Higher Education (HE) research community. This issue is not confined to the UK, and is often a feature of community–university partnerships. While clearly an essential part of CUP work, and to some degree explained by the fact that, in the UK at least, Principal Investigators accountable for projects must be academics, focusing just on the value to the HE research community can lead to a number of problems. For example, what the community partner values may be hidden or may not be recognised in an equitable way, or the way the research is assessed may fail to encompass the learning and knowledge created throughout the process of doing research together. Furthermore, there is a potential danger that privileging the HE researcher viewpoint could undermine the dynamics of the CUP and its work, and therefore the quality of the research done. Given the assessment of research excellence in the UK encompasses the notion of impact (HEFCE, 2014) it makes sense to us to consider whether more equitable consideration of all of the partners' views about the research impacts and value can lead to even more excellent research. There is a growing body of evidence to suggest that in order to develop high-quality research with impact, there is a need to find effective ways to partner others (ESRC, 2016).

One of the challenges is defining who the non-academic partners are. Many before us have struggled with this too. We find the CCPH's (2016) definition helpful:

> What we mean by community is dynamic and inclusive. There is no one definition of community. Community need not be defined solely by geography. It can refer to a group that self-identifies by age, ethnicity, gender, sexual orientation, disability, illness or health condition. It can refer to a common interest or cause, a sense of identification or shared emotional connection, shared values or norms, mutual influence, common interest, or commitment to meeting a shared need. Defining community in a community-campus partnership is more about the process of asking and answering key questions than about a strict definition of who is community or represents community ... the purpose of the partnership drives the definition, therefore each effort must ask for the definition of community. (CCPH, 2016)

Clearly there are a diverse range of communities that can be involved in CUPs, representing a variety of people, places and purposes. Communities can be formally and informally involved in CUPs, some may be individuals, groups or organisations named as partners, some may be involved as research participants, while others may be affected by the research but not directly involved. People can frequently be using the same terms to mean very different things. This messy area of definitional chaos makes exploring the dynamics of CUPs all the more difficult.

While academics may be driven by creating excellent research, with a pressure to evidence the value of their work through peer-reviewed publications or through an impact assessment process, community partners may have other priorities. We believe that it is equally important for the expectations and accountabilities of community partners to be made explicit and valued in the collaboration. In her work, Kim Aumann uses a simple framework to plan, monitor and test the potential changes that might occur at the individual, the organisational and the societal levels as a result of a specific intervention or project (Aumann, 2011). Building on this we developed a table to make visible the wide range of benefits that might accrue over time from a CUP (2016) working across these three areas.

Focusing specifically on community-based partners, Table 1.1 shows the benefits the CUP might include.

Table 1.1: Benefits of community–university partnerships

	Individuals	Organisations	Society
Skills	Learn and develop various research skills; research demystified	Integrate research activity appropriately into their way of operating	Positive impact of improved evidence-based service delivery
Knowledge	Affirm their expertise as they contribute to study and tacit knowledge is articulated and tested; gain new insights relevant to their work; broaden perspectives from drawing on other sources to contextualise experience	Develop areas of service delivery in response to research findings; reputation enhancing	Issue or theme represented competently at policy table
Confidence	Increased confidence and competence gained from both involvement in and knowledge generated by research study	Integrate learning from research findings into their strategic work; grow proficiency/confidence to champion the issue or theme	Changed policies or services at local and/or national level
Practice	Alter their practice as a result of new understandings from the research study	Embed new or improved activities or services as a result of research findings	Change in attitude about ways to support or respond to the group, issue or theme
Networks	Access new networks with shared interest or shared values, which enhances quality and support for the work; ideas and experiences shared with others	Increased social capital as new high-status HE supporters are secured; expertise enhanced and acknowledged	Improved recognition, increased understanding and awareness raised of profiled group, issue or theme
Funding and resources	Secure evidence to argue value of their work; daily activity and decision making supported via published documents	Secure additional evidence to improve funding applications; reports to share findings with colleagues	Review and reallocate government spending; published reports used to champion issue; outputs accessible to wider groups to inspire new ways of thinking

In our experience those actively participating in CUPs see value in this way of working (NCCPE, 2013a) (Martikke, Church and Hart, 2015) but what is interesting is where they locate and how they weight that value. This is often different for the partners involved. The framework provides a useful starting point for conversations between academics and community partners in the initial stages of planning a collaboration; as well as when considering or assessing the value of CUPs with those either directly involved in the research, research participants, or those likely to encounter and be affected by the research activity

We also need to recognise the powerful influence of the different cultures of academia and of community-based organisations, which can have an effect on individuals and the dynamics of these partnerships, including how people articulate their value. For example, the pressure on academics to be able to publish research, and to claim ownership of these outputs, sits in tension with the nature of the collaboration that has contributed to that research. In addition, many peers may not understand or value CUPs. The issues affecting how CUPs flourish and operate need to be addressed at a meta level – encouraging institutions to reward and recognise engaged research alongside more traditional forms of knowledge making (Hall, Tandon and Tremblay, 2015).

More positively, the potential of CUPs to change the attitudes and practices of academics or community-based colleagues is also important to recognise, while not assuming this is the main focal point of the interaction. For example individual researchers involved and invested in CUPs are a critical part of the academic landscape, offering a kind of seasoning to the academy by exploring different ways of knowledge making. This is a less well-recognised but important collective value they can offer the academy.

Mature CUPs tend towards delivering mutual benefit, with the academics and community partners working together to deliver outputs, outcomes and impacts that are relevant to each party. However when a new partnership develops between a community organisation and a research team, taking the time to consider what each partner needs from the partnership can be overlooked, with assumptions being made about where the value lies, and who will validate what matters. Community partners have reflected that there can be a tendency for the researchers to assume they are the final arbiters of assessing the value of a piece of work – which undermines the notion of equitable partnership working. It is therefore important to consider how at least those community partners directly involved in the partnership have a say in identifying or measuring the value of the research.

In addition to those formally involved in the partnership, there are many others who are influenced by the research process and outcomes who will also have a useful perspective on the value of the work undertaken. This includes members of the community involved indirectly in the project, who may well have strong views on if and how the work being undertaken has value to them, and to wider society. As the majority of CUP working is publically funded in the UK, and is focused on delivering excellent impactful research, the widening of the group of people able to assess this could be a useful way of improving the effectiveness of these ways of working.

For many involved in CUPs, value has to be meaningful to a wider group of people than those individuals invested in the project – not least the funders of the work. Therefore we need to seek ways to communicate and clarify the value. One of the challenges currently is that articulating the social value of a piece of work is more challenging than being able to articulate the economic value – which in the UK is really important to the Department of Business, Energy and Industrial Strategy, whose funding supports research. Without engaging in this, we run the risk of undermining the very approaches to engaged research that we believe matter. There is much universities can learn from attempts in the charitable sector to capture the impacts of their interventions, for example the work by Ní Ógáin, Lumley and Pritchard (2012).

Can the value of CUPs be evidenced?

So how do we evidence the benefits of this way of working – both to understand better and thereby improve what we are doing, but also to justify to others the funding invested? This is challenging territory and it is worth noting that while much value is explicit, some is implicit and less easy to articulate.

Lots of the people we talk to, both academics and community partners, are vehement about the value of this way of working, but really struggle to describe why it is so important. Strong values often drive their work and motivation to get involved and they can find it hard to realise the importance of evidencing something that to them is so very obvious. In turn they can struggle to ask hard questions about the effectiveness of this work. The current evaluation literacy in the sector is relatively low – with summative evaluations assessing activity at the point of intervention often being the primary focus of effort. Our language and tools of evaluation are not yet fit for purpose, especially when engaged in these more emergent complex ways of working. In 2012 a UK study concluded that evaluation of university public engagement in the UK was small scale and project based, with the primary focus on advocacy. The report called for a more rigorous, long-term approach to researching the dynamics of engagement, drawing on the breadth of disciplinary expertise (Facer, Manners and Agusita, 2012). A more recent global study of CUP drew a similar conclusion. With a few notable exceptions (for example Indonesia) there is little attempt to develop effective approaches to evaluating the social impact of CUPs (Hall, Tandon and Tremblay, 2015).

Unfortunately, much of the legacy of CUP working seems impossible to measure due to the resources available and the time frames afforded to measuring it. With funding strongly bound to the time frame of the grant, it is difficult to put in place mechanisms for assessing impacts that are realised long after the grant has been spent. This is aggravated by the fact that the CUPs will often be one contribution among a wide range of other factors that might lead to the legacy being claimed. The challenge of this can be seen in the recent UK Research Excellence Framework (REF) exercise. When asked to evidence the impact of their research, academics struggled to do so, in part because the request to evidence this impact was made retrospectively, and therefore few had collected the necessary evidence. The literature on assessing research impact identifies a host of other factors which make the ambition to identify impacts arising from research very difficult to claim definitively. The table in the box below (adapted for this chapter from the NCCPE's work (NCCPE, 2013a)) identifies just some of these challenges.

ATTRIBUTION: How to determine what specific intervention led to what specific impact

TIME LAGS: Impact can take a long time to show – many years in some cases

CHANGE OVER TIME: the nature of impact changes over time

DIFFUSION: the impact of the research becomes more diffuse over time as it permeates into society

ADDITIONALITY: what would have happened anyway if this specific research was not carried out?

DISENTANGLEMENT: how to be clear about the impact of your research, rather than your existing expertise or knowledge

DEPENDENCIES: many other activities, not derived from the research, are required for the research to make an impact

NON-POSITIVE IMPACTS are possible (but rarely considered) and any risks of achieving impact are not either

EXOGENOUS FACTORS: High quality and highly relevant research may not make an impact for reasons beyond the researcher's control

While the table is specifically created to consider impacts from the REF, the challenges of looking at how a CUP has generated value to all involved are similar.

How might that value be evidenced?

Evaluating the impact of collaborative research projects is currently very difficult to do in any meaningful way, as outlined above. However, if we are tasked with assessing the value of these ways of working, we would be wise to create a reflective culture, where evaluation tools are used intelligently to capture the significance of the changes being made. Following a global study of CUP working, Hall, Tandon and Tremblay (2015) conclude that evaluation is a critical step in developing effective CUP work.

As advocates of effective and appropriate use of evaluation, the NCCPE have developed a range of resources to support people to consider how best to use evaluation tools to inform their approach and assess its value. Through training people to develop their approach, it is clear that there is much more that needs to be done to inculcate the types of reflective practice needed to really evidence the value of these types of approach.

One critical dimension to developing more effective evaluation is considering the approach right at the start of a CUP project. This enables all those involved to make collective decisions as to where best to expend evaluative effort. Being clear about the purpose of an evaluation and whether, for example, it is to satisfy funding requirements, to learn about effective practice, or to research the appropriateness of particular ways of working in a given context, are specifics worth discussing and agreeing on.

Working together to develop a 'theory of change' is a valuable approach which can support partnership development. Community partners we have spoken to state that it is imperative to describe the aims, objectives, potential outputs, outcomes and impacts from a collaborative project at the beginning – and to do this together. By starting here, assumptions about how change happens, what matters, and how to recognise value are all on the table from the start of the project. This necessarily means that you need to invest time right at the beginning of the project, and continually reflect on how and whether your assumptions change as you work together. It also helps decide what types of methodology to use to assess how the process is working, and what value it has delivered. Done well, evaluation can provide a critical mirror by which to assess how the process might need to be adapted in light of evaluation findings. Given the often emergent nature of CUP work, the evaluation approach needs to be flexible enough to capture things that were not originally deemed important.

The issues at the heart of CUP working play out in evaluation, particularly with respect to power imbalances, previously acknowledged by others such as Hart (Hart et al, 2013). We have been sad to see many community partners unable to share their real experiences of CUP working within the formal evaluation processes that have been put in place. For instance, interviews with community partners to encourage them to reflect on their experiences are often held alongside the academic partner, and some people involved in these are anxious not to jeopardise the work or the relationship with the university, or inadvertently criticise a valued colleague. There are, as a consequence, community partner stories that don't get formally recorded. Reflecting on the tensions that exist in CUPs and how these might be worked with constructively provides useful pointers for ways to evidence the value of collaborative working. However, creating a reflective culture can prove challenging when the partners in a CUP have too much at stake to be able to honestly reflect on all aspects of the work.

One potential way of addressing this is to recognise the power differential in the partnership, and find effective tools to identify different expectations and provide formal opportunities to reflect constructively together on the collaboration. For example, a Memorandum of Understanding can help partners to develop a sense of their expectations from the partnership and regularly reviewing this provides a space for challenges to be faced. Many universities now employ engagement brokers, who can help provide a more effective space for community partners to reflect on what is happening and draw attention to challenges that are not being addressed effectively. There has been some useful work done by the UKCPN (CUPP, 2012) and CCPH (CCPH, 2015) in North America to highlight common issues in these ways of working, and the Productive Margins project has created 20 top tips for academics and community partners working together (Productive Margins, 2015). These tools help highlight the common nature of the challenges, open up things that are not working for either partner and can lead to creative solutions that maximise the potential of the partnership.

The REF attempted to lay out a framework where academics could evidence the impact of their research through providing an impact case study. These are now available for study online (HEFCE, 2016). The REF required academics to consider impact in terms of reach (how widely the impact was felt) and significance (how much difference was made to the beneficiaries). While clearly these are helpful parameters to consider, there was a concern that local CUP work could be undervalued as the reach is often local rather than national or international. This is compounded by an assumption that impact generation is a linear process, an 'outcome' from the activity rather than seeing it as a 'praxis – a collaborative process of critical reflection on reality in order to transform it'(Centre for Social Justice and Community Action, 2011).

We also need to be careful not to only value the things that can easily be measured. The work of the ESRC (2009) is helpful as it explores the potential use of proxy indicators of impact. These are things that can be measured at the time of the project that enable you to be more confident that the project will lead to impact. The use of these indicators encourages people to examine the dynamics of the process, and suggests that if the key ingredients are managed properly there is a much stronger likelihood that impact will be achieved in the long term.

The ESRC's *Taking Stock* report (ESRC, 2009) identified the following 'proxies':

- established relationships and networks with user communities
- involvement of research users at all stages of the research
- well-planned user-engagement and knowledge exchange strategies
- portfolios of research activity that build reputations with research users
- good infrastructure and management support
- where appropriate, the involvement of intermediaries and knowledge brokers as translators, amplifiers, network providers

Proxy indicators of impact are a real help when planning projects and making sense of whether and how they might lead to impact. They concentrate on the things that are within our control, and help us to ensure the processes we use are as effective as possible. They also help to address the issues that exist within partnership working as they provide a frame to think about how to develop effective ways of working that are most likely to achieve the desired outcome and impacts.

When to sustain or not sustain CUPs?

A key indicator of the value of the work done together could be whether the partnership is sustained. Plainly, an unanticipated outcome might be a community group so badly burned by the partnership that they no longer want to work with the university. However a long-term sustained partnership could be the most desired outcome, when the partnership has clearly led to significant value for both partners. Our work exploring CUPs has made us aware of how complex the area of sustainability is and in this section we explore some of the challenges.

Given it takes a lot of time to set up and build trusting links (most community partners say they totally underestimate the hours involved) ongoing partnerships represent good value for the community sector. Most organisations are not in a position to reinvest hours to build new partnerships every time they set out on a new piece of work.

While sustained partnerships indicate that participants believe there is value to their working together, this opens up wider questions about the equity in this type of working. To what extent should public funding be restricted to those people lucky enough to have found each other, and to what extent should there be access to other organisations that might be a better fit for the research partnership being explored? However, if CUPs were always comprised of partners new to this work it is unlikely that the issues of sharing power or resources more fairly would ever be addressed.

In addition, the changes being sought might be achieved through a one-off partnership and therefore the need to work in this way over multiple projects should not necessarily be a measure of success. Indeed, with vested interests from academics and community partners there is a danger people might sustain work that has already served its purpose. In contrast, working with the same partners over time can often be the best match, justifiably helpful and an efficient use of everyone's time and resources. This tension between the efficiency of longer-term sustained partnerships and equity in those accessing these opportunities is not easy to resolve. A healthy ecosystem would clearly support both.

We are also interested in whether there is a point when a partnership loses its value. Participating in a serial community–university research partnership could normalise people to the others' ways of thinking. For example, languages, codes of practice and ways of thinking might change to such an extent that partners would no longer be different enough to be challenging or contribute alternative ways of knowing. This is an interesting point to reflect on, as long-term sustained partnerships do help us get into the shoes of others. By considering how comfortable the partnership has become, it opens the question of how to introduce other people into the partnership to refresh it, while maintaining its value.

Is a CUP the best way?

Assessing the value of these ways of working, and exploring to what extent the various purposes have been achieved raises the question as to whether a CUP is always the best way. Some partnerships fail to ask the question and assume collaboration is the best every time, however CUPs can be very labour intensive, and while at their best achieve amazing things, at their worst can be inefficient and unfit for purpose. Therefore it is important in the early planning stages to consider whether the knowledge or changes sought by the individual partners are served well by working together, or whether a different approach could be more efficient or lead to more effective outcomes. Given CUPs may be a site of creative potential, whose value is realised in the doing, this is all the more difficult to do.

This also assumes capacity to explore these various options. For many community partners the promise of working collaboratively with a university outweighs the need to explore other mechanisms to achieve their ends, and even were they able to do so there is little guidance available. This begs the question, how can we support community partners and academics to decide whether a CUP is the right intervention for them? What questions should we be asking about the efficacy of any particular approach and its applicability to our context?

Were community partners to do a cost–benefit analysis of this way of working, many would avoid it altogether because it could prove an expensive way of getting some things done, particularly in the current economic climate. Measuring the extent to which the legacies sought from CUPs are proportionate to the investment in them is a significant challenge, especially given the different weighting people place on what has value.

One useful tool for CUPs could be Socially Modified Economic Value (SMEV), a technique which enables you to weight certain outcomes based on the purpose and aims of your organisation (Kelly, 2012). The technique enables you to quantify any intervention in monetary terms – for example time spent doing consultancy is costed on the basis of how much it would cost to employ a consultant for that time. Rather than taking this as the 'value' of that piece of work, a social modification is employed, which allows you to value some things more than others, depending on alignment with your institution's mission and role. Applying SMEV to CUPs could be helpful because it would be a clear way to recognise the different value placed on things by the university and the community partner.

A related challenge is that CUPs miss out multiple actors who could help inform long-term systemic change – with the partnerships sometimes rushing to fill a perceived gap in service which other organisations, not participating in the project, are already seeking to serve. If one of the sought legacies is change in society, in our understanding and practice, or in policy then a CUP might be one part of a much more sophisticated partnership that brings a range of different stakeholders to tackle the challenge together. While collaborative research can help shift and achieve some changes, it can be more effective if perceived as part of a bigger jigsaw with other players, so that lots of things happen simultaneously with parallel processes all focused on the same issue at the same time.

Principles of good CUP working that lead to value

So far in this chapter we have explored the challenges of assessing the value of CUPs. Here we want to share some of the positive steps that can help people create the conditions for generating value that are relevant to all those invested in the project.

We have seen, written and contributed to many guides to partnership working (for example NCCPE, 2011). However many of them try to set out guidelines for a trouble-free partnership and fail to value the culture of difference. When looking back on a partnership it is easy to look at times of conflict as times to be managed and overcome, and then glossed over. However one of the most effective ways to develop new ways of thinking, knowing and doing is to work with people who have different perspectives and insights. This inevitably is difficult and will lead to conflict. In our experience, disunity or conflict can be sites of great creative potential and – if handled well – can build strength in the partnership.

So what tips would we offer community partners and academics about how to maximise the possibility of successful CUPs that also maximise the potential to leave a positive legacy? Our suggestions are in the box that follows.

Guidance for understanding and creating legacy

Tip Number One: Be clear and make space to understand the purpose of others, as well as your own. Be prepared for these conversations across the duration of the partnership, and try to focus on the mutual benefit of working together. Don't assume what you value will be the same as what your partner values, and respect that difference.

Tip Number Two: Plan out what you are looking to do together, and the potential outputs, outcomes and desired impact from the activity. Review these regularly, using evaluation as a tool to help inform your approach. Make sure you don't miss unexpected outcomes or impacts from your work together! It can help to recognise that others (your partners and your colleagues) may have more knowledge of evidencing impact than you do – and draw on their expertise and experience.

Tip Number Three: Consider what the partnership might look like at the end of the project. Are you hoping that it will be sustained, and if so what do you hope it will go on to achieve? Start out as though you expect to be working together forever as it might influence how you interact at the start!

Tip Number Four: Consider the proxy indicators of impact when planning your project: to what extent are you ensuring the processes you are using are appropriate to the impact you seek to have?

Tip Number Five: If you are looking for a change, make sure you are aware of other people working in this space, and build appropriate links where you can – otherwise you could inadvertently waste effort duplicating the work of others, or miss out on key insights that would be invaluable to the process.

Tip Number Six: Change happens across all levels of a partnership – and the impacts are not always easy to quantify or link back to the original CUP. This is true of all projects that seek to have impact over a long period of time. It helps to track what you can – capturing the outcomes of specific interventions; changes in ways of thinking within the individual team members and so on. It can be surprisingly difficult to remember these once the project ends.

Tip Number Seven: Terminology can be misleading. Make sure the terms you are using are understood across the partnership, and be prepared to ask your partners what they mean when they use particular words.

Tip Number Eight: Think about the type of partnership that best suits your resources and ambitions. Consider the power at play within your partnership, and to what extent you want to have equal agency in the partnership. While co-production is currently in vogue, remember that there are a range of types of partnership – and pick the one that's right for all involved. Consider articulating your expectations in a Memorandum of Understanding (or similar) and review this regularly.

Tip Number Nine: Community–university research partnerships are only one mechanism by which changes can happen – so consider carefully whether the investment of time and energy in this type of approach is right for your context.

Conclusion

CUPs provide a particular way of working and can create significant positive outcomes – at an individual, organisational and societal level. However these cannot be taken for granted. We need to develop a more effective way to value these ways of working for all those involved – to ensure that collaborative research processes lead to high-quality research with impact. So how can we find better ways of deepening our own understanding of what makes for valuable CUPs – and how can we convince funders and policy makers to better incentivise and resource these?

While we recognise that 'not everything that can be counted counts, and not everything that counts can be counted' (Cameron, 1963) we should not be daunted by the task ahead. We need to move towards an honest and reflective culture of evaluation, ensuring we think about this from the start of a project, and utilise evaluation tools effectively to help us navigate this territory.

There are several things that could help us do this. Some are project focused, supporting more effective ways of partnering across the lifetime of a project. These might include co-writing of research funding applications, time spent at the outset planning projects and evaluation strategies to ensure that all partners have had the opportunity to articulate the outputs, outcome and impacts that they value; and ensuring that the project team regularly reflect on this throughout the project.

Some are more systemic – linked to how this work is funded, and tensions between collaborative working and the highly competitive culture within the academy that makes evidencing the impact of CUP working problematic. Inevitably, these are less easy for project teams to address locally, but they do need to be recognised. Collectively, we need to find ways to recognise that community partners have much to contribute to the process of identifying and measuring the value of collaborative research. Requirements to involve and reimburse them need to be stipulated by funders to lead to the types of change we seek.

Some of the challenges are about how we articulate what value we seek, how we create a culture where this value can be realised, and how we measure it. Given that the legacies of these ways of working operate at multiple scales, we need to ensure that we consider what we might expect to change at each of these levels – recognising that our assumptions about how change might happen may not be valid, and may need to be renewed and refreshed as we do the project. Creating a space for these conversations at the outset of a project will enable partners to consider whether working collaboratively has the potential to deliver more value than working in other ways, or with other people.

A key opportunity for the community is to consider how to platform difficult conversations, without the concern that the relationship will be adversely affected in the long term. By inculcating a reflective culture, and utilising some of the tools available that highlight common issues of these ways of working, we encourage partners to find the space to reflect together on how their practice is supporting or undermining those that they are working with. By recognising that working across difference is necessarily difficult, we may open up the potential to have these conversations in a more effective way.

Engagement brokers can play a critical role in this. Those working in these ways formally and informally are a critical part of the engagement ecosystem – ensuring that partnerships are better supported throughout the process (Hall, Tandon and Tremblay, 2015: 274).

Measuring value is a challenge but help is available. The UK academy is currently reflecting on the outcomes of the 2014 REF exercise, where evidence for impact was provided for a range of claimed impacts arising from research. Proxy indicators of impact are also a real help when planning projects and making sense of whether and how they might lead to impact. One key thing that it helps to consider is if and how the partnership might be sustained once the funded part of the programme is over. However, we should not assume that sustainability is always an effective measure of success. The challenges are replicated across the world, with approaches to the evaluation of CUP working being developed in a range of contexts. In partnership with colleagues at the University of Victoria in Canada, the NCCPE has developed an international framework that highlights the critical need for evaluating impact expertise from different country contexts to be shared and to build a stronger base of tools and evidence that can be utilised to support this work (NCCPE, 2013b) and *Research for All* (NCCPE, 2016), a new open access international journal, has been launched to share theoretical and practical reflections on the nature of engaged research.

CUPs thrive on difference (different ways of being, knowing, doing and seeing the world) and recognising this is key to developing effective ways of working. Our work has convinced us of the huge potential in CUPs. We have seen how they can generate multiple legacies – embodied in individuals, performances, practices, publications, networks; tangible and intangible; short lived or long lived; important to one or important to all; societal, organisational or personal. These types of legacy are passed between people, they grow and adapt at every interaction – and have potential to make a positive difference in the world.

We are also clear that we still have much work to do to find better ways to ensure all types of value and legacy can be recognised and valued, respecting different ways of making sense of the world. CUPs remain – thrillingly, sometimes frustratingly – work in progress.

References

Aumann, K. (2011). Project Decision Checklist. *Internal document*. Brighton: Amaze

Aumann, K. and Duncan, S. (2015). *Connected Communities Consultation*. NCCPE

Aumann, K., Duncan, S. and Hart, A. (2014) 'What Have We Learnt? A Year On from the First UK Community Partner Summit'. *Gateways: International Journal of Community Research and Engagement*. [Online] June 19. 7:1

Cameron, B. (1963). *Introduction to Causal Sociological Thinking*. Random House

CCPH (2015). *Principles of Community University Partnerships*. https://ccph.memberclicks.net/principles-of-partnership

CCPH (2016). *FAQ*. Retrieved 03 12, 2016 from CCPH. https//ccph.memberclicks.net/faq

Centre for Social Justice and Community Action (2011). *Community-based Participatory Research: Ethical Challenges*. Centre for Social Justice and Community Action, Durham University

CUPP. (2012). *Working in partnership with local communities*. Retrieved 3 12, 16 from NCCPE: http://www.publicengagement.ac.uk/do-it/who-work-with/working-with-local-communities

ESRC (2009). *Taking Stock: A Summary of the ESRC's Work to Evaluate the Impact of Research on Policy and Practice.* http://www.esrc.ac.uk/files/research/evaluation-and-impact/taking-stock-a-summary-of-esrc-s-work-to-evaluate-the-impact-of-research-on-policy-and-practice/

ESRC (2016). *Impact Toolkit – How to Maximise Impact.* http://www.esrc.ac.uk/research/impact-toolkit/

Facer, K., Manners, P. and Agusita, E. (2012). *Towards a Knowledge Base for University-Public Engagement: Sharing Knowledge, Building Insight, Taking Action*, Bristol: NCCPE

Hall, B., Tandon, R. and Tremblay, C. (2015). *Strengthening Community University Research Partnerships: Global Perspectives.* Victoria: University of Victoria Press

Hart, A., Davies, C. Aumann, K., Wenger, E., Aranda, K., Heaver, B. and Wolff, D. (2013). 'Mobilising Knowledge in Community-university Partnerships: What Does a Community of Practice Approach Contribute?' *Contemporary Social Science: Journal of the Academy of Social Sciences* 8(3): 278–91.

HEFCE (2014) *REF: Assessment Framework and Guidance on Submissions.* London

HEFCE (2016). *REF Case Study Database.* http://impact.ref.ac.uk/CaseStudies/

Kelly, U. (2012). *Through a Glass Darkly.* UK: NCCPE

Manners, P. and Duncan, S. (2016). *Evidencing the Impact of Engagement: An Analysis of the REF 2014 Case Studies.* NCCPE

Martikke, S. Church, A. and Hart, A. (2015). *Greater Than the Sum of Its Parts: What Works in Sustaining Community-university Partnerships.* Greater Manchester Center for Voluntary Organisation/Imagine

NCCPE (2011). *Working in partnership.* http://www.publicengagement.ac.uk/do-it/working-partnership

NCCPE (2013a). *Measuring Impact for the REF.* NCCPE

NCCPE (2013b). *Draft International Framework for Collaboration.* NCCPE. http://www.publicengagement.ac.uk/sites/default/files/publication/draft_framework_for_international_collaboration_april_2014_0.pdf

NCCPE (2016). *Research for All.* UCL Institute of Education, IOE Press and NCCPE. http://www.publicengagement.ac.uk/work-with-us/current-projects/research-all-journal

Ní Ógáin, E., Lumley, T. and Pritchard, D. (2012). *Making an Impact: Impact Measurement among Charities and Social Enterprises in the UK.* http://www.thinknpc.org/publications/making-an-impact/

Productive Margins. (2015). *Top tips for Academics and Community Organisations.* www.productivemargins.ac.uk)

UKCPN (2012). *UK Community Partner Network Resources. Getting Started, Potential Problems.* http://www.publicengagement.ac.uk/work-with-us/uk-community-partner-network

Evaluating legacy: the who, what, why, when and where of evaluation for community research

Peter Matthews, Janice Astbury, Julie Brown, Laura Brown, Steve Connelly and Dave O'Brien

Introduction

In this research we understood legacy in terms of how the projects served the community involved and delivered outcomes for them. We sought to use evaluation to understand this legacy. Within policy analysis, evaluation studies have a long history of extensive methodological and theoretical work. Over 60 years, a whole academic industry of policy evaluation has emerged. Much of the literature is dominated by epistemological debates regarding the measurement of change and causation. For instance, while methodologies such as the randomised controlled trial (RCT) dominate the mainstream, and are seen as the 'gold standard' among some scholars (Haynes et al, 2012) and bodies such as the UK Treasury and UK Civil Service (Government Social Research Unit, 2007; HM Treasury, 2011), there is also a broad critical literature highlighting the methodological and epistemological weaknesses of such approaches (Pawson and Tilley, 1997). As will be explored below, evaluation and evaluative approaches make us focus our attention on ontological and epistemological questions about researcher positionality, power and knowledge, how we understand social objects, and how we understand and interpret causation.

This contrasts with ways the legacy of academic research may traditionally be evaluated, for instance through the number and quality of journal papers submitted for audit exercises such as the Research Excellence Framework in the UK (see Introduction to this book and Research Excellence Framework 2012). The outputs of research co-produced with communities, such as the projects in focus discussed below, often fit uneasily within the audit regimes of contemporary academic practice (Pain et al, 2011). In evaluating the co-produced research, our research created an artificial experiment, as many evaluations do, to consider the strengths and limitations of academic-led evaluative studies, and the strengths and limitations of a study led by community partners supported by a university-employed researcher. It thus had two purposes – first, to deliver substantive evaluations of three earlier, co-produced, social 'interventions' and secondly, to compare different approaches to evaluation. In this chapter we do two things. First, we report on the findings of the evaluations to explore what the legacies of co-produced research are. Secondly, we use the collective reflection on doing evaluation to provide a rich account of how we might embed evaluation into community co-produced research.

Ultimately, we argue that evaluation for community research should be 'utilisation-focused'. Patton (2008) argued that the success of an evaluation should be judged primarily by how it is used and it should be designed to meet the needs of users. An evaluation of legacy should thus serve the community involved, helping them make good decisions and maximise the benefits of their activities to as many people as possible. Extending this, we also suggest the key questions that evaluation makes you ask – are we making a positive difference and how? – should be part of the ethical practice of research co-produced with communities. If ethical research is premised on causing no harm, evaluation, and particularly embedded developmental evaluation, takes this further to become an ethics in action: identifying potential harm, and identifying positive benefits that can be maximised.

Key resources for thinking about legacy

We used evaluation to understand legacy. This opened up a focus on what specific outcomes were developed within the community that co-produced the research. It also led to a consideration of causation and attribution: how strong was the evidence base for saying the projects in focus had caused the resulting change, or might cause change in future?

Patton, M.Q. (2008). *Utilization-Focused Evaluation*. London: SAGE Publications

Pawson, R. and Tilley, N. (1997). *Realistic Evaluation*. London: Sage

Mayne, J. (2008). *Contribution Analysis: An Approach to Exploring Cause and Effect*. Maccarese (Fiumicino), Italy: Institutional Learning and Change (ILAC) Initiative

The 'problem' with evaluation

There are two challenges in taking an evaluative approach to co-produced research: an epistemological challenge around identifying causation; and an ontological challenge regarding the status of evaluative knowledge. Before we consider these challenges, we should state there are practical reasons why evaluation is a useful tool for community co-produced research. For instance, funders and academic partners usually find it useful to know if particular funding or methodologies were effective in attaining their aims and outcomes. If an intervention was based on academic theory or research, an evaluation would also add to academic knowledge by testing underlying theoretical predictions. Community actors may also want to be able to judge whether to pursue future opportunities for collaboration with academic partners. These community actors are likely to be primarily engaged in action on the ground and their main focus is on how to continue to do effective work in their communities, that is, to deliver positive outcomes for individuals and groups to improve their well-being – and so evaluation is, or can be, of direct use to them to inform their planning.

Despite this potential, evaluation is often seen as anathema to co-produced research. One of the reasons is that methodologies such as RCT have increasingly come to dominate evaluation, seen as the 'Gold Standard' (Haynes et al, 2012). Derived from testing of medical interventions, RCTs can focus solely on simple interventions, determining causality, but in a simplistic way. A key critique of this sort of evaluation is that it presumes X intervention causes Y outcome. It might be that B factor also causes Y outcome, but under this methodological paradigm, B is seen as a problem and must be controlled for (Pearce et al, 2015). Social interventions, and the types of interventions that might be developed in co-produced research, are messy and complex, seeking to deliver numerous outcomes in complex contexts: A, B, C, X and n number of contextual variables might help or hinder the development of a Y outcome. Causal mechanisms not considered by the initial designers of the intervention might be at work, or feedback loops might be supporting, or preventing, the delivery of outcomes (Pawson and Tilley, 1997).

Thus the key epistemological challenge in all evaluations is identifying attribution; that is identifying that an intervention caused a particular outcome. The typical RCT achieves this by controlling for as many possible external influences as possible. At the end of a well-designed RCT, the outcomes *must be* caused by the intervention or variables that cannot be easily measured – the intangibility of the relationship between individuals or communities often falls into this category. In social interventions, this latter category is often extensive and has led to approaches such as realist evaluation or contribution analysis (Pawson and Tilley, 1997; Patton, 2012). These approaches aim to develop a plausible story that can identify attribution, or just some contribution. For example, Patton (2012) suggests the aim of a contribution analysis should be to produce a plausible argument such as a lawyer would provide in court.

As we discuss below, different approaches to evaluation can resolve some of the epistemological challenges of attribution within interventions in complex systems. However, the ontological challenges of evaluation – the main problem for many people – are more difficult to overcome. Essentially this is a problem of power: when an evaluator is appointed, they are put in a position of power. They have the authority to decide whether a project or intervention is successful or not, and often whether it should continue to receive funding.[1] More subtly, evaluation can become embedded within organisational practices with perverse effects. As Colebatch (1995) suggests, evaluation can become part of organisational culture, going on to frame behaviours. For instance, as suggested in Chapter Eight, for many in academia the REF has become this sort of evaluative practice, distorting priorities in contradictory ways. This aspect of power makes evaluation seem contrary to the values and ethics of co-produced research.

Yet at its heart, evaluation harks back to an essential practice of the public sphere – to make people accountable for their actions and provide a reflexive critique – asking the very basic question of who is accountable to whom, how and for what? Evaluation also bring things into social reality – it makes aspects of an intervention that might have been unexplored visible and thus a subject for discussion (O'Brien and Lockley, 2015). Ordinarily in policy evaluation it is a project that is accountable to a public imagined as taxpayers in a consumerist role wanting value for money. It is this that is often so problematic about evaluation – the endless evaluation associated with meagre funding that is the bane of community organisations across the world is testimony to this.[2] However, rather than blaming individuals or organisations for failure, good evaluative practice, as elaborated here, allows a shared accountability to be developed between communities and professionals (Durose and Richardson, 2013).

Importantly for co-produced research the core questions at the heart of evaluation open up new arenas for reflexive practice. For example, in co-produced research, webs of accountability are complex: researchers are accountable to their universities, the research councils funding them, to ethics committees, and disciplinary norms and standards (Beebeejaun et al, 2015). Community organisations are accountable to their boards, funders and wider community. Opening up questions around aims, definitions and success criteria helps surface these issues and develop reflexive practice. Ultimately, in the pragmatic tradition (see Chapter Five), there is nothing inherently wrong with asking 'is this the right thing to do?'. In fact, it should be a central part of a praxis that aims to minimise harm.

In the rest of this chapter, we discuss the evaluative practices we deployed to explore how these epistemological and ontological tensions played out in evaluating the interventions delivered by co-produced research.

What we did

In understanding legacy, we sought to address some of the critiques of evaluation. We aimed both to provide knowledge of what had worked in terms of the projects in focus, and to answer the methodological question of which approach(es) to evaluation produced the most useful knowledge to community partners and why. We therefore created an artificial experiment, running concurrently an academic evaluation, made up of four sub-projects, and a community-led evaluation. In a somewhat artificial fashion, the academics used their disciplinary epistemological backgrounds to frame the focus of their evaluation without a consideration of what the community partners might need, or want to understand. In practice, this meant the academic evaluators planning their evaluations without regular input from the community partners, although there was initial input so the team knew what they were evaluating. Further, one of the team (Matthews) was heavily involved in the research that produced the projects in focus, a point discussed further below. However, the disciplinary background of the academics framed the questions that would be asked and the methods used to collect data.

For the community-led evaluation, community partners were supported to define their own problems and work with a researcher to explore their own lines of inquiry and methods. Our projects were centred on an area called Wester Hailes, which is south-west of Edinburgh, in Scotland. Wester Hailes includes a large housing estate and on statistical measures is one of the most deprived neighbourhoods in Scotland. We involved a number of community partners from the neighbourhood. These community partners had all been involved in the previous projects: WHALE Arts, a local community development and arts organisation; Wester Hailes Health Agency a voluntary sector organisation tackling health inequalities; local housing provider Prospect Community Housing Association (Prospect CHA); and a local community activist.

A logic modelling workshop among the community partners determined the evaluation focus and questions. Logic models are a common tool in project management and evaluation in many sectors, helping partners in a project consider what outcomes they want to achieve over the short, medium and longer terms and then linking specific inputs (money, people and so on) through to outputs (a specific intervention), while considering the evidence that links these to outcomes. These can be produced by individuals – this was the experience of the community partners who had used logic models before[3] – in this case, however, the logic model was produced by a facilitated workshop with the community partners. This immediately surfaced assumptions about what the projects were meant to be doing and why and it allowed different perspectives to surface within the group. The logic model thus helped guide the evaluation process and the workshop itself helped to create a more reflexive space within the evaluation process. It did not confine the evaluation to a linear process as a traditional logic modelling exercise by an individual might do. Rather than focusing partners on a small number of strategic outcomes, it allowed for a multiplicity of outcomes and different outputs (some spun off from the original project but not directly attributable) to be identified.

Table 2.1 outlines the contrasts between the questions the academic evaluations and the community-based evaluation sought to ask of the projects in focus. The different standpoints of the evaluators, or evaluation teams, is also apparent. The box that follows outlines the projects that we were evaluating.

Table 2.1: Comparison of academic and community evaluation questions

Community evaluation	Academic evaluation
Have the projects in focus helped revive local democracy and engagement?	*Engagement evaluation*: what were the barriers to wider citizen engagement being delivered through the projects in focus? (Peter Matthews)
To what extent have the projects in focus helped develop personal and community resilience?	*Well-being evaluation*: did the projects in focus improve the health and well-being of local residents? (Laura Brown)
To what extent has the community participated in the projects in focus?	*Cultural value*: what was the cultural value of the projects in focus for the local community? (Julie Brown)
To what extent have the projects in focus and the projects that delivered them helped develop partnership working and how?	*Partnerships*: how did the projects in focus help the community partners develop external partnerships and lever in resources and influence? (Dave O'Brien)

Projects in focus in this chapter

Digital totem pole: This was a 5 metre-high wooden totem pole erected in Wester Hailes, a neighbourhood of Edinburgh, Scotland, in 2012. It included 'quick response' (QR) codes so people could access information about the neighbourhood from smartphones. The idea came from the community partners to an earlier project and it was carved as part of a community workshop in 2011 and raised in 2013.

Code books: These booklets described routes of social history walks around the neighbourhood and were produced by a local community activist with an interest in the history of the neighbourhood working with an academic researcher. They also included QR codes that took people to galleries of historical photographs of the area provided by the Royal Commission on the Ancient and Historical Monuments of Scotland. They were distributed through partner agencies in the neighbourhood and the local library.

The Digital Sentinel: The Digital Sentinel was an online 'hyperlocal' or neighbourhood-focused news source, inspired by the previous community newspaper, *The Wester Hailes Sentinel*. This ceased publication in 2008 when funding was withdrawn by the City of Edinburgh Council. The Digital Sentinel began in 2013. The idea came, again, from the community partners, supported by the resources, expertise and enthusiasm of academic partners.

From There to Here ...: This was a social history Facebook page set up by Prospect CHA in 2011 allowing people to comment on historic photos of Wester Hailes. This emerged prior to the co-produced projects but became integral to their operation and thinking about them.

Valuing Different Perspectives aimed for equality of status and resources between the two approaches to evaluation. The community evaluation had the resources of a full-time researcher. The £10,000 that was allocated to the community evaluation to support the research was matched by a similar sum in the academic evaluation to cover travel and accommodation for the academics. The community researcher assisted the academic evaluations, for example in organising and assisting with focus groups and interviews. The size of the team of academics on the academic evaluations meant their resources were stretched further and practical challenges such as travelling distances and other commitments meant they could not commit fully. This is a finding in itself – to successfully know what outcomes co-produced research is producing an evaluation needs to be adequately resourced. If, as we suggest below, evaluation should be a core part of ethical co-produced research with communities, then resources are needed for this.

A final stage was two workshops held with community partners to present the findings of the evaluations. This allowed for collective reflection on how the community and the academic evaluators had captured legacy and then what the further legacy of the evaluations could be. Final interviews with the community partners were also carried out to understand what they had got out of the evaluations and what lessons they had learnt.

What we found out and how

Although the academic and community evaluations came from different perspectives, many key findings were shared. In this section we outline what these were – the legacy of the previous co-produced community research projects – and explore how knowledge of these outcomes was created in the different evaluations. The findings covered three areas: place making; partnership working, both internally and externally; and engagement.

Place-making outcomes

Both academic and community evaluations found that the totem pole had place-making value. The well-being evaluation found that, of all the projects in focus, it had been noticed by some residents, with a high familiarity score. Residents who engaged in a focus group appreciated it, noting it had not been vandalised and as one said: "the young ones like it, they think it's, 'cool', is the word?" There was no evidence of negative feelings towards the totem pole. It also had recognised potential to improve perceptions of the area to outsiders. The evaluation of cultural value found that community partners highlighted that after being in a prominent location for three years the totem pole had not been vandalised at all, taken as anecdotal evidence that it was either valued, or was not broadly recognised. The evidence could not definitively say either way, but there was not substantial evidence of negative feelings towards the totem pole. This suggested that the totem pole might have had a number of different values ascribed to it by different people (many not necessarily picked up by the evaluations) that were positive for the community. The well-being evaluation also suggested that these place-making activities were showing some evidence of increased place attachment, which could contribute to increased health and well-being among residents. However, the totem pole had fallen short in terms of linking online stories of the neighbourhood to the totem pole itself.

The community evaluation identified some indirect effects from the social history activities on place identity and attachment. Many people in Wester Hailes expressed a strong and positive connection to the neighbourhood and it is probable that the opportunities offered by the initiatives to tell and share stories, and come together in a range of ways, had reinforced this sense of place and community. As discussed below, this was not the experience of all in the community. Despite differences in data collection methods, and questions asked at the outset, between the evaluations, there were few substantive differences in findings in terms of place-making outcomes. The academic-led evaluations used specific methods of data collection (a postal survey, focus groups, interviews) and the community evaluation used this data supplemented by further ethnographic data from observation, less-formal interviews and being in the neighbourhood.

Partnership working

A finding across the evaluations was that working together on the original projects served to cement collaboration among local organisations. The external funding and support to plan and carry out complex projects over several years left a legacy of strong relationships and potential for future collaborations. The existing constellation of anchor organisations provided a base for developing broader community-wide partnership, where the existing group of partners acted as inspiration, backbone and facilitator. The elite interviews academic evaluation demonstrated that partnership with the academic collaborators on the original project raised the national profile of the neighbourhood, community partners and the projects in focus. This was through the social networks of academic partners and the legitimacy afforded by these connections. Outputs, such as photographs of the totem pole, featured prominently in documents produced by the funder. Additional connections were made by the community organisations leading to further research partnerships. The collective process of reflection garnered through the evaluation also revealed that the community partners felt empowered to ask directly for resources from academic partners as part of co-producing research proposals.

The academic support for the original projects in focus also contributed to making a collaborative, open, flexible and thoughtful space. The story of one of the projects that led to the totem pole, recorded through the academic evaluations and the workshops, is a good example of this. From an original idea of using the online concept of 'hacking' applied to understanding offline community relations and practices, the projects in focus evolved in emergent ways. An initiative premised on the potential of 'community hacking' stayed true to its nature by being continually hacked as new relationships and opportunities surfaced. The outcome of this was the creation of the totem pole. One of the earlier community hacking activities was a 'memory shed', where archival photographs inspired people to record their memories. The memories were then linked to the photographs using QR codes leading to the recorded memories on a website 'Tales of Things'. The full title Tales of Things and Electronic Memory was abbreviated as TOTeM; this led to musing about a totem pole and ultimately one being carved and erected in the neighbourhood.

One key difference between the academic and community evaluations was what was immediately done with the knowledge created. When the findings on partnership and collaboration were reported by the academic evaluations it provided a plausible story that the community partners could recognise, but little else happened with the knowledge – it may become useful if it helps justify future co-produced research. In comparison, when the community evaluation identified good partnership working it could build on this, extending the partnership working. The resource of an individual's time (the community researcher) enabled relationships with SCORE Scotland, a local group that works with the black and minority-ethnic community, to be strengthened.

Engagement

Finally the evaluations produced knowledge on the extent of community engagement with the original projects in focus. Ultimately, all the evaluations identified a low level of digital engagement with the projects in focus. This had been tacitly noted by the community partners prior to the evaluation. What is interesting here is what the range of methods used in the evaluations tell us about the nature of evaluation and the role and status of knowledge.

Through a postal survey the well-being evaluation identified very low engagement with all aspects of the projects in focus. However, the response rate to the survey itself was very low: of the 500 questionnaires that were distributed with the housing association newsletter and rent statements, only 22 were returned. During the reflective workshop discussions, the community partners highlighted that the questionnaire, with a lengthy statement on the purposes of the study and consent and confidentiality, was probably alienating to many people. These two factors highlight how difficult engaging a wider community in co-produced research can be, particularly in a deprived neighbourhood. It also highlights the necessity of embedding researchers within communities for evaluation so they can learn more about what research processes are most effective.

The community evaluation and the well-being evaluation also found that efforts to digitally engage residents had not been successful. Many active citizens in the community continued to make little use of email let alone newer social networking sites like Twitter or QR codes. Some contributors to the Digital Sentinel did not go online to read it. While time banks and other 'sharing economy' mechanisms are expanding worldwide using digital platforms, the local West Edinburgh Time Bank operated through face-to-face meetings and phone calls. The projects in focus were further complicated by the use of a medium most appealing to younger people to address issues of greater concern to an older demographic. There were many, mainly young, people in Wester Hailes who were regularly online but appeared to engage in gaming and social networking without links to local engagement. Some respondents pointed out that ICT and social history were a challenging combination, with older people being interested in the latter while younger people are more skilled in the former.

Unlike the community evaluation, the academic evaluation of engagement in the Digital Sentinel could put this lack of engagement in a broader context. It accessed survey data showing widespread digital engagement across Scotland, including using smartphones, but a clear socio-economic digital divide: those in low-income households, older people, people who live in deprived neighbourhoods and people who socially-rent their homes had lower rates of smartphone ownership and access to broadband internet (Ofcom, 2013; Scottish Government, 2014; Matthews, 2015). This is a similar finding to that of the community evaluation, but it provided an understanding of why people were not engaged. The lack of digital engagement was an outcome of broader socio-economic inequalities and barriers. The community evaluation just understood this as a lack of digital engagement without further elaboration as to why this was the case.

How useful were the evaluations?

The contrast between the findings on engagement brings us to consider the usefulness of different types of evaluation. Four of the evaluations sought to understand community engagement: the community evaluation, the engagement evaluation; the cultural value evaluation; and the well-being evaluation, as discussed. The well-being evaluation sought objective knowledge (through a survey) that the digital engagement initiatives had, or had not, been successful. Both the community evaluation and engagement evaluation began from some degree of immersion and co-production with the community (Matthews had been involved in co-producing the projects in focus). Therefore both of these evaluations could accept the premise from the community partners that the projects in focus had little wider engagement. This could be said without causing hurt by saying 'you have already failed in your intentions' as a degree of trust and embeddedness had already been established. Unlike in the previous research, Matthews initially tried to maintain a degree of separation from the community partners, as a purely academic-led evaluation. Therefore the engagement evaluation focused on what the barriers were to wider engagement and sustainability within hyperlocal web-based news services, learning from other successful projects in focus.

The community evaluation, accepting the failure to engage, could use the immersion within the neighbourhood and close working with the community partners to discuss possible activities and small experiments to increase engagement. If these were successful then they could be rolled out. If they were not successful then the question became, how could we learn from this failure? What barriers to engagement were there? This focus on barriers to engagement in these two evaluations showed that barriers for engaging with the Digital Sentinel hyperlocal news service were high for most people. The earlier projects in focus had presumed the technology itself would overcome these barriers, but this was not the case and further support was required. This helped support an application for ongoing funding for a development worker and a different approach that recognised and overcame these barriers.

Evaluation as a developmental and embedded practice

The discussion above on the power of evaluations might suggest that, if evaluations by academic experts are oppressive to communities – judging their activities as 'good' or 'bad' – then communities should be empowered to challenge findings. This flipping of power relations was present when the evaluations were presented to community partners. The academic leads for the research reported that they felt more nervous presenting their findings to community partners than the lead for the community evaluation did. Stating difficult findings, such as that low levels of engagement by community members suggested the projects in focus had 'failed', was a difficult message to communicate, particularly for someone who had parachuted into the neighbourhood to tell people this, without a working relationship of trust.

To conclude, we want to take a productive approach to evaluation, using the contrast between the community evaluation and the academic evaluations to recommend the use of evaluation as a way to create and embed processes of group learning within co-produced research. This is a fruitful way first to understand what the legacy of co-produced research is, and secondly to maximise that legacy. However, there are differences in the possible approaches to evaluation that should be considered. Returning to evaluation methodology, as summarised in Table 2.2, evaluations can be summative, that is they weigh up a project or intervention, usually at the end, stating what has, or has not, been successful; or formative, that is, they improve understanding of how the implementation of an intervention or project is proceeding and help overcome any barriers or issues as they emerge. Ultimately both summative and formative evaluations may provide evidence to cease or alter an intervention if it is shown to be of little benefit.

Carrying out a summative evaluation (which was the normal practice of the researcher leading the well-being evaluation) was difficult here as there were not appropriate baseline measures, such as psychological well-being indicators, that could be used to see if the projects in focus had created quantifiable change. The evaluation of engagement in the Digital Sentinel was more formative – it aimed to provide future guidance on the development of the site. Ultimately, all the evaluations

Table 2.2: Types of evaluation (Gamble, 2008)

Type of evaluation	Appropriate situation
Summative evaluation – renders judgments about the merit, worth and value of an intervention	At the end of a programme or initiative when key decisions about its future are going to be made When judging the model's merit or worth for continuation, expansion, going to scale, or other major decisions
Formative evaluation – helps a programme become an effective and dependable model	When fine-tuning a model When a future summative evaluation is expected and baseline data will likely be needed
Developmental evaluation – supports the process of innovation within an organisation and in its activities	When working in situations of high complexity When working on early-stage social innovation

became formative as the community partners did adjust their activities based on the findings.

The findings described above relating to the embeddedness of the evaluator and the immediate usefulness of findings, suggest that a developmental approach to evaluation – the final row of Table 2.2 – is most appropriate in the context of research co-produced with communities. The community evaluation took a developmental approach recognising its usefulness within complex contexts. As Patton writes (2010: 1):

> Developmental Evaluation supports innovation development to guide adaptation to emergent and dynamic realities in complex environments. Innovations can take the form of new projects, programs, products, organizational changes, policy reforms, and system interventions. A complex system is characterized by a large number of interacting and interdependent elements in which there is no central control. Patterns of change emerge from rapid, real time interactions that generate learning, evolution, and development – if one is paying attention and knows how to observe and capture the important and emergent patterns. Complex environments for social interventions and innovations are those in which what to do to solve problems is uncertain and key stakeholders are in conflict about how to proceed.

As illuminated in the rest of this book, this is an accurate description of much co-produced research. Developmental evaluation responds to a widespread reality rather than fixed points in time. Interventions keep developing as the context and situation they are in changes and the intervention can be adjusted as new needs and opportunities arise. It subsequently has the potential to create or remove barriers, and provide opportunities to roll out new interventions that might even make the ones being evaluated less relevant. This approach requires and stimulates continuous learning among all partners in complex contexts, and the strengthening of a learning culture can be a key outcome.

As noted above, in Wester Hailes, the academic and community evaluations found that the previous co-produced approach (in terms of being both creative and open-ended) had created space for creative capacity to come to the fore in a way that may be smothered by grant support in voluntary sector organisations. As discussed in the evaluation workshops, this was a key reason that all the interventions, including the evaluations discussed, were valued. The community partners were not constrained by policy goals of funders or their reporting and evaluation requirements. The outputs and outcomes could be directed by the community partners and be useful for them. The use of developmental evaluation in the community-led evaluation demonstrated that by developing collective reflexive learning, this open creative space could be extended.

Arguably, this meant the developmental community-led evaluation was more useful for the community. The frame of inquiry was developed by the community itself through the logic modelling session, questioning whether the co-produced projects in focus had been of benefit to them. This presumed that the community is the arbiter of the usefulness of knowledge. In order to be fully immersed in the 'community frame' and fully address the community's questions, the researcher/evaluator needed to be embedded in the community. As already touched on, embeddedness is important in terms of developing a relationship of trust and openness which allows understanding and helps people accept the researcher's understanding and eventual findings; it's easier to tell people something isn't working if you have been working along with them and they trust you. Embeddedness also allowed the researcher to seize opportunities as they arose and participate in community activities or conversations and better understand community dynamics and identify effects and outcomes, including surfacing unexplored outcomes and legacies.

This did not necessarily mean all findings were accepted uncritically. When asked about the projects in focus, many respondents associated them with a particular individual whose efforts they appreciated, but they did not feel any ownership of them. For the individual this was a difficult finding to accept and it meant some relationships were strained. Just because an evaluator is embedded, this does not mean difficult findings are necessarily easy to convey or easy to accept, particularly for residents or individuals who have invested heavily in interventions. However, in such a situation a summative evaluation, or evaluator, would walk away, leaving the community to deal with the tensions and unhappiness. The developmental approach left a more trusting relationship between community partners and the evaluators. The finding could be broadly accepted, while recognising the individual's hard work, and the projects could be changed and new partners brought in to develop wider ownership. The academics could work with community partners to hand over this challenge, using the skills of partners as community development workers and greater knowledge of the community and its dynamics and relationships.

Similarly, the academic evaluations were not of less use to the community partners because they were not embedded, or did not use developmental evaluation. None of the academic evaluation findings came as a big surprise to the community partners; in reaffirming what they already knew from their tacit knowledge they were useful in guiding future decision making. To return to the discussion of power dynamics within evaluation, the community partners could use the evaluations because they had power and legitimacy. The findings had the legitimacy of coming from researchers in universities and could be presented as being 'objective'. They could be used tactically by the community partners to add legitimacy to arguments they were making, for example to secure further funding.

Conclusion: research, evaluation and the university in the community

Ultimately, we found a broadly positive legacy of the original co-produced research projects within Wester Hailes – they had delivered outcomes for the community. One of the elements of this not yet discussed was the 'not-yetness' of these outcomes; for example, there was evidence that the totem pole had a positive place-making value for residents and this *would* probably lead to better psychological health and well-being. However, it was too early to tell definitively. Similarly, the Digital Sentinel had the potential to garner widespread reader engagement and create a voice for the community, but it required more funded support from community journalists and workers to become sustainable in the longer term. This 'not-yetness' was partly a result of the study designs – particularly that the evaluation happened a short while after the projects had begun – but also reflected the barriers to successful co-production and community empowerment. Wester Hailes is one of the most deprived neighbourhoods in Scotland. Many of the residents experience individual challenges, for example poor mental health, disability or poverty, that take up most of their energies. In a country where the state is increasingly making such people and groups abject (Tyler, 2013), it is going to be difficult to get people in such situations to engage in projects such as those developed in Wester Hailes, with numerous barriers to overcome.

However, we do not see this as a reason to discontinue co-produced research with the most deprived and marginalised communities, and only focus on those who can successfully engage. Indeed evidence shows those communities that are good at engaging already use these skills to accrue substantial benefits to themselves (Matthews and Hastings, 2013). Rather, to return to the discussion at the opening of the chapter, we see evaluation as an essential part of ethical practice in co-produced research. Many guides to the ethics of participatory or co-produced research focus on minimising harm. We believe taking an evaluative approach takes this a step further, moving beyond the traditional harm-minimising approaches of institutional ethics committees that often sit uneasily with co-produced research (Beebeejaun et al, 2015). Asking the evaluative questions of who benefits from an intervention and how, and also what positive outcomes are produced, can make co-produced research address far more searching ethical questions. The challenge of evaluative questions is not just 'has this research caused harm?' but also 'has this research caused benefit or has it caused dis-benefit or costs?'

Applying this test to our evaluations means we have to ask the question: how can we ensure a legacy of positive outcomes in communities from broader research? O'Brien and Matthews (2015: 203) argue that: 'It is only by offering guarantees of genuine partnership that universities can avoid repeating the inequalities engendered by the profiteering of consultants, businesses and government ministries'. The broader legacy of our evaluations is that the collaborative learning environment engendered by the approaches should become a more mainstream part of the activities of our universities in a modern settlement movement (Benson et al, 2000). Small pieces of research using the outsider role of academics and their skills can help organisations reflect and learn, while longer-term co-productive partnerships might transform outcomes in communities, and universities should invest in building trusting relationships with their local communities.

Guidance for understanding and creating legacy

Try to create further legacy through your evaluation

Evaluation can be a useful focus to ask ethical questions around what is the best way to produce positive outcomes in communities

Developmental evaluation can help collective learning in complex environments

Formal 'university' outputs can be very useful for community partners – they have added legitimacy with many external partners

The resources in people and funding of an evaluation can themselves be useful for partners and produce further legacy

---

Notes
[1] Equally, evaluations might just be ignored, and a great deal of methodological work on evaluation involves understanding how to improve practices so that the outcomes are actually used by policy makers and others.
[2] The authors sought a reference for this point, but it seems such an accepted truism of evaluative practices in the voluntary sector that there is no source for it.
[3] This was apparent in this case, where a collective logic modelling workshop was a new experience and was welcomed. Logic models developed by evaluators are also one of the first stages in Theory-of-Change evaluations.

References
Beebeejaun, Y., Durose, C., Rees, J., Richardson, J. and Richardson, L. (2015). 'Public Harm or Public Value? Towards Coproduction in Research with Communities'. *Environment and Planning C: Government and Policy* 33(3): 552–65

Benson, L., Harkavy, I. and Puckett, J. (2000). 'An Implementation Revolution as a Strategy for Fulfilling the Democratic Promise of University-Community Partnerships: Penn-West Philadelphia as an Experiment in Progress'. *Nonprofit and Voluntary Sector Quarterly* 29(1): 24–45

Colebatch, H.K. (1995). 'Organizational Meanings of Program Evaluation'. *Policy Sciences* 28(2): 149–64

Durose, C. and Richardson, L. (2013). *Who is Accountable in Localism: Findings from Theory and Practice*. Swindon: Arts and Humanities Research Council

Gamble, J.A.A. (2008) *The Developmental Evaluation Primer*, Montreal: The J.W. McConnell Family Foundation.

Government Social Research Unit (2007). *The Magenta Book: Guidance Notes for Policy Evaluation and Analysis*. London: HM Treasury

Haynes, L., Service, O., Goldacre, B. and Torgerson, D. (2012). *Test, Learn, Adapt: Developing Public Policy with Randomised Controlled Trials.* London: The Cabinet Office

HM Treasury (2011). *The Green Book: Appraisal and Evaluation in Central Government*. London: TSO

Matthews, P. (2015, in press). 'Social media, community development and social capital.' *Community Development Journal*

Matthews, P. and Hastings, A. (2013). 'Middle-Class Political Activism and Middle-Class Advantage in Relation to Public Services: A Realist Synthesis of the Evidence Base'. *Social Policy & Administration* 47(1): 72–92

O'Brien, D. and Lockley, P. (2015). 'The Social Life Of Cultural Value'. In L. MacDowall, M. Badham, E. Blomkamp and K. Dunphy (eds), *Making Culture Count: The Politics of Cultural Measurement*. London: Palgrave, 87–103

O'Brien, D. and Matthews, P. (2015). Chapter 13 – Conclusion. In D. O'Brien and P. Matthews (eds) *After Urban Regeneration: Communities, Policy and Place*. Bristol: Policy Press, 199–204

Ofcom (2013). *Communications Market Report 2013*. London: Ofcom.

Pain, R., Kesby, M. and Askins, K. (2011). 'Geographies of Impact: Power, Participation and Potential'. *Area* 43(2): 183–88

Patton, M Q. (2008). *Utilization-Focused Evaluation*. London: SAGE Publications

Patton, M.Q. (2010) *Developmental Evalustion: Applying Complexity Concepts to Enhance Inovation and Use*, New York: Guildford Press.

Patton, M.Q. (2012). 'A Utilization-focused Approach to Contribution Analysis'. *Evaluation* 18(3): 364–77

Pawson, R. and Tilley, N. (1997). *Realistic Evaluation*. London: Sage

Pearce, W., Raman, S. and Turner, A. (2015). 'Randomised Trials in Context: Practical Problems and Social Aspects of Evidence-based Medicine and Policy'. *Trials* 16(394): 7

Research Excellence Framework (2012). *Assessment Framework and Guidance on Submissions.* Bristol: REF

Scottish Government (2014). *Scotland's People Annual Report: Results from 2013 Scottish Household Survey.* Edinburgh: The Scottish Government

Tyler, I. (2013). *Revolting Subjects: Social Abjection and Resistance in Neoliberal Britain.* London: Zed Books

THREE

Implicit values:
uncounted legacies

Julian Brigstocke, Elona Hoover, Marie Harder, Paula Graham,
Sophia de Sousa, Andy Dearden, Ann Light,
Theodore Zamenopoulos, Katerina Alexiou, Gemma Burford,
Justine Gaubert and Colin Foskett

Introduction

University–community collaborations are often complex, fraught, emotional affairs. Participants devote a lot of time, energy and emotion to bridging differences, improvising solutions, and making things work. This can be difficult and sometimes frustrating, but can also have a transformative legacy for the participants and the wider communities they are part of. These legacies, however, are not always easy to observe, identify and authorise. As we will explore in this chapter, some of the most important legacies of community–university partnerships are intangible and refer to emotions, affects, ongoing processes and emerging potentials: for example, inspiration, confidence, friendship, as well as knowledge, ideas and networks. These legacies are at least as important as projects' harder, more tangible and easily measurable legacies.

Our exploration of legacies started with a shared interest in the role that values play in collaborative research, and in the way in which we understand related outcomes. Exploring this through the concept of legacy was particularly relevant as it allows for a more fluid understanding, and one that can be shaped by the local project context. Thus, the theoretical starting point for this work was that making the values within collaborative projects explicit would allow for the identification and evaluation of those, 'less tangible', legacies. Our University of Brighton authors Harder, Burford and Hoover previously established that a values-based approach could be very successful for evaluating 'intangible' outcomes and achievements projects led by civil society organisations (Burford et al, 2013). They brought the approach, named WeValue, as a raw starting point to the members of two complex partnerships called Scaling Up Co-Design and the Authority Research Network (ARN), and then collectively as a consortium we co-explored, co-developed and co-generated a localisable, values-based approach for a new purpose: to identify and legitimise legacies (not only outcomes) from partnership projects (not projects from a single group or organisation).

By 'starting from values', we mean starting with what participants consider *valuable, meaningful and worthwhile* in the context of their group or partnership. An explicit values lens is first locally constructed, and then used to view, identify and evaluate legacies. The WeValue approach was previously developed to allow a formal, rigorous evaluation of 'soft' or 'intangible' achievements. It uses a 'menu' of values statements that are intended to trigger, novel local-values statements by participants, which become their bespoke values-based indicators. The *legacies* work reported here built on and significantly adapted the WeValue approach for *partnerships*.

The approach of starting from values, we will suggest, did indeed help to identify new, less 'tangible' outcomes, as well as to articulate deeper dimensions of already known ones. In addition, by further developing that approach for partnerships and legacies, we moved well beyond specific outcomes to identifying culturally situated legacies which had *values* as an explicit starting point, with unexpectedly clear articulation and detail. By acknowledging and seeking out different values perspectives, we also revealed multiple definitions of legacy for each single collaborative research project, leading to large numbers of identified legacies for each. In addition, we later found that explicitly linking legacies to values led us to understand much more clearly the conditions necessary for achieving these legacies – which could not help but immediately feed into future strategic planning of the groups.

The chapter is divided into four sections. First, we offer a theoretical account of our approach to legacy and its relation to values and co-produced knowledge. Second, we describe how we elicited values from groups, and facilitated them to identify and evaluate their values-based legacies. Third, we introduce the two main case study projects, with descriptions and analyses of some of the most important legacies, such as new types of knowledge, inspiration from project partners and deep friendships. Finally, we draw out key insights for the context of collaborative projects before concluding. We propose that a values-based approach to investigating legacy can provide a rigorous approach to critically assessing a broader spectrum of outcomes from collaborative research projects, moving beyond the punctual concept of impacts to multiple culturally situated legacies.

Key resources for thinking about Legacy

Alexiou, K., Zamenopoulos, T. and Alevizou, G. 2013. *Valuing Community-Led Design*. AHRC Discussion Paper

Podger, D., Velasco, I., Amezcua Luna, C., Burford, G. and Harder, M.K. 2013. 'Can Values Be Measured? Significant Contributions from a Small Civil Society Organisation through Action Research Evaluation'. *Action Research* 11(1): 8–30

For more detail on the WeValue approach, visit the WeValue website at: http://blogs.brighton.ac.uk/wevalue/. Short films from the Starting from Values project also provide additional detail for some of the steps described: http://arts.brighton.ac.uk/projects/starting-from-values-evaluating-intangible-legacies/project-videos.

Theorising values and intangible legacies

The project discussed in this chapter starts from the assertion that the community partners and academic researchers who carry out research should have the space to articulate the legacy of their work through frameworks that derive from their own value structures, and that this can ultimately help create new, more participatory, forms of accountability. We argue that it is precisely a shift to making the values underpinning such decisions explicit that makes this type of investigation of legacy particularly fruitful. We are proposing an unapologetically multiple, heterogeneous and 'inside-out' approach which accepts the culturally situated nature of project impacts and focuses on 'legacy' as something that implies an inherent values judgement. As we will see, different legacies are revealed when projects are viewed through different lenses. Our method for capturing legacies aims to be as faithful to this variety as possible, by taking as a starting point the premise that the research partners and participants should themselves define what potential legacies are most important. This means that the project can be evaluated according to criteria that are immanent to the project's own multiple value structures such as those of the academics, separate partner groups and wider community members. Achieving this would make it possible for legacies to be evaluated according to a very broad set of social and political values, including values that do not necessarily sit entirely comfortably with those of the funders. This is not to say that public funding does not need to be accountable to the public, but to recognise that additional forms of accountability are needed that engage with community organisations as equal partners.

Our approach does not offer a pre-defined notion of what legacy is, but reflects that the many different senses of what legacy is can be captured by grounding it in the values of the people involved in co-producing the project. Starting from values, therefore, is a way of uncovering legacies that may otherwise remain hidden, marginalised or denigrated. We are not claiming to come from a position that escapes theoretical or normative assumptions. Indeed, the approach is explicitly aimed at contributing to a wider social goal, shared across much co-design and participatory research, of redistributing the authority relations in academic research, and recognising, to the greatest extent possible, the authority and expertise of the communities, often silenced or underrepresented, who participate in research activities.

The aim of the project is not to replace overly objectivist, rationalised approaches to evaluation with purely subjective definitions of legacy. Rather, the aim is to redistribute the authority to define the nature of desirable legacy to project participants, by grounding part of the definition of legacy within their own values. Values, far from being merely subjective, are complex socio-cultural constructs that are rooted in social power relations (Hitlin and Piliavin, 2004). Grounding legacies in the authenticity, coherence and persuasiveness of a locally shared set of values is a way of redistributing the authority to define what legacy is in a particular context. Thus we are contributing to an effort to demonstrate that co-produced research, far from flattening out standards of knowledge and objectivity, has the potential to create stronger, richer, more authoritative knowledge that challenges conventional, historically specific, divisions between subjective and objective knowledge (see Blencowe et al, 2015), and enables knowledge to be used in more effective ways in novel contexts and across new community networks.

A key theoretical challenge, however, lies in developing a clear theory of the nature of values and their link to legacies (or in more general terms, the link between values and action). The use of the concept of 'values' in social-scientific analysis has proved controversial in recent debates, due to the great difficulty of clearly defining what 'values' actually are. As Hechter (1993) observes, studying values presents many problems. For example: values are not visible; the link between values and behaviour is unclear and hard to determine; the formation of values is poorly understood; and, it is very hard to measure values.

Whereas much social-scientific research has assumed values to function at a largely cognitive level, existing as abstract ideals that are (perceived to be) outcomes of individual choice, we would emphasise the affective and emotional aspects of values and valuing. Values are not necessarily abstract or philosophical principles; they are outcomes of social processes of valuing, which occur routinely as we encounter the world through our embodied practices. Valuing is done through the senses and emotions as much as it is done through reason. Valuing occurs when the world puts something into question, when it invites people to consider or reconsider their orientations, perspectives and approaches to (particular aspects of) the world. Values are 'evaluative beliefs that synthesise affective and cognitive elements to orient people to the world in which they live' (Marini, cited in Hitlin and Piliavin, 2004).

Values, then, are not stable and static. What is more, value systems are rarely systematic or internally coherent, since different values are often brought into play in different kinds of social context and social practice. Everyday life often does not force people to develop carefully articulated and internally differentiated systems of values; rather, we actualise different values at different times in relation to different demands. The values I prioritise at home are not necessarily the same as the values I prioritise at work or in the public sphere. Conflicting or competing values may coexist quite happily until a particular situation translates this conflict into a problem that needs resolving. Values, therefore, are relational achievements of specific practices, events and situations. In this sense, values are always shared in some way, since they emerge from shared social practices. In the context of groups and organisations, shared values are co-created (whether explicitly or implicitly) through the development of shared practices, problems, achievements and failures. Given the heterogeneous nature of such groups, however, these shared values may be very hard to make explicit and tangible.

It is no wonder, then, that efforts to define values have proved challenging, and approaches vary widely across disciplines. There is a disparate body of work on values elicitation that spans many different academic disciplines. The methods used to elicit values range from deductive approaches which use pre-established definitions of values, which people have to rank, rate, evaluate or classify, to inductive approaches which seek to develop a context-specific understanding of values (Shilton et al, 2013). Proponents of different approaches have shown their respective advantages and disadvantages. Deductive approaches can be accused of reductive rationalism, assuming values to form clear, singular, relational structures. Inductive approaches tend to be time consuming and only applicable to a given context. In contrast, our method for eliciting values (and evaluating legacies based on these values) acknowledges both the performative aspect of eliciting values (playing an active role in forming values judgements, not neutrally measuring them) and also the affective aspects of them (acknowledging the rootedness of values in emotional and affective social life), while using an approach that can be transferred across context by noting that many locally expressed group values can be considered variations of items in a 'fuzzy framework' previously elicited from other groups. We describe our approach for achieving this in the next section.

What we did

Our 'starting from values' approach involves creating a space for participants to reflect on what they value in their collaborative work, and then to articulate this through a facilitated discussion, in a collective valuing process. This began with eliciting local statements of 'what is meaningful, worthwhile and valuable' to partnership members through brainstorming, storytelling, photo-elicitation, mapping, and diagramming. This produced 'values statements': articulations of values-in-action in the partnership. See examples in the box.

Examples of 'values-based statements' (where the level of specificity is purposeful)

"People have a sense of power that they can effect change"

"People feel they will not compromise their personal beliefs/values by participating in the organisation's activities"

"People reflect critically on what is necessary to learn"

"Differences of opinion are acknowledged and valued through dialogue"

Second, participants were introduced to additional values statements from other groups. These were used to trigger participants to actively explore *their own* unarticulated values by collectively rephrasing and prioritising those that represent what they collectively valued most.

Third, participants were asked to loosely organise their values-based statements into a framework (also noting unshared values). Seeing previously 'intangible' concepts specified, and related to each other, created a new overall frame, or lens, with which to view their work.

Fourth, by using their new values lens, the partnership was assisted to identify actual or intended legacies. The values-based statements included aspects that might usually be considered awkward to articulate or evaluate; but because they were very specific – like deep friendships – it made it easier for these aspects to be openly considered.

Fifth, groups were asked to devise creative ways of 'measuring', capturing or expressing these legacies. We identified that the legacies could not be adequately represented with a series of bullet points or text alone. Thus, we assessed evidence for different legacies and represented these through illustrations, mind-maps including text and images, narratives and stories, and audio-visual material. Some projects developed documents and objects to identify and record evidence for intended legacies, such as a 'value and legacy box'.[1]

Sixth, the processes above were repeated separately for groups which were members of the Scaling Up consortium, to reveal the legacies from their values viewpoint. This revealed different, but sometimes overlapping, sets of legacies – and many more than previously envisaged by looking at the first partnership perspective alone.

This approach was further developed, modified and extended through several iterations, in response to the experiences of the consortium members in a series of co-learning exercises (not reported on further here). A number of critiques and ideas for change were developed, summarised as follows:

- *Partnerships beyond consensus*: the original WeValue process was designed for use with organisations or groups, rather than partnerships where there typically will be less expectation of an entirely shared set of values. This led to a redesign of the WeValue approach, to allow better identification and acknowledgement of unshared and even diverging values, and the expansion of the trigger set to include some more focused on aspects of partnerships.
- *Materiality matters*: the use (or non-use) of material artefacts affected the process. For example, using spatial representation and mapping tools could help guide discussions about shared or not shared values, having pre-printed examples of values statements could discourage editing for authenticity, while blank cards could create barriers to starting to write. Different fonts, cards, post-its and lists were all found to influence voice and authenticity, as too was participants' ability to manipulate concepts. All of these raised new issues of ethics. Creative or arts-based methods were found to be key: in order to produced rich values elicitation material, on which the process depended, non-cognitive methods were key such as photo-elicitation, storytelling and sensory recording.

Projects studied

The ARN is an international, university-based research collective which engages with questions of authority, positive power and participatory democracy through developing strong social theory and links with practice. Initiated by a group of academic researchers, the network developed as a collaborative space where deep thinking and theorising could be done through friendship and a supportive environment. Members of the network collaborate through week-long residential reading and writing 'retreats' and joint research projects. The ARN has recently participated in or led several university–community projects exploring issues including: community forestry; democracy and non-human life; law and debt; and violence in marginalised communities. It has also developed new theoretical frameworks for understanding participatory practice.

Scaling Up Co-Design (Scaling Up) is a collaborative project between academics and six UK community organisations, exploring how the impact and reach of civil society work can be scaled up through co-design practices. By sharing experiences and connecting existing knowledge and resources together, partners created new opportunities for innovation, built their capacity to address complex issues, and thus achieved more with less. Legacies were explored separately for each of the collaborating community organisations, and for the partnership.

Evaluating and identifying legacies: through a values lens

The Starting from Values project yielded a rich set of data about legacies from the two projects, and these have been represented through audio-visual production, illustrations and diagrams[2]. Both partnership teams had taken time to consider what their legacies were before they joined our consortium and developed their 'values' framework. This provided a new lens with which to view their project landscape of outputs, achievements and impacts to evaluate which combined to form legacies now identifiable to them. More detail can be found in learning and outcomes from the project, including non-text representations that display them more richly and appropriately (see Starting from Values, 2016; Hoover et al, 2016), but we highlight some points below.

Legacies for the Authority Research Network

Values agreed to be central to the research network, whose members engage in numerous community–university projects, including:

resisting superficiality and creating deep, lasting connections and collaborations; valuing creativity; adopting an experimental attitude towards research and knowledge; and contributing to the thinking and practice of equality and the making of the commons.

Both tangible and intangible legacies were then identified that specifically linked to these values. A key legacy was that the network itself had developed very strong, close links with an expanded network of community activists, artists and academics. The network strongly values prioritising quality over quantity, and focused on building deep and meaningful collaborations with a relatively small number of people and groups. These close connections were productive of many new ideas, academic collaborations, projects and forms of activism and engagement. For example, ARN projects enabled participants to set up community reading groups, new community–university networks such as the Soils, Seeds and Social Change network, and new partnerships with groups such as the Bolivia Democracy Centre, a centre for marginalised children in the Bronx in New York, the Citizens Advice Bureau in the UK, and Redes da Maré, an NGO working with deprived communities in Rio de Janeiro.

Another important legacy was the emerging skills in arts-led forms of research practice. Network members and community partners explored new forms of 'creative listening' and creative writing, and are now incorporating new arts-led methods into their research practice. One project also produced a book of accessible essays on participatory democracy, aimed at a general activist audience, which was downloaded by several thousand unique users (Noorani et al, 2013). In brief, ARN's community-engaged projects and activities led ARN to develop its more theoretical work in community-engaged ways: to move their academic work 'into the world'. That is a legacy which has transformed the network, its members and its outputs, and is now embedded in their core research and practice.

One of the crucial legacies identified by ARN members was previously intangible and thus not appropriately valued: the new friendships that emerged out of these close collaborations. The 'retreat' method, which involves living, cooking and cleaning together for a week in a remote rural location, is conducive to generating close bonds with project participants. Participants in these retreats were struck by the space they allowed to create new forms of thinking, novel ideas and new friendships. This was perceived to be extremely valuable as research participants frequently felt alienated from the process and products of university research. Developing these new ways of working together was a way of experimenting with new relationships between life and work, and between play and scholarship. Such close friendships enable an enabling environment for generating new ideas and impossible-sounding projects, as well as generating support networks (or even 'magic circles'!) to protect themselves from the sometimes poisonous atmosphere of the neoliberal university and its gruelling schedules, demands and frequent impersonal (and personal) rejections.

In that sense, the new friendships produced by working closely together can have a positive legacy on developing future community–university partnerships. However, participants were keen to insist that not only should such legacies be viewed instrumentally, in terms of the new projects and partnerships they make possible, but that an *intrinsic* value of such projects is the friendships, new forms of life and new forms of joy to be found in working collaboratively, across boundaries, in new and sometimes challenging contexts. This is an important legacy in and of itself.

Projects didn't only generate new knowledge, but also created new affective relations, new practices of relating work to everyday life, and experiments with living differently. At the time of writing, project participants were beginning to imagine an ambitious, long-term project that would involve contributing large amounts of time, resources and energy to a collective, community-based project that would encompass, but far exceed, academic research. Plans such as these, whether or not they come to fruition, were possible only within a context of having generated close friendships through collaboration (including collaboration across university–community boundaries) over a number of years.

Legacies of Scaling Up Co-design

The Scaling Up team identified three key (shared) values that drive action for the members:

- *Collaborate*: collaboration offers opportunities and resources to test ideas and approaches.
- *Cross-pollinate*: cross-fertilisation of ideas inspires new practices and ways of thinking.
- *Make a difference*: the ambition to make a clear difference for communities and broader society encourages trust and further collaboration.

Associated with these values was a set of three legacies:

- *New ways of thinking and doing*: the team found that people individually were able to do new things, or do things differently in their own organisations as a result of scaling up.
- *Growing connections*: the project created connections or networks between organisations and individuals that otherwise would not have connected, and these last beyond the end of the project.
- *Cascading co-design*: the project's activities and messages influenced practice and behaviour beyond the project group/partners.

Although the team already held some of the data that provided evidence for these legacies, the values approach gave team members the space and processes to think more deeply about values and the importance of the resulting legacies from the different perspectives of individuals and participating organisations. It also gave the opportunity for the team (academics and project partners) to better understand and make more explicit the meaning and implications of these legacies, and to understand each other's perspectives. A characteristic moment of this process was during the first workshop of the Starting from Values project, when the term 'openness' arose as an important value and legacy of the project. This then helped the team to explore a series of interpretations for this commonly used term. It gave the opportunity to articulate various nuances and views about openness, for example regarding the boundaries of the network of people and ideas that form the project; the movement and dissemination of ideas; but also the flexibility (or incompleteness) of the ideas and infrastructures that this project created. These discussions gradually led to the legacy statements that appear above.

Legacies of Scaling Up Co-design: from the perspective of its community partner organisations

The Scaling Up project involved community partners, who also separately explored their own values and created their own bespoke values lenses to examine the Scaling Up project and its legacies. A key aspect of our approach was to ensure that this multiplicity of voices had a place, and to lend authority to the legacies from different partners' perspectives. We found that these both relate to and differ from the legacies defined by the project partnership itself. In some cases new legacies, in others similar legacies, were identified, but using different language to describe them. In one case, a partner articulated new legacies after viewing them 'in reverse' through the values lens of the Scaling Up partnership: the value 'people do new things or do things differently' helped Silent Cities identify that they now use research and have even recruited research students. Below we present the values and legacies identified from the perspectives of the community partner organisations.

The Glass-House community-led design

The Glass-House is a national charity bringing together hands-on support for community groups and organisations with developers and local authorities to help them work more effectively together to create better quality places and spaces. They had already done significant analysis and capture of legacies and impact of their action research within the communities in which they worked. However, starting from a values perspective helped them make sense of a very long list of outcomes by identifying how each contributed to their mission and values, and what they should focus on for further work. Their new bespoke values framework helped to identify a number of strategic organisational legacies as well as shifts in actual project delivery and professional practice, which included: a more complex and richer set of definitions and approaches around scale, impact and reach; greater clarity around what The Glass-House seeks from and can contribute to partnership working, with a stronger emphasis on co-designed collaborative projects; and cross-pollination across areas of work and disciplines as a key organisational aspiration and approach, both across The Glass-House programmes and with partners. Staff also noted individual-level legacies of new confidence and inspiration, aligned both with organisational values and their own personal values.

The Glass-House further identified three main practice-based legacies: refocusing on and developing new tools for the use of sensory and emotional connection with place as a tool to support place making; the building in of research approaches and tools developed in the Scaling-Up project (such as a workshop resource book that helps gather data as well as being a facilitation tool), and bringing artistic production into their place-making work with communities in new ways. This last legacy includes new layers and deeper personal aspects, such as shifts in personal perceptions of the inherent worth of these kinds of outputs: valuing them as artistic productions in their own right (and not only as a useful tools for place-making processes). The bespoke values framework developed within the Scaling Up partnership has become a legacy, in its own right, and is now used by The Glass-House as a valuable strategic tool.

Silent Cities

A very significant, and already identified, impact of the Scaling Up project was the wining of a city-wide Age Better Big Lottery bid for £6m to reduce isolation and loneliness among 12,000 of the most isolated older people of Sheffield, UK, in which Silent Cities played a key role (see also Light and Akama, 2014). Starting from Values highlighted the importance of the bid's integration of co-design principles – a key value of the partnership. But from the perspective of Silent Cities' values, further legacies were identified: the director acquired energy and confidence to speak about co-design in an authoritative way, inspiring her to integrate newly cross-fertilised methods, strategies and approaches. These legacies allowed for potentially much broader and longer-term impacts, for example not just integrating co-design into the bid, but also facilitating its permeation into other organisations in Sheffield involved in the development and future delivery of the project.

Other values-based legacies for Silent Cities were: a renewed strategic focus for the organisation; expanding networks; developing a lasting partnership with one of the other community partners; and building capacity in community media through their community journalists' programme, and the personal and professional transformation this led to for those involved. To explore third-order perspectives of the latter legacy, two community journalists were asked to consider their values-based legacies: they reported that it developed and enhanced their confidence and skills in community media practice (for example vox popping, editing) and education; it enhanced their employability and professional experience; it gave them the courage to do things that were personally important to them; and it led to new friendships.

Blackwood Foundation

The Blackwood Foundation's mission is to support people who have been affected by disability to live independently. Previously, legacies of new partnerships and the transfer of co-design principles into Blackwood Foundation had been identified. The process of starting from values led the Blackwood Foundation to better articulate its legacies in its own terms, and, perhaps crucially, to legitimise and strengthen them. For instance, a key legacy was that through the embedding of co-design principles within their organisation, the project helped them to reconnect with the spirit of their founder, and to go on to advocate for co-design practices within regional health and social care policy reforms. Other legacies included transforming the work of several community partners by raising awareness of accessibility and disability issues in their practice, as well as integrating these issues into the product design curricula at Brunel University; and new practices and enhancing activities on the foundation's in-house community network through integrating multi-media approaches (digital stories, video conferencing). Figure 3.1 shows a summary of these legacies represented through illustration.

Figure 3.1: Visualisation of legacy from Scaling-up Co-Design project for the Blackwood Foundation

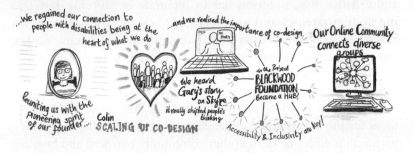

Fossbox and Flossie

Prior to the values approach, the director at Fossbox had identified that the most important legacies of the project were increased social capital and networks. The process of starting from values provided new insights on outcomes: Fossbox had contributed to empowering women to use technology; inspired individual women to integrate co-design into their practices; and allowed their network of women in technology to gain profile and participate in workshops focused on international issues. These contributed to building confidence within the organisation, expanded contacts and enhanced their profile as a training provider for women in technology. Finally, while the Scaling Up partnership project led to reflection on strategic direction generally, the values-based approach greatly enhanced this process by clarifying the importance of co-design in Fossbox's strategic direction, and triggering thinking about a lack of consistency between their service delivery and advocacy work: they had used co-design with the former but not the latter. They realised that advocacy should be 'designed' by and for all stakeholders as much as – perhaps more than – service delivery. As a result, Fossbox collaborated with community organisations Common House and Furtherfield to develop a series of free critical design workshops to explore what many see as a democratic deficit around new technologies such as 'quantified self' and 'future cities', which has since opened up new avenues for exploration.

Insights from values to legacies in collaborative and interdisciplinary work

In this section we briefly outline learning from the 'starting from values' approach, in particular relating to the context of collaborative and interdisciplinary work, and discuss possible limitations of the approach.

The project team spent time reflecting on the benefits and added value of the values-based approach. This was conducted by referring back to discussions prior to the first reflection meeting and questioning the insights each partner gained from the process. This reflection was captured by a visual artist at the last iteration of our reflective meetings. Some of the key insights were that our co-evolved approach:

i) leads to identifying previously unarticulated outcomes or impacts;
ii) helps partners gain a deeper understanding, identify new layers of meaning and articulate deeply personal (for individuals and/or organisations) aspects of project legacies: though not all projects found 'new' legacies, all developed deeper understandings of existing ones. Making multiple values perspectives explicit was important to achieving this, for instance community partners revisited the impacts of the project in a new way, linking to their values;
iii)provides an explicit values lens through which to analyse project impacts, thus moving from a mere collection of outcomes or impacts towards a culturally situated understanding of legacies;
iv)through a rigorous articulation of legacies through locally relevant values frameworks, legitimises and authorises legacies that partners had previously not considered valid, in many cases, less 'tangible' legacies such as energy, friendship or new ways of thinking, which were now perceived to be significant and valid;
v) incorporates creative and critical approaches central to Arts and Humanities research as an acknowledged key component to articulate shared and conflicting values in collaborative and interdisciplinary work, as well as to effectively identify and articulate new, deeper and 'less tangible' types of legacies.

In addition to the insights above, we looked across all of the legacies identified during the course of the project and identified two themes that we suggest are of interest in the context of collaborative and interdisciplinary work: (a) new knowledge, ideas and inspiration linked to the nature of the cross-boundary, interdisciplinary work, and (b) friendships, networks and connections that are qualitatively deep and lasting. The ubiquitous evidence of legacies relating to these themes is perhaps important. Finding shared ground in collaborative and cross-context research is challenging, and when this happens successfully it is probably because a lot of effort, work and carefully allocated time and space has been put into building such relationships. Thus, depth of connections between collaborators is an important kind of legacy from this kind of work, and we need to find appropriate ways of expressing and representing this. Relationships and networks were not formed in all cases, and projects usefully attended to conflict in their values systems and relations between members, or ignored them at their peril. But, when it was there, the depth and endurance of these relationships, often characterised by the term 'friendship', was a crucial dimension.

Last, the consortium identified several design principles needed in order to use a values-based approach in a way that is appropriate to collaborative research. We are still refining these ways of building capacity within community and academic partners for facilitating this process. Some of our remaining questions include whether the process should (or can) take into account wider social contexts which may influence or bring particular challenges to organisations or individuals with certain types of values. We also would like to explore the potential for this approach to hold differences in values perspectives open, and to what extent condensing around shared values is important for the process. In doing so, we recognise that an openness to the development of values is a value in itself (see Light's concept of metavalues (Light, 2011)).

Conclusion

Using the values-based approach described in this chapter, the projects evaluated in this project identified intangible legacies including new knowledge, ideas and inspiration, as well as new friendships, networks and connections. The research found that these softer, intangible legacies are an extremely important dimension of community–university collaborations.

The values-based approach used in this project opened up deeper and more personal legacies for the partnerships we worked with. This led to a deeper understanding of traditional output-related legacies and identification of new legacies, as well as reflections on the specific value of the projects to multiple parties. In this sense, by reaching to deeply personal realms through values discourse, partners could re-evaluate their own involvement in the collaborative research projects and make new sense of them in terms of their own organisational and personal values. In most cases, this brought new depth, breadth and multiplicity to the legacies of the projects. En route, the approach made different values perspectives explicit, providing a rigorous mechanism for articulating multiple perspectives and recognising their situated validity.

We propose that these findings are particularly important for the context of collaborative research for a number of reasons. First, only one of a few values perspectives (for example funders, academic investigators) is commonly the basis for evaluating the outcomes or impacts of such projects. By starting from values we set a new balance, allowing diverse values perspectives (academics, community partners, institutions, collectives, individuals) to share authority. Secondly, in doing so and creating a space for reflection through values, we have identified dimensions of legacies that had not previously been considered legitimate or even seen to exist as valid impacts from collaborative research. Our legacy project gave authority to new ways of articulating legacies that we propose are inextricably linked to the nature of collaborative and interdisciplinary research, and which warrant acknowledgement as such, despite their unfamiliar typology. Collaborative partnership projects involve connecting ideas, knowledge and/or practice from often 'distant' domains – this connection and collaboration takes time, effort, safe space and careful attention. It is thus not surprising that an important legacy of these projects should be new ways of thinking and knowing through deep connections (or friendship) that are qualitatively different from other types of collaborations.

Key messages for others interested in understanding legacy

- When we think about the legacies of a project, we are defining those by what we value. Thus, legacies will be different if we identify them from different values perspectives.
- Try *starting from values*: first clarifying the locally defined values of a group, and then using them as a lens through which to investigate legacy.
- Using carefully developed values statements from other groups (used in the WeValue approach) can help to rapidly identify where values are shared, not shared or even contested.
- Use carefully developed values statements to challenge how values are defined, through slight disruption and reconsideration.
- Consider the multiple viewpoints for legacy, and acknowledge plural views.

• Do not limit expressions of legacy to words: explore different ways of representing them.

Notes
[1] Additional detail about legacies found and approaches used to identify and represent these can be found in the project report (see Hoover et al, 2016).
[2] Various representations are available on the project website, learning and outcomes section (see Starting from Values, 2016).

References

Blencowe, C., Brigstocke, J. and Noorani, T. (2015) 'Engines of alternative objectivity: Re-articulating the nature and value of participatory mental health organisations with the Hearing Voices Movement and Stepping Out Theatre Company', *Health*, early online

Burford, G., Velasco, I., Janoušková, S., Zahradnik, M., Hak, T., Podger, D., Piggott, G. and Harder, M.K. (2013). 'Field Trials of a Novel Toolkit for Evaluating "Intangible" Values-related Dimensions of Projects'. *Evaluation and Program Planning* 36(1): 1–14

Hechter, M. (1993). 'Values Research in the Social and Behavioral Sciences'. In Hechter, M., Nadel, L. and Michod, R.E. (eds), *The Origin of Values*. Picataway: AldineTransaction, 28

Hitlin, S. and Piliavin, J. (2004). 'Values: Reviving a Dormant Concept'. *Annual Review of Sociology* 30: 359–93

Hoover, E. and Harder, M. (eds) (2016). *Starting from Values: Evaluating Intangible Legacies*. Project report. Retrieved 29 11, 2016 from University of Brighton website: http://arts.brighton.ac.uk/__data/assets/pdf_file/0003/198444/Starting-from-values_multimedia-report_FINAL_2016.pdf

Light, A. (2011). 'HCI as Heterodoxy: Technologies of Identity and the Queering of Interaction with Computers'. *Interacting with Computers* 23(5) 430–8

Light, A. and Akama, Y. (2014). *Structuring Future Social Relations: The Politics of Care in Participatory Practice, Proceedings of the 13th Participatory Design Conference: Research Papers-Volume 1*. ACM, 151–60

Noorani, T., Blencowe, C. and Brigstocke, J. (eds) (2013). *Problems of Participation: Reflections on Democracy, Authority and the Struggle for Common Life*. Lewes: ARN Press

Shilton, K., Koepfler, J.A. and Fleischmann, K.R. (2013). 'Charting Sociotechnical Dimensions of Values for Design Research'. *The Information Society* 29: 259–71

Starting from Values (2016). *Starting from Values – Evaluating Intangible Legacies*. University of Brighton, http://arts.brighton.ac.uk/projects/ starting-from-values-evaluating-intangible-legacies

FOUR

Socialising heritage/ socialising legacy

*Martin Bashforth, Mike Benson, Tim Boon, Lianne Brigham,
Richard Brigham, Karen Brookfield, Peter Brown, Danny Callaghan,
Jean-Phillipe Calvin, Richard Courtney, Kathy Cremin, Paul Furness,
Helen Graham, Alex Hale, Paddy Hodgkiss, John Lawson,
Rebecca Madgin, Paul Manners, David Robinson, John Stanley,
Martin Swan, Jenny Timothy and Rachael Turner*

Introduction

At some point during our inaugural research team workshop we started
to generate many different ideas about how to increase participation
in heritage decision-making. We tried to keep track as the questions
flowed by writing recurring words on pieces of paper, to be linked,
connected and ordered at some later point. The words were in some
ways not surprising. Heritage, of course. Stewardship. Custodianship.
Expert. Leadership. Institutions. Ownership. Differences/Tensions.
Scale. Personal. Values. Voice ('+ not heard', was added in another
hand in biro). So far, so predictable. These words, after all, index the
big conceptual challenges that have been identified to a greater or
lesser extent in heritage policy, practice and its research for the last
four decades. Yet as we spoke, each of these terms started to change in
dimension. As the different people around the table gave examples, and
checked they understood each other's contributions, the familiar words
were in the process of gathering new uncertainties and ambiguities as
well as new colours, textures, shapes and potentials.

We were brought together by a funding scheme that supported not
just collaborative research, but also its collaborative design.[1] While we
did have a shared interest in our overall question 'how should heritage
decisions be made?', we – as you will see by how we describe ourselves
– came to this question, and our first workshop, from quite different
places and different trajectories.[2] To frame it in the language implied by
this book, we carried with us different inheritances – legacies – from

our disciplines, professional backgrounds, organisations and places. As such, the other crucial thing we had in common was an interest in the potential for rethinking 'heritage' offered by drawing on many different perspectives and working across hierarchies and institutional boundaries. We used both these shared commitments *and* our different perspectives to collaboratively design our project.

In this chapter we tell the story of our project with the aim of showing how our research emerged through dynamic connections between *know-how* generated through practitioner reflections, *dialogue*, characterised by conversations between us as a project team and *conceptual innovation*, in terms of the way this allowed us to think about heritage and decision making differently. In theorising further our approach, we explore how our project navigated two connotations of 'social': *social* as people, relationships, feelings and 'the social' as the conceptual reifications and tools that have given us a language to talk about the world and which have defined debates about 'heritage'. The inheritances we take back to our many different places of work and life include making more malleable and amenable to participation the old and persistent conceptual challenges posed by heritage and the ongoing effect – as we act, work and write – of hearing each other's voices in our heads.

Project in focus in this chapter

This chapter explores the legacy of the 'How should heritage decisions be made?' project. The project was funded to include collaboration from the beginning, including defining research questions and research design. The social dynamics which helped us define our research question have also influenced our approach to legacy.

Co-designing the research: thinking and acting systemically

It is again no question of expediency or feeling whether we shall preserve the buildings of past times or not. We have no right whatever to touch them. They are not ours. They belong partly to those who built them, and partly to all the generations of mankind who are to follow us (John Ruskin, [1849] 1865: 163).

The words we generated in the first workshop were prompted by John Lawson, Kathy Cremin and Mike Benson (who have worked together at Ryedale Folk Museum and Bede's World) presenting their approaches to involving many more people in decision making. Through flipcharts, hand-drawn illustrations, videos of a Middlesbrough football match, of the Portuguese Fado sung by students at the University of Coimbra and of a volunteer explaining her transformational experiences of volunteering at the Tenement Museum in New York, John, Kathy and Mike argued that museums could only become a meaningful part of their communities through conceptualising heritage differently. As they put it in our end-of-project booklet:

> We believe that folk engage with heritage everyday probably, in truth, in spite of, and not because of, heritage professionals. If we use the metaphor of heritage as a river that flows every day then one choice is to contain the river and constrain its possibilities and box off opportunities. However, for us, it is the ecology that sustains the river, which is critical. The more streams that feed into the river, big or small – all carrying stories, all playing their part in making the river flow – the better. Then the river, and its ecosystem flourishes and begins to sustain the places and spaces through which it flows (Heritage Decisions, 2015: 10).

John, Kathy and Mike's presentation became a shared reference point throughout the rest of the project. As can be seen in John Ruskin's quotation, the logic of 'heritage' can leave those of us in the present with very little right to be involved at all: the medieval buildings Ruskin evokes are 'not ours' and we have 'no right whatsoever to touch them'. Yet from the first workshop John, Kathy and Mike showed how their practice unseats, and imagines in radically different ways, the Ruskinian notion of heritage and makes space in the here and now for people to play an active role.

Like John, Kathy and Mike's river of heritage, our research project needed a design that would also emphasise action and plural ways of contributing. In developing our design we drew on what Danny Burns has termed 'Systemic Action Research', which fuses complexity theory and action research. Drawing on ideas of ecosystem also evoked by John, Kathy and Mike, Burns argues that 'complex issues cannot be adequately comprehended in isolation from the wider system of which they are part' (2007: 1). We saw this as a useful means of recognising heritage as 'complex' and bound up with the intermeshing of ideas, language, buildings, objects, people, memories and emotions. The project team were interested in the ways in which we actively construct knowledge from experience: know-how. We put the practice of different team members – many of whom had long experience of increasing participation in heritage – at the heart of our approach and identified detailed case studies in specific places in the UK (Leicester, Stoke and York) and within heritage-focused organisations (Bede's World, MadLab, Royal Commission on the Ancient and Historical Monuments of Scotland and the Science Museum, all in the UK).

Having identified the case studies, we then developed tailored research methodologies. For example, semi-structured interviews were used to investigate already completed decision-making processes and approaches drawn from systemic action research were deployed within 'live' projects where decisions were being made at all moments by many different people. The research was structured to recognise that 'each situation is unique and its transformative potential lies in the relationships between interconnected people and organizations' (Burns, 2007: 32). We regularly came back together as a team to make sense of the project as a whole. In designing our project, we already knew that the conceptual ideas we jotted down in our first workshop would play a key role in our research.

The two socials of heritage

In both of the images John, Mike and Kathy produced – the first an account of how their thinking and practice developed at Ryedale Folk Museum (an open air museum with a focus on rural life based in North Yorkshire, UK – Image 4.1), and the second, more recent innovations at Bede's World (a museum based in South Tyneside, UK, dedicated to the work of the monk known as the Venerable Bede – Image 4.2) – there are specific and iterative connections drawn between how to conceptualise heritage and how to increase participation, and vice versa. The illustration in Image 4.1 shows an iterative relationship between 'know-how' and the ethos of heritage as dynamic and social.

Both illustrations show how John, Kathy and Mike draw on ideas of heritage as living and adaptive: 'heritage as a living stream', 'museums in the heritage ecosystem', 'museums must understand their role as nourishing the heritage ecosystem not containing it', museums as a living and 'social space'. Yet, as the flow of illustrations indicate, these ideas not only enable, but have been generated by, specific actions, *knowing how* to open up and devolve decision making. These practices include 'creating a medley of voices' and 'unleashing the talents of volunteers and activists'. As the illustrations indicate, these, in turn, enable and are enabled by cultivating what John, Mike and Kathy call 'feltness' (signified by beating hearts), identifying levers for change and turning upside down the traditional decision-making triangle

Image 4.1: Ryedale: the story of how John, Kathy and Mike's thought developed at Ryedale Folk Museum

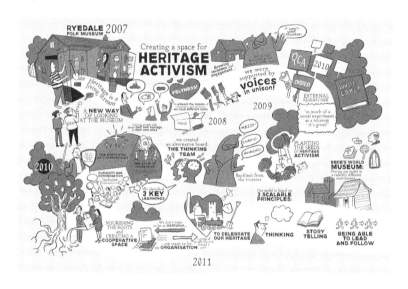

Image 4.2: Imagining museums as part of the heritage ecosystem

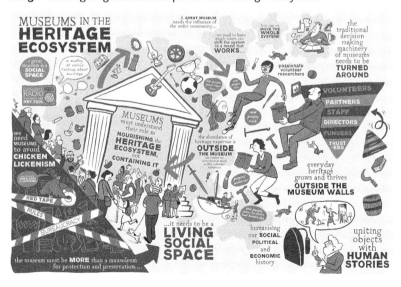

and thinking of leadership not as fixed in the Director or trustees but as a 'spinning atom' with different people leading and following at different times.

Two different connotations of 'social' are navigated in John, Mike and Kathy's work. The first is the way they use 'social' in terms of museums as a 'social space'. This is 'social' in its more familiar and everyday meaning: people, relationships, living, sociable, fun, feltness. Yet in certain theoretical literatures 'the social' is also associated with the particular form of knowing about the world that is secured from a distance, the 'view from nowhere', as historian Mary Poovey has put it:

> Organized from the standpoint of a nonparticipating, objectifying observer, it has become possible to think about social structures, relationships, and processes as entities, as relatively autonomous, and as sufficiently systematic to warrant scientific descriptions – which are systematic as well. Whatever individual theorists mean by the term, 'the social' has become thinkable as part of the long history of reification that we call modernity (Poovey, 2002: 125).

Poovey here talks about the social as in social theory, sociology or social policy: the methods by which we seek to know about, and change, the world.

The way the term 'heritage' has been conceived draws heavily on the traditions of the social, as is clear in the conceptual issues we identified in our first workshop. As is widely diagnosed in the critical heritage studies literature, and as Laurajane Smith has argued, there is a dominant approach to heritage in the West which 'privileges monumentality and grand scale, innate artefact/site significance tied to time depth, scientific/aesthetic expert judgment, social consensus and nation building' (2006: 11). Through this, Smith argues, an 'authorized heritage discourse' can be detected which seeks to disconnect heritage from the present and sets up experts as stewards working on behalf of posterity and future generations and specifically disengages 'certain social actors in the present (that is non-experts), from an active use of heritage' (Smith and Waterton, 2009: 291). The classic example of this is the National Trust's slogan 'for ever, for everyone'.

The conceptual challenges we generated in the first workshop indicated our need to try and make sense of the relationship between meta-concepts which have defined the professional and policy imaginary of heritage and John, Mike and Kathy's approaches to heritage. In others words, how our research might rework 'the social' with the imaginative and conceptual capacities 'unleashed' by 'social spaces'. As we developed our research methodology, we became interested in how new ways of thinking at an abstract level can generate, and be generated by, the flows of insight that come through everyday life and interaction with others. Participation in heritage decision making could be better enabled, we thought, if there was a more dynamic interaction between ideas and social practices.

Paul Carter deploys the metaphor of weaving to indicate the relationship between big and persistent ideas and 'practice'. Although working in very different traditions both Carter and Danny Burns draw attention to the role of process in producing research. Carter indicates a productive relationship between 'grand narratives', which in our project we could read as concepts of posterity, stewardship and scale, and 'local invention', which creates a 'new place' or new understanding, through drawing overly general abstractions into new relationships:

> With the weaving image in mind, these propositions constitute respectively the woof (or weft) and the warp of material thinking. The warp is composed of the threads extended lengthwise in the loom. These can be thought of as culture's myth lines, the grand narratives in terms of which it defines its sense of place and identity. But these linear narratives can neither cohere to form a pattern nor be subverted and overturned, unless the shuttle of local invention is at work, casting its woof-thread back and forth, over and under the warp-threads. Only in this way can cultures collectively gain agency over their story lines learning to become themselves at this place. But to take control this way, to represent a society locally reinventing itself, the shuttle has to advance creeping progressively crosswise along the warp (Carter, 2004:11).

For us the words we developed in the first workshop – Heritage. Stewardship. Custodianship. Expert. Leadership. Institutions. Ownership. Differences/Tensions. Scale. Personal. Values. Voice/ Not heard – became the structure, the woof/weft, across which we began a new horizontal and social weaving. The specific contribution of the know-how of team members in their practice (as well as our project's forms of collaborative dialogue and action research) may be seen as 'local invention' through persistent actions which rework and imagine differently the 'storylines' of heritage.[3] The following short sections show how our research methods (know-how, dialogue, research experiments) *socialised* – in the sense of making more acceptable, more malleable and more useable for our focus on participation – the storylines, the linear narratives and the abstract ideas we noted in our first workshop.

Key resources for thinking about legacy

Thinking of legacy as a social process has enabled us to articulate both our methodology for making 'change from where you are' and our own project's impact. We drew on theoretical traditions that recognise that knowledge becomes legitimate through being built relationally and enabling it to adapt and grow in new contexts. The project's methods were informed by systemic approaches to action research combined with sustained dialogue and sense making between team members. This enabled us to see our own work and our research questions through 'others' eyes' and to use action, and building new networks beyond the research team, to generate new insights.

Burns, B. (2007). *Systemic Action Research: A Strategy for Whole System Change.* Bristol: Policy Press
Carter, P. (2004). *Material Thinking.* Melbourne: Melbourne University Publishing
Smith, L. and Waterton, E. (2009). *Heritage, Communities and Archaeology.* London: Duckworth

Socialising 'stewardship' and 'scale'

As indicated by Laurajane Smith and Emma Waterton, 'scale' – the monumentality of temporal and spatial imaginaries ('for ever, for everyone') – has the effect of putting a great deal of power in professionals' hands (Smith and Waterton, 2009; see also Hertzfeld, 1990; Kirshenblatt-Gimblett, 2006). If heritage has to be managed for imagined constituencies (and for those that do not even yet exist), then the implication is that people in the here and now must be held at arm's length with no right of action or use while professionals act as custodians or stewards. Although this has been highly contested in both academic and practice contexts (not least the Heritage Lottery Fund's definition of participation as 'taking decisions about heritage' (2010: 3)), the legitimacy of participation in heritage is still often questioned on the basis of ideas of stewardship and scale.

In one strand of the project, Karen Brookfield (Heritage Lottery Fund, UK), Danny Callaghan (Potteries Tile Trail) and Helen Graham

(University of Leeds), worked together to explore Danny's approach to the heritage of the Potteries. The Potteries is an area of Staffordshire, UK, known for his history of ceramics. As part of this Danny took Helen and Karen to specific stops on the Potteries Tile Trail, which Danny had developed as part of a Heritage Lottery Fund 'All Our Stories' project. One stop on the trail was a building which used to be a shop called Snapes and it had a beautiful tiled door well depicting the name of the owner of the building, A Allterton. Danny came to know about the door well because the grandson of the proprietor of Snapes had got in touch, worried about a development to turn the shop into flats: would the door well survive? In conversation with Karen and Helen sat in the car, Danny explained how they went about making sure the door well was not removed:

> 'Even in terms of the Local Lists and certainly in terms of the Conservation Team. No. You are not going to get anywhere near it. ... [A door well] is the last thing the conservation officers would be able to get into their field of vision when there are Grade 1 and Grade 2 buildings that they are struggling to protect.[4] But at the same time it is a unique piece of ceramic.
>
> Best thing you can do is Step 1: preserve it virtually. Take a photo. Then capture the stories. So first we've got this family – the Snapes – talking to each other. They've agreed for it to be in the public domain. It's on the Tile Trail on Historypin. Then you've got a dialogue happening locally. [As part of the Tile Trail] we had a walk through and a little tour. 'Ah Snapes, I remember Snapes'. ... Then I said – have you talked directly to the builders? Tell you what, if I'm that way I'll find out about the development. So I went and spoke to the builders. ... I explained about the doorstep. Told them the story about Snapes. Do you know the histories of mosaic production? All made in local bottle kilns. They are local builders. 'Wow, makes you proud'. They've not been told to dig it up. I said, "It's on our trail". "Oh I'll tell my boss. Be a shame to dig it up". You give it an alternative value. One of the guys connected with us is a Master Tiler. I suggest "maybe we could do a restoration class". You create a public event.'

Here you can see the emerging thinking that a year on became the DIY Manifesto (Image 4.3).

Image 4.3: The DIY heritage manifesto

One of the aims of the manifesto was to expand what might count as a heritage decision, who might make such a decision and how.

Danny's work uses experimentation and action to reconceptualise heritage as social, living and dynamic. Inverting Ruskin, Danny suggests *it is* yours, and *it is* your responsibility. Danny's practice also explicitly addresses the problems of 'stewardship' and 'scale'. Even when the heritage is material and even when there is a focus on its physical survival, Danny's work shows that 'preservation' need not be delegated to the stewardship of monumental-type institutions or legal frameworks. Rather 'preservation' is inseparable from both action now and the relationships through which it can be known about and valued. Danny's work, along with the approach of John, Kathy and Mike, reconceptualises scale. Scale is not *scaled up*, as in the vertical and hierarchical 'on behalf of' structures. Instead new special and realisable constituencies are developed and are then *scaled out* more horizontally, whether that is the spinning atom at Bede's World or the micro networks of knowing, caring and sharing created around 'A Allerton'. In Carter's terms what we have here are 'local inventions' reworking long-standing heritage storylines.

Socialising 'expert' and 'voice (+ not being heard)'

'The expert' remains a crucial figure in current debates in heritage. Indeed, many people are employed by heritage agencies, local authorities and museums to designate buildings or collect things deemed significant. This approach has seen decision making about heritage as a technocratic exercise best legitimised by expertise rather than democratic process. Yet in the last 30 years what counts both as 'expertise' and 'significance' has been radically contested and ideas of public or community expertise are recognised in many policy documents (for example Historic England Conservation Principles; Museum Association Code of Ethics). As a result you could say that today there is a legitimacy deficit in both directions. Community groups do still often need, and want, to draw on professional and expert knowledge. But professionals now also often seek further legitimacy for any decision by trying to engage communities.

As part of our experimental action research method in the historic city of York, UK we set up a mini-project called 'York: Living with History' and explored heritage and its decision making in the city, thinking of it as a complex system. The York team – Martin Bashforth (York's Alternative History), Peter Brown (York Civic Trust) and Helen Graham (University of Leeds) and which expanded in the research phase to include Paul Furness and Lianne and Richard Brigham from York Past and Present Facebook group – recognised that members of the public having a greater 'voice' was bound up with networks, who you know, which in turn was related to whether you, and what you know, could be seen as 'legitimate'. Peter, reflecting on his involvement in the wider project noticed a change in thinking in his organisation about 'expertise' and 'voice' as a result of the research project:

> 'My organisation [York Civic Trust] has, until recently, functioned in "silo-mode", considering itself one of a small number of "experts" engaged in the heritage decision-making process in York. Involvement in the [Heritage Decisions] project, however, has shown the benefits of a

more democratic and inclusive engagement with a broad spectrum of opinion, thereby offering a more measured view on issues of common interest.'

Peter indicates that there is a relatively small group of people, framed as 'experts', who wield much of the influence within and across official structures of decision making in the city, as was borne out by a social network analysis conducted in the first few months of our work in York. We decided to try to expand the number of people who are part of those networks, both as a research method and as a tactic for change. This action revealed something of how legitimacy is created and the social textures of any individual's or group's ability to act and make a difference:

Lianne: When we first had the meeting at the café (with Helen), although it was something that we wanted, I seriously thought that we were all just getting high hopes that we'd actually be able to get somewhere; that we'd actually be able to chip away at the Council. So, I did come away, not disillusioned, but a bit cynical to be honest. I did think, this isn't going to happen, this isn't going to work. But looking back, good things have happened. Because for us as a group it's opened up so many opportunities that I don't think we would have been able to get. And working as a team we've opened up a lot of people's eyes that actually we're not going to go away; we have a voice and we can be heard now.

Peter: You've suddenly become legitimate.

Lianne: Yes, exactly. Not just two people.

Richard: It's allowed us to meet people like John Oxley [City Archaeologist], Richard Pollitt [Mansion House, Guildhall and Civic Services Manager], yourselves [Peter and Helen]; people we wouldn't normally meet. So, if we have a question we have these different people that we can contact. I think that's probably the most important thing is the different people you have to meet that will help you in every different direction.

The York team's discussions suggest that if you want to make a difference, other people need to see you as legitimate. However, what has also become clear through our experimental research is that there are different routes to legitimacy. Over the lifetime of the research project, York Past and Present has grown from hundreds to over 12,000 members. Lianne and Richard's ability to work with key people in professional roles – and to get replies to their emails – has run in step with their growing constituency and increasing twitter presence. As such the discussions between Peter, Lianne and Richard indicate that democratic claims can be used to challenge a narrow reading of professional expertise in ways which organise claims to 'legitimacy' differently, through diverse and plural networks. Indeed, owing to the requirements of the Heritage Lottery Fund and other funders that bids demonstrate community involvement, the professionals they work with need groups such as York Past and Present as much as York Past and Present might need them. The York research indicates how we might more systemically recognise the connection in current policy and funding contexts between 'expertise' and 'voice', with both professionals and community groups seeking relational – socialised – forms of legitimacy for action and decision.

Socialising 'significance'

Defining significance – and whether something should be listed, designated or collected – has been one of the key tasks of heritage professionals and is often imagined as a stable and fixed part of the planning process. In the context of the historic environment, the reasons why a building is important are then supposed to shape its management and any development that might happen

Rebecca Madgin (University of Glasgow) and Jenny Timothy (Leicester City Council) worked together to question how ideas of a building's significance are understood through researching the various points of view of those involved in the development of a particular listed building, College Court in Leicester. Rather than the significance of College Court being fixed, Rebecca and Jenny were able to show how the collaboration between Jenny, as the Conservation Officer, and the team of architects and developers enabled the meaning of the building to be developed and adapted through the process of working together. Rebecca and Jenny reflected on this:

'[A] theme running through the interviews was people's emotional response to both the project and the building and how this governed their responses, and their perception of other people's responses. This is interesting as arguably the planning system was put in place as a reaction to people's positive emotional responses to their past. But it is a system which tries to take emotion out of the decision-making process. Making the subjective objective, it tries to make decision-making fair and transparent. But the biggest criticism of the planning system is that it is neither of those things.'

The object – College Court – far from being stable became described by all involved as shifting and growing:

'[The architects and developers] did all the stuff that you need to do for your application. Yet the building's significance never felt like it was explicit, it kind of seemed to grow as the project went along. And it wasn't actually until it was kind of all finished and we were stood there that people actually then started to explicitly say, actually this is really important, it's a really beautiful piece of architecture, it's a really nice building. But all the way along you could feel people's attachment to the building growing, and the understanding of the significance of the building growing; and by turn, how much they cared about it kind of growing.'

Equally the research process played a role in this as it gave the different collaborating members – Jenny, as well as the architects and developers – a chance to recognise that the structures of law and policy (the woof, to return to the metaphor of weaving) – came to work better when both became woven with 'local invention' comprised of emotional attachments to the building and to each other.

Socialising 'the future'

The idea of 'posterity' – future generations or forever – plays an active role in heritage practice. Regularly decisions are made not to display or loan museum objects, or make them available to touch, because they are too delicate. While there have been examples of museums making objects accessioned into the collections available for use – such as Glasgow Museum's loan boxes or the Science Museum's working objects (such as trains and clocks) – how to make decisions about balancing between use now and preservation for the future is a very active problem in museum practice. As such a key issue for our project became how to rethink the 'future'.

Another of the project's experimental strands of work, alongside York, was at the Science Museum where Tim Boon (Science Museum), Richard Courtney (Leicester University) and Helen Graham (University of Leeds) worked with a group of musicians, composers, journalists and fans of electronic music – Jean-Phillipe Calvin, David Robinson, John Stanley and Martin Swan – to explore questions of collaborative museum collecting, with a focus on electronic music. Yet the conversation very often turned to the problem of synthesisers and conservation. There emerged through the group's discussions a very clear sense that the synthesisers should not to be treated as artefacts to be preserved. Instead, as their intent was to make music, they should be treated as instruments to be played, allowing them to come alive for the networks of fans and enthusiasts which give them meaning:

> 'I ended up feeling very strongly that some of the objects in the Science Museum stores, particularly the rarer synthesisers, needed to be powered on again. The longer they sit in the dark with the capacitors slowly failing, the less likely they are to ever make sound again, and ultimately, the less meaning could be assigned to them. It seemed that a limited project to bring them back to life, if that was possible and fundable, would be a excellent way of using the knowledge of interested communities, engaging with the objects and the general public' (John Stanley).

> 'If you engage the network of geeks out there then you create a community with "a curatorial head on". They will say – "we will look for those things". You're creating a community of curators. But as soon as you stop playing them, synths start to decay. They become less and less the thing that made them worth collecting. As they become less and less viable as instruments, they also become less and less interesting to the geeks, the very people who would want to enthuse about the objects to other people. And these are also the people who could maintain them and could get them going again' (Martin Swan).

John and Martin reimagine ideas of what it means for something to be preserved; what the 'it' being kept safe through preservation logics might be. The argument developed within the group was that the synths were collected for a specific reason (they are electronic musical instruments), which the methods of their preservation (no longer using them) itself occludes. Also, more powerfully, the very community that enthuses about the collections themselves lose interest as the objects are no longer allowed to be what originally gave them purpose. Preservation is often defined broadly as keeping something in unaltered condition or to maintain it unchanged. The group's conversation developed different nuances offered by conservation – not 'keeping unaltered' but as 'wise use' 'not using up'. Martin's comments here frame the idea of 'being used up' not in material but in *social* terms. This reimagines the future as something which unfolds socially from the now. A key point, that we will take over into our final discussion about the legacy of the Heritage Decisions project, is that the structured monumental and posterity-style approaches to legacy fail if they are not enlivened by ongoing and unfolding social dynamics.

Legacies of heritage decisions: interacting 'socials'

Through drawing out the techniques for 'increasing participation from where you are' – which are more generally techniques for creating change – we realised that we were also identifying a methodology for sustaining our own research project's legacy.

Act: make change from where you are

Act came about in defiance of the idea that those of us in the present have no agency or that individual people cannot make a difference in their organisations or places. This has also proved good advice to ourselves in developing an ongoing life for the ideas we developed together. For example, Alex Hale (Royal Commission on the Ancient and Historical Monuments of Scotland) – who worked with Rebecca Madgin to undertake organisational reflective practice around the Source to Sea project – describes that starting from where you are, and being in dialogue with colleagues, has had positive organisational effects:

> 'Working with a diverse group of people within the team has enabled me to recognise how you can make little changes, "tweaks" if you like, to your working practices. These are often through collaborative partnerships that will effect positive change to your work and could also engender greater changes from within the system that you work in.

Taking colleagues along is a vital part of this. Keeping others informed and telling them about the pitfalls and progress that you've made is a very important aspect of this way of working.'

Connect: cross boundaries and collaborate

A key idea we identified was the power of networking – Richard Brigham refers to this as the 'magic path' of people who also want change (Heritage Decisions, 2015: 4). After reading one of the drafts of this chapter, Lianne Brigham and Richard Brigham emailed a comment for inclusion:

> 'Coming from a non-academic background Richard and I found at the beginning working with everyone a little bit of a language barrier.
> The project has not only given us confidence … It has also given us the opportunity to build a bigger network. We have learnt so much. Everyone gave us the time to talk and listen, we both thought at first "what could anyone learn from us, as we are just 'Joe Public'?" (which we did state in one of our earlier meetings). … we all have our own voice but from that we have been able to come together in the end of project booklet.'

Rachael Turner (MadLab) also drew attention to the challenge of communication across boundaries as well as its potentially transformative benefits:

> 'Finding people who want to work with each other is not difficult. Finding people to work together across different sectors, from different points of view is an altogether harder proposition. It takes time to develop networks, and trust – especially with a large and (by design) relatively disparate community, such as the one we have at MadLab. Language is key. Different communities within our community naturally speak *different* languages. Where is heritage in this? The answer is that it lives (or dies) on the same established (or nascent) networks.'

When we were developing our end-of-project booklet we recognised it would be most meaningful if we also *socialised* its dissemination and tried to be a kind of connection point between our different worlds. That is, we each took on the task to pass it to people we worked with and saying why we thought they might be interested – a process we are tracking in the post-project phase. Karen Brookfield led an exercise at one of our workshops where we each listed all the people we'd spoken to about the project. It was an enormous list, each of us tapping into our quite diverse networks. A metaphor Danny Callaghan used to evoke our approach to dissemination was that of a diamond. We had each brought our different perspectives – inheritances – into the project, in order for the ideas to be impactful they had to be reflected back at lots of different and targeted angles back to our home places, organisations and disciplines.

Reflect: see your work through other people's eyes

A common theme of the team's reflections on the project was the transformative potential of conversations. For example Martin Bashforth reflects:

> 'Diversity was present in the Heritage Decisions group itself, opening up the potential for greater collective wisdom. After the first workshop in Jarrow, the event which for me most captured this quality was the workshop in Manchester, where we invited in an equal number and equally diverse range of "critical others" to reflect and comment on our work up to that point. I continue to absorb and reflect on the intellectual impact of that workshop. Apart from that, the deepest influence has come from one-to-one discussions with team members, each of whom has helped me appreciate different viewpoints and perspectives in ways I could never have expected.'

Or as Paul Manners remembers about an exchange between Rebecca and Danny:

> 'Rebecca, one of the academics on the team, was talking about how the project had influenced her practice. She said: "I'll never be able to approach a piece of work on this topic again without hearing Danny's voice in my head." Danny is one of the "community activists" recruited to the project. Prior to this project, neither he nor Rebecca had met – they worked on heritage in separate worlds. This project

encouraged a wonderful form of "social learning" – where different kinds of expertise and insight came together. This process is captured beautifully by the Russian psychologist, Vygotsky [1978: 88] who talked about learning as a social process "by which we grow into the intellectual life of those around us". Not only did this mean we could think better collectively – but long term, these connections will continue to animate our practice and our ways of making sense of heritage: like it or not, each other's voices will continue to echo in our imaginations and challenge our thinking – even when we're sat in splendid isolation, working back in our own heritage worlds.'

A legacy for us all will be each other's voices – and we will carry that inheritance from the project with us into our future work. We might be working with the same ideas and policies as we did before the project, but are now able to address the blocks to participation in heritage decision making generated by 'scale', 'stewardship', 'expert', 'significance' and the 'future' differently.

Situate: see your work in context

The final of our four ideas refers to systemic thinking and we have also sought to use 'seeing our work in context' for identifying specific levers (as John Lawson, Kathy Cremin and Mike Benson call them) for our project's legacy. We have sought to develop 'working pictures' as a way of being able to act and invent within our contexts, local and national. Yet to bring us back to the two types of social, a final context is 'the social' thinking which animates debates in heritage policy and practice. We've taken the opportunity in this chapter to see our work in the context of live debates in heritage policy and practice and heritage studies. We think conceptual insight has come from the social, felt, lived and relational work we've done. It comes from listening hard to the practical knowledge of people in the team – what we've called *know-how*. Karen Brookfield drew attention to this in her reflections on situating the insights of the know-how of Danny Callaghan in the context of the strategic issue of deployment of Heritage Lottery Funding:

'The Heritage Lottery Fund supports hundreds of small community projects every year, but only rarely am I able to spend time with a "heritage activist" like Danny, to begin to understand how an individual's knowledge and passion for heritage makes great things happen locally. This has been invaluable to my professional practice, particularly in stimulating ideas of how HLF might invest differently to enable people to take ownership of their heritage and realise their vision for the future.'

As Karen's quote suggests, what we've done is to research 'the social' of heritage *socially*, from a position that foregrounds how knowledge is constructed through interactions and dialogue. A crucial part of this has been to socialise heritage abstractions unfriendly to participation in heritage decision making. Through our case studies above we have shown how the conceptual ideas of 'stewardship', 'scale', 'expert', 'voice', 'significance' and 'future' might be made more amenable to open, inclusive and participatory use by practitioners and activists.

The potential for our method – that of holding *social approaches* and 'the social' in relationship – was there from the first workshop. As words were written on pieces of paper. As people tried to see, understand and feel what everyone else was saying. As stories and ideas tumbled out. As what our project would become started to emerge.

Guidance for understanding legacy

From the start: Build legacy into the project from the start. Are the people who really care about and can carry forward the research ideas involved?

Act: Knowing is enabled through action and action enables knowing to adapt and grow. See research and its legacy as the same process.

Reflect: Develop legacy throughout the project. Check the resonance of what you are doing and allow feedback to shape your trajectory.

Connect: Always increase the number of people you are engaging in your thinking and keep in touch with them.

Situate: Understand your project's wider context but also get involved and actively create contexts within which your research can thrive and develop.

Notes

[1] An Arts and Humanities Research Council Connected Communities pilot, 'Co-design and Co-creation Development Awards'.

[2] A full list of the Heritage Decision team with our chosen descriptors: Martin Bashforth, radical family historian and York's Alternative History; Mike Benson, Director, Bede's World; Tim Boon, Head of Research and Public History, Science Museum; Lianne Brigham, York Past and Present; Richard Brigham, York Past and Present; Karen Brookfield, Deputy Director (Strategy), Heritage Lottery Fund; Peter Brown, Director, York Civic Trust; Danny Callaghan, independent consultant (public art, history and engagement) including *The Potteries Tile Trail* (HLF All Our Stories); Jean-Phillipe Calvin, composer and researcher; Richard Courtney, School of Management, University of Leicester; Kathy Cremin, Director, Hive; Paul Furness, writer and historian; Helen Graham, School of Fine Art, History of Art and Cultural Studies and Centre for Critical Studies in Museums, Galleries and Heritage, University of Leeds; Alex Hale, archaeologist, Royal Commission of Ancient and Historical Monuments of Scotland; Paddy Hodgkiss, Riccall Archive co-ordinator; John Lawson, storyteller, Loftus; Rebecca Madgin, urban studies, University of Glasgow; Paul Manners, Director, National Co-ordinating Centre for Public Engagement; David Robinson, technical editor and musician; John Stanley, writer and electronic musician; Martin Swan, musician and educator; Jenny Timothy, Senior Building Conservation Officer, Leicester City Council; Rachael Turner, Director, MadLab and *The Ghosts of St Pauls* (HLF All Our Stories).

[3] Representational democracy (as a form of decision making recognised as holding at least some legitimacy) could also be thought of as an achievement of the 'reifications we call modernity' (Poovey, 2002). 'We might say that the problem of democracy is never simply that of making collective decisions, but is also, indissolubly, the problem of bringing "the collective" into being at all' (Gilbert, 2014: 24).

[4] In England, Historic England has responsibility for recommending and regulating buildings recognised as having heritage value. This process of called 'listing' and buildings can be listed as Grade I, II* or II.

References

Burns, B. (2007). *Systemic Action Research: A Strategy for Whole System Change*. Bristol: Policy Press

Carter, P. (2004). *Material Thinking*. Melbourne: Melbourne University Publishing

Heritage Lottery Fund (2010). 'Thinking about … Community Participation'. http://closedprogrammes.hlf.org.uk/preApril2013/furtherresources/Pages/Thinkingaboutcommunityparticipation.aspx

Hertzfeld, M. (1990). *A Place in History: Social and Monumental Time in a Cretan Town*. Princeton. NJ: Princeton University Press

Gilbert, J. (2014). *Common Ground: Democracy and Collectivity in a Age of Individualism*. London: Pluto

Kirshenblatt-Gimblett, B. (2006). 'World Heritage and Cultural Economics', In Karp, I., Kratz, C.A., Sawaja, L. and Ybarra-Frausto, T. (eds), *Museums Frictions: Public Cultures/Global Transformations*, NC: Duke University Press

Poovey, M. (2002). 'The Liberal Civil Subject and the Social in Eighteenth-Century British Moral Philosophy'. *Public Culture* 14(1): 125–45

Ruskin, J. ([1849]1865). *Seven Lamps of Architecture*. New York: John Wiley and Son

Smith, L. (2006). *The Uses of Heritage*. London: Routledge

Smith, L. and Waterton, E. (2009). *Heritage, Communities and Archaeology*. London: Duckworth

Vygotsky, L.S. (1978). *Mind in Society*. Cambridge, MA: Harvard University Press

Performing the legacy of animative and iterative approaches to co-producing knowledge

Mihaela Kelemen, Martin Phillips, Deborah James and Sue Moffat[1]

Introduction

Various modes of research such as *engaged scholarship* (see Van de Ven and Johnson, 2006; Van de Ven, 2007), *relational scholarship* (Bartunek, 2007) and *dialogical research* (Beech et al, 2010; Lorino et al 2011; Avenier and Parmentier Cajaiba, 2012; MacIntosh et al, 2012) have been advocated as forms of collaborative research in which academics and practitioners work together to co-produce knowledge about a complex/problematic/sensitive phenomenon. The collaborative work discussed in this chapter shared many of these engaged, relational and dialogical features and involved a variety of people from three countries (academics from diverse disciplines, community partners from local and national level organisations) all with different ideas about how collaboration should work and what change it should achieve. In this chapter we introduce five theoretical perspectives (theatre studies, American Pragmatism, critical theory, actor network theory (ANT) and Deleuzian studies) which we used to make sense of our collaborative efforts. We then provide a short account of the research projects undertaken, their creative methodologies and resulting artistic outputs (two interactive installations, a game and a documentary drama). We examine how our chosen theories have shaped the processes by which we co-defined and co-evaluated the legacies of our research projects. We conclude that any attempt to define legacy of collaborative research involves a strong element of performing it with the community partners.

Making sense of collaboration: five theoretical lenses

Collaborative research and co-creation processes in general (Denis and Lomas, 2003; Shani et al, 2008) are seen as forms of research that facilitate examination of the dynamic relationship between academic and community practice. As outlined below, we made use of five theoretical perspectives to help make sense of our collaborative, co-creative research endeavours and their resulting legacies. Building on Nicolini's (2009) work, we switch theoretical lenses and repositioning in the field so that certain aspects of practice are grounded while others are bracketed. A common thread across our theoretical lenses is that they challenge disciplinary boundaries, emphasise everyday performance, and create safer spaces for thinking about existing challenges and about how to tackle them by making visible the creative possibilities that exist within individuals and communities. By adopting an agonistic pluralist stance (Mouffe, 2007), our approach has been to reflect and embrace rather than suppress difference and to find skillful ways to acknowledge and accept that conflict can be co-generative in collaborative efforts.

Theatre studies

A key collaborator in many of the collaborative projects being discussed here was the New Vic Theatre, in Newcastle-under-Lyme, UK, wich has a 50-year documentary and theatre-in-the-round tradition. Its productions reinvigorated and radicalised British theatre in the 1960s, with working in the round bringing new ideological and creative possibilities such as 'verbatim theatre' and the opportunity to create documentaries concerned with the everyday life struggles and stories of the community. The rigour of the research undertaken for a piece of documentary theatre and the respect for the way people tell their own stories dovetailed well with a methodology of knowledge co-production known as 'cultural animation' (Kelemen and Hamilton, 2015). The director of New Vic Borderlines and pioneer of cultural animation in the UK, Sue Moffat, describes the theatre's involvement in the Connected Communities (CC) programme as follows: "we've never done any research before being involved in the CC programme and never connected our stories with existing theories and insights. Working with academics lent credibility to what we had been doing for a decade, providing a powerful language that resonated deeply with our own ambitions and agenda." Cultural animation's main ambition is to create a democratic space, where hierarchies can be dissolved at least temporarily. Playful experiential exercises which draw on a range of theatre traditions including Stanislavski, Brecht and Boal (Bishop, 2006) are adapted to hasten the reduction of barriers and insecurities and to create connections which grow throughout the process. Using cultural animation as a research tool allows 'tricky', contentious and potentially difficult themes to be explored in such a way that opposing narratives can exist side by side and common concerns can be identified.

American Pragmatism

The emphasis on the formation of trusting and genuine relationships, based on equality between academics and community partners, finds resonance with strands of American Pragmatism, such as John Dewey's democratic experimentalism. His democratic experimentalism rejects the idea that science has a special method to access reality, which is different from the way in which we gain knowledge in our everyday lives (Dewey, 1938 [1991]). Thus, scientific inquiry follows the same pattern as common-sense inquiry as there is methodological and content continuity between science and commonsense. Ordinary experience can produce from within itself questions and criteria of judgement that constitute legitimate knowledge. Just like the theatre tradition above, Pragmatism views academic expertise, commonsensical intelligence and practical knowledge as equal partners in the research conversation. As such, the relationship between researchers and community partners during the research process is necessarily democratic. In Dewey's ideal, experimentalism and democratic behaviour become fused (Gouinlock, 1990). Democratic experimentalism does not aim to produce knowledge that represents the truth about the world. Rather, its main ambition is to provide intellectual instruments and practical tools for people to think and act more effectively in a world shot with contingency and ambiguity (Watson, 2011).

Critical theory

The processes of intersubjective interactions facilitated by our collaborative research connect to many aspects of the critical theory of commentators such as Jürgen Habermas, Max Horkheimer and Axel Honneth, which draw on, and distance themselves from, the philosophy of American Pragmatism (for example see Rehg and Bohman, 2001; Aboulafia et al, 2002). Horkheimer argued that the purpose of theory should not be to 'simply ... increase knowledge as such' but should have as its goals 'emancipation', 'the happiness of all individuals' and the achievement of 'all their potentialities' (Adorno and Horkheimer, 2002: 245–8). In relation to our projects, important shared features included 'an understanding of rationality as intrinsically dialogical and communicative' (Bernstein, 1992: 48) and a performative or consequentialist understanding of truth, whereby truth is established through, and often operates within, people's practices.

Actor network theory

Our collaboration was also influenced by actor network theories where the 'truth' or 'power' of an interpretation is seen to lie in the connections it can sustain (for example see Callon, 1986; Latour, 2005). Such work has frequently claimed that knowledge is produced by networks of heterogeneous human and non-or more-than-human entities, or 'actants'. There are clear parallels to the emphasis in American Pragmatism on the practical judgement of knowledge, although arguably this places greater emphasis than ANT does on conceptual revisions and the improvement of the conditions for the thriving of life. A striking feature of our research project was that the research themes and the methodologies of the original projects were able to transfer into new contexts, enrolling support from new participants in the UK but also in other countries: Japan, Canada and Greece.

Deluezian studies

The writings of the post-structuralist philosopher Giles Deleuze (for example see Deleuze, 1994) advance the notion of 'difference within repetition', which was a central aspect of our collaborative work, which relied on various forms of iteration. For Deleuze, even within the apparently identical there are always differences: even if the outcome of creating an understanding is simply a repetition of some earlier understanding, the creation of this understanding has been a unique event or series of events, or as Abel (2002: 234) puts it, each interpretation is 'a new voyage, one that repeats some of the old movements but [always] introduces new ones'. Five modes of iteration have underpinned our collaboration, namely iteration as 'refinement of ideas', 'deepening description', 'inter-subjective engagement with others', 'enrolment', and the 'detailing of difference within repetition'. These modes of iteration are by no means mutually exclusive, although they can produce quite different outputs and can be connected to quite different, and arguably quite incommensurable, epistemologies.

Key resources for thinking about legacy

The suggested sources encourage the readers to approach the concept of legacy through a plurality of theoretical lenses and challenge disciplinary boundaries when exploring the performative nature of research impact and legacy.

Aguinis, H., Shapiro, D., Antonacopoulou Gnosis, E. and Cummings, T. (2014). 'Scholarly Impact: A Pluralist Conceptualization'. *Academy of Management Learning & Education* 13: 623–39

Beech, N., MacIntosh, R. and MacLean, D. (2010). 'Dialogues between Academics and Practitioners: The Role of Generative Dialogic Encounters'. *Organization Studies* 31 1341–67

James, D. (2015). 'Evaluating the Legacy of Animative and Iterative Connected Communities Projects: Reflections on Methodological Legacies'. https://www.keele.ac.uk/media/keeleuniversity/ri/risocsci/thelegacyofconnectedcommunities/FINAL%20EVALUATING%20LEGACY%20REPORT%20NCVO%20300915%20(1).pdf

Kelemen, M. and Hamilton, L. (2015). 'The role of creative methods in redefining the impact agenda'. *CASIC Working Paper* No. 1, https://www.keele.ac.uk/casic/workingpaperseries/

Nicolini, D. (2009). 'Zooming In and Out: Studying Practices by Switching Lenses and Trailing Connections'. *Organization Studies* 30: 1391–418

Projects in focus and their methods: cultural animation and iteration

We provide in Table 5.1 a short summary of the four research projects whose legacy we have evaluated, followed by a summary of the key points of the cultural animation methodology that underpinned the first three projects and of the iterative methodology that led to the development of a community co-produced interactive game called *Glossopoly* in the fourth project.

Cultural animation lies within the broad field of Creative Methods (Gauntlett, 2007), which include an array of techniques of a visual, performative and sensory nature (Barone and Eisner, 1997). Yet cultural animation eludes simple narrative. Nonetheless, we can summarise it for our present purposes as a form of community arts engagement which literally animates, or 'gives life to', the underlying dynamic of a community (Reynolds, 1984). It is this enlivening process that makes this approach a valuable method of social enquiry as well as a

Table 5.1: Projects referenced in Chapter Five

Project Title	Aims and Methodologies	Type of collaboration	Interdisciplinarity	Outcomes
Exploring Personal Communities: A Review of Volunteering	Explore how personal communities contribute to the public good via a scoping review Documentary Theatre	Co-design of a documentary drama with community members	Community studies Organisation Studies Sociology Theatre Studies	Literature scoping study: http://www.keele.ac.uk/exploringpersonalcommunities/ Documentary drama: 'Little Act of Kindness' performed in Newcastle-under-Lyme and London
Untold Stories of Volunteering: A Cultural Animation Project	To explore volunteering experiences with a wide range of stakeholders Cultural Animation Documentary theatre	Co-design and co-production with community members and other stakeholders (such as NCVO)	Philosophy Theatre studies Human geography Management studies Community art	Documentary drama: 'Untold Stories of Volunteering', performed in Newcastle-under-Lyme, Leicester and London Mini-performances Songs Shadow puppet theatre Installations http://www.keele.ac.uk/volunteeringstories/
Bridging the gap between academic rigour and community relevance: fresh insight from American Pragmatism	To explore how communities in the UK and Japan respond to different types of crisis Cultural animation	Co-production with local communities, NGOs, local businesses and government agencies	Management Design studies Theatre studies Community studies Philosophy Business Communication	Collaborative workshops The *Tree of Life* installation The Bridging the Gap Boat installation http://www.keele.ac.uk/bridgingthedivide/
Revisiting the mid-point of British	To explore the relationship between place, affect and affordance Iterative methodologies	Co-production with community members, community arts and heritage organisations	Human geography Sociology Community studies Philosophy Community arts	*Glossopoly*: an interactive board game http://www2.le.ac.uk/departments/geography/research1/projects/ConCom/glossopoly

powerful way of representing and communicating important issues. Through a variety of drama-based techniques and artefact making, the methodology helps to accentuate the relational, processual and emergent nature of collaborative research and its networks. In a relatively straightforward sense, then, it aims to make the voice of the community more central rather than assuming academic privilege in simplifying and categorising the world for scholarly purposes. Cultural Animation is heavily influenced by theatre studies and American Pragmatism, in particular Dewey's principle of the experimental iteration.

Iterative methods have been defined, at least in relation to data analysis, as a set of reflexive processes that spark insight and help us develop meaning (Srivastava and Hopwood, 2009). The research project 'Revisiting the mid-point of British community studies' came to focus on a range of iterative movements, including between various moments of engagement with people in a community. For example, it considered how initial engagements with people through a household survey involving questionnaires and semi-structured interviews compared to later engagements through follow up psycho-social interviews. It also explored the iterations between people and their environments during mobile interviewing, in which people's responses, and indeed the interviewer questions, were frequently prompted by things that were seen or otherwise sensed as one moved through space. However, a focus on iterative methods came to particular prominence in the development of *Glossopoly*. The iterative process of playing the game enabled refining of views and helped generate new themes for discussion and analysis. Though iterative and animative methods are different, they have several things in common in terms of their approach and value base:

- They are highly participatory, group-based methods. In common with other participatory research methods, the process (engagement of participants with the themes, activities, and, importantly, with each other) is valued alongside the output.
- They are at heart creative, drawing on play, imagination, and art and games as ways to energise people to articulate ideas and experiences in new and different ways.
- Objects, artefacts and creative tasks serve an important purpose as a way to stimulate imagination and conversation.

Given their embodied nature, these methodologies have been effective across national cultures. Indeed, Japanese and Canadian academics and community partners have been quick to embrace their ethos. While critics may argue that these methodologies are forms of play, our collaboration taught us that 'you can discover more about a person in an hour of play than in a year of conversation' (Plato quoted in D'Angour, 2013: 296). Thus, our collaborative methodologies linked to problem solving in a rather innovative (and playful) way because they complicated the very idea of significant research problems just as they challenged traditional methods for tackling them.

Artefacts co-produced in these projects

We now briefly consider a few artistic artefacts which were co-produced in cultural animation workshops and iterative activities, respectively. We start by focusing on two 'installations' and a documentary play and then move on to introduce *Glossopoly* (a game that resulted from iterative collaborative research). It is important to explain how these emerged because this demonstrates the performed and co-creative nature of the collaborative process in close-up and is relevant to our subsequent analysis. *The Boat* installation (see Image 5.1) is a 7-foot wooden 'barge' on wheels with sails made out of silk imprinted with images produced in cultural animation workshops that focused on creating 'new worlds' in Stoke-on-Trent, a UK city experiencing the aftermath of decline in primary industry (coal mining, steel and pottery production) and with a number of pressing social problems including widespread unemployment and poverty. In seeking to co-design and co-create a physical artefact for imagining new worlds from the 'lost worlds' of industry and production, *The Boat* takes participants on imaginary voyages of discovery, inviting them to make artefacts and write poems or songs about a lost past and an imagined future.

The second art form we describe here is the *Tree of Life* installation, which was created during a field trip to Minamisanriku, Japan following the 2011 Tsunami. In Japanese mythology the tree is a symbol of endurance and longevity (see Image 5.2). Thus, the tree became a useful anchor to base the workshops around. The workshops included a variety of government and community partners (Minamisanriku City Government, Isatomae Fukko Shoutengai Shopping Street Cooperative, Heisei-no-mori Temporary Housing Residents' Association, comprising 248 houses, Iriya Yes Craft, and Minamisanriku Fukko-dako-no-kai or the Citizens' Association for Town Reconstruction). Here, cultural animation approaches facilitated storytelling through object making: such objects (dolls, flags, poems, and so on) were 'hung' onto the bare branches of the tree filling it

Image 5.1: *The Boat*

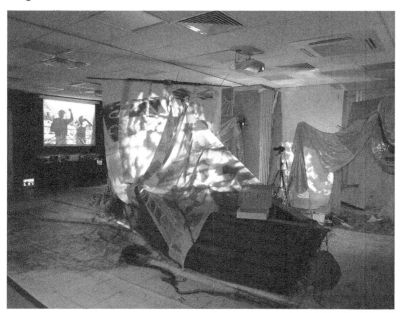

with stories of survival and hopes for the future. Like *The Boat*, this is an installation themed around lost worlds and imagining new ones with communities in crisis.

The third art form is an interactive documentary drama about volunteering performed by project participants and theatre practitioners. Entitled, 'Untold Stories of Volunteering', the drama focused on the role of volunteering in our communities, exploring the dynamism and challenges of individual volunteering journeys and organisational practices relating to volunteering (see Image 5.3). It was co-designed using volunteers' testimonies from 20 interviews, as well as ideas that emerged and artefacts created in five cultural animation workshops with diverse community partners and other institutional stakeholders. The performance included voice-over (interview clips), songs and poems written by original participants in the project.

Image 5.2: *Tree of Life*

Image 5.3: Documentary drama on volunteering

Finally, *Glossopoly* developed as a game-based method of engaging people to interact with each other to reflect on and discuss notions of community. The game was derived from the popular board game *Monopoly*, but has been redesigned to act as an instrument of iterative research (see Image 5.4). Specifically, the game involves people interacting with the views of other people, as expressed through face-to-face discussions with other players of the game and with the comments and images made by people and expressed in images on the board on which the game is played and a series of cards players pick up as they move counters, or themselves in a floor-based version of the game, around the *Glossopoly* board. The images and words were derived from earlier research, such as the questionnaires and interviews discussed above, but also incorporated materials derived from earlier enactments of the game or produced as part of the current game.[2] The game is seen to be an expression of iterative research in that there are repeated movements between people's initial viewpoints and the views of others. There was also, in some variants of the game, iteration between the expression of problems and the formulation of potential solutions, as well as interactions between different community constituents. Though initially a board game, *Glossopoly* evolved into a floor game during the course of this legacy project as seen in Image 5.4.

Image 5.4: *Glossopoly*

In setting out some of the artistic outputs that were co-produced in our projects, we suggest that a more refined view of collaboration and change is possible. This, we argue, offers a distinctive way to transcend disciplinary, social and national culture borders and, in a practical way, enables us to reconceptualise what is meant by the legacy of our research. In the next section, we discuss this in more detail by drawing on the nascent literature on 'legacy' and by outlining the collaborative work undertaken in our legacy project.

Co-evaluating legacy: methodological insights

Deborah Jones, a senior evaluator from the National Council for Voluntary Organisations (NCVO) worked alongside project partners and community members from the outset. One of her main ambitions was to ensure that the historiographies of the community partners came to the fore and were heard as loudly as the disciplinary backgrounds of the academics.

Our aim was to understand, create and perform legacy from these four projects. To that end we organised a number of UK-based showcase and taster activities (delivered over five separate events: see Table 5.2) and the two supported pilots where researchers new to cultural animation and iterative methodologies tried them out with community members (see Table 5.3). Other evaluative activities took place including meetings with policy makers and practitioners (for example, at the Department for Communities and Local Government) and a field trip to Canada involving showcasing the activities via talks and workshops that reached almost 100 delegates (members of a non-profit network, a business school, local academics and members of local communities).

Table 5.2: Showcase and taster activities

Session	Audiences
Drama performance and cultural animation workshop: a performance of the 'Untold Stories of Volunteering' play followed by a taster workshop to introduce the methods that went into creating the stories.	A mixed audience interested in volunteering and the original research findings [47] and a smaller group of volunteer managers, researchers and policy makers [11] interested in findings and methods (cultural animation).
Summer camp for community organisers: one cultural animation and one iterative taster workshop (supported by the *Boat* and the game) and an interactive installation (*Tree of Life*) during a summer camp for community activists.[3]	Community organisers on their annual weekend summer camp [50] with an interest in the methods as potential tools to engage communities, as community development/planning tools.
National volunteering workshop: a taster cultural animation workshop organised by the National Association of Neighbourhood Management for people interested in engaging with volunteers in Big Local areas[4] preceded by a presentation and Q&A on Untold Stories of Volunteering.	Residents of Big Local areas – volunteers and members of partnerships engaging their communities to improve local areas [20] with an interest in the findings of the research as well as in the methods as potential tools to engage with volunteers.
Big Local learning events: two short taster cultural animation workshops with residents of Big Local areas preceded by a presentation and Q&A on Untold Stories of Volunteering and cultural animation methods.	Residents of Big Local areas – volunteers and members of partnerships engaging their communities to improve local areas [27]. Interest in methods as tools to engage community members and/or to energise planning processes within local partnerships.
Legacy project upscaling event: four intensive half-day tasters – 2 × cultural animation and 2 × *Glossopoly*.	Mixed audience of academics/practitioners to give in-depth experience of methods [55]. This audience was interested in the methods for engagement and research purposes.

Table 5.3: Research pilots with new partners

Session	Audiences
Green Keele research workshop. A cultural animation workshop delivered in partnership with researchers involved in a university campus-based sustainability project[5] – using cultural animation to explore environmental issues and the relevance of sustainability to different groups and disciplines within the university.	Students and lecturers. The group involved 3 researchers and 20 participants and was a part of a wider research project on sustainability.
LGBT research workshop. A *Glossopoly/* cultural animation workshop undertaken in partnership with Middlesex University and an LGBT people's group based in Stoke.	13 researchers and members of an elderly LGBT group took part in this session, which was conceived as part of a wider exploratory piece of research into ageing, sexuality and identity.

A series of evaluations based on mixed techniques (see Table 5.4) were carried out. This data, which had a story-like shape, was subsequently analysed in light of the five theoretical lenses introduced earlier to shed light on the meanings and dynamics of collaboration and resulting legacies.

Table 5.4: Evaluation methods and outputs

Methodologies and artefacts evaluated	Evaluation methods	Outputs
Cultural animation (*The Boat*, the *Tree of Life*, 'Untold Stories of Volunteering' drama)	Observations Semi-structured interviews Informal conversations Feedback forms On-line follow up questionnaires	Stories and artefacts
Iterative methodologies (*Glossopoly*)	Observations Semi-structured interviews Informal conversations Feedback forms On-line follow up questionnaires	Stories and artefacts

The data analysis suggested that legacies can be both intended or unintended, tangible or intangible, positive or negative. Such views build on both popular understanding and existing literature which links the term to notions of continuation and sustainability (as in the legacy narrative of large-scale projects and events such as the Olympics or Live Aid).[6] The latter importantly adds the consideration that legacy is not just what is left behind but what is being used, or 'living', adding weight to the idea that legacies are performative and processual.

Legacy-as-performance

Our research adopted performance in literal senses in that not only were some of the activities focused around creating a documentary drama enacted on a stage, but also, more frequently, involved people speaking or doing things in front of others. More generally, participants involved in showcase and taster activities and the pilots were immersed in an embodied experience that linked together thinking and artistic processes. Thus, these activities made an impression on those involved precisely because of the embodied and sensory nature of their involvement. But performance carries further theoretical dimensions of meaning, bound up in questions relating to the so-called 'crisis of representation' and associated movements away from viewing knowledge as simply some form of reflection of the world. Applying this to issues of legacy implies that legacy is never something simply to be outlined or mapped, but is always something that has been created, or performed, and the degree and form of its performance reveals the extent to which people as actors (be they academics or practitioners) have made judgements about the worth of the project activities in regard to their own research/practice contexts (Mason et al, 2015).

Moreover, in making sense of these performances, we have found all five theoretical perspectives highlighted in this chapter helpful. For, when participants in a workshop are requested to reflect on a particular problematic such as 'volunteering' or 'crisis' for example, they are being encouraged to think, feel, do and reflect in collaboration with others and it is this co-creative process which can be characterised as performative in nature; knowledge is being created by being performed into life. In the case of *The Boat*, for example, principles of theatre studies ensured that participants felt included and able to 'play a part'; critical theory facilitated reflection on social problems and truths; American Pragmatism allowed for an unfolding and iterative process of refinement to take place in creating the artefact, Deleuzian approaches focused on how participants iterate thoughts and actions in order to arrive at new meaning or form closer relationships, while ANT provided the framework for thinking about collaboration as a growing connectivity of actors held together over time because of their shared creative goals.

In light of the theoretical lenses that informed our legacy work, we define legacy in five specific ways (see Table 5.5).

Table 5.5: Legacy definitions

Theoretical perspective	Definition of legacy
Theatre studies (Boal, Stanislavski, Brecht)	The reproduction and transformation of a theatre tradition for new contexts such as research.
American Pragmatism (Dewey, James)	Changes in ideas or practices (or both).
Critical theory (Habermas, Horkheimer, Honneth)	The empowerment of individuals and groups through the intersubjective development of understandings.
Actor network theory (Callon, Latour)	The enrolment of new actants into a network.
Deleuzian studies (Deleuze)	Novelty and change through repetition.

Legacy as the reproduction and transformation of a theatre tradition

The collaborations facilitated by the CC projects allowed New Vic Borderlines to develop its creative processes into a recognisable methodology, which is no longer just useful for the theatre in their outreach work, but is also a tool of research which encourages academics and community members to collaborate and co-produce knowledge. In the words of Sue Moffat, Director of New Vic Borderlines:

'Cultural Animation allows researchers and communities to stand shoulder to shoulder, exploring things together, in order to create meaningful questions through which the search for answers brings genuine and useful insights. These answers as well as being co-produced are co-owned, and therefore available to be used to begin the process of making the changes communities identify as being needed. The playful processes used in Cultural Animation can sometimes seem at odds with the seriousness of the issues explored, but the process of collaborating, creating and connecting accelerates the formation of genuine relationships which do not evaporate as the research ends, but remain an important living legacy in contrast to "hit and run" research.'

The methods at the heart of cultural animation are accessible and flexible, and community members as well as the researchers are able very quickly to learn how to use them in different contexts for their own purposes. They worked well across different national cultures such as Japan and Canada. Through these projects, a theatre-based methodology has been transformed to become useful and meaningful for different contexts, in particular the research context. This particular legacy was not intended, and yet it is probably the most powerful legacy that our collaborative research led to. The nature of the relationship between academics and practitioners encouraged by animative (and iterative) activities was according to the participants unexpected, amazing and democratic. One community organiser said: "It encourages people to work in a democratic way and share their experience, vision, ideas, which might be helpful for community planning," while a manager from a national charity suggested that "it creates an opportunity for people of different status to work together and make best use of their experience and creativity ... " A volunteer described the unexpected, yet democratic nature of our collaboration which made room for a diversity of voices: "One thing I like about this approach is the way that, being slightly unexpected, it levels the difference between residents and managers. In any setting you may get some voices heard more than others, but I felt with this methodology people who may not normally do so, feel safe."

Legacy as change in ideas or practices (or both)

The research has inspired many participants to reflect on their ideas and practices and to consider different ways of engaging in their communities. Participants to the showcase and taster activities talked about how *Glossopoly* helped them to think differently, suggesting that it "challenged me to think creatively beyond the boundaries of current systems" (public sector manager); "I thoroughly enjoyed last year's workshop and though I can't strictly say I've used any of the specific practices from the day, it did influence how I understood community organising and how creative practices can tie into it, which meant I felt more comfortable using creative practices in my community setting" (community organiser). Researchers also commented on the long-lasting effects of the animative exercises: "I'm sure that the moments of genuine worry, whilst scavenging for objects during the time pressure, will have done much more for changing minds and reinforcing ideas than any poster or fact-receiving session. This morning was a great way of exploring the concept. Fantastic" (early career researcher). "It was a very unusual experience but very worthwhile. I keep thinking back on various things we did/I thought which I'm surprised at. The experience seems more persistent than I'd expect for a workshop" (lecturer). Other participants reflected on how the experience has changed how they may do things in the future: "I will use this technique to encourage co-operation, idea-sharing and community engagement" (local authority employee); "I liked the dramatic aspect, as it gave scope for different skills and creativity. I will take that away and think about new ways to enliven group work" (charity manager).

Legacy as empowerment of individuals and groups

The 'Untold stories of volunteering' project grappled with a number of issues that are not usually reflected in current discourses of volunteering. 'Voluntolding', for example, is a word that refers to unpaid labour undertaken as an alternative to a prison sentence, or as a result of being on benefits. Paula, a participant in the project, describes herself as being 'sentenced' to do volunteering as part of her community payback sentence, whereby she avoided a prison sentence. Initially she was a 'voluntold' in a charity shop while simultaneously taking part in a local theatre project called 'Next Chapter'. After this project finished, she continued to volunteer with the New Vic Theatre and became part of our CC project, as well as becoming a volunteer at the Citizen's Advice Bureau. Paula's story was enacted on stage as part of the 'Untold stories of volunteering' documentary drama, which toured in Newcastle-under-Lyme, London and Leicester. In conversation, Paula frequently exclaimed "look at me now!" and speaks of her volunteering activities as something that gave her a new life. She said: "I have registered for a pre-access course and one day I'll come to Keele to do a degree." For her voluntolding turned quickly into volunteering and this helped her to "network and expand my mind and vocabulary and meet decent people, hard-working, caring people. In the past I was hanging with the wrong crowd but not anymore." Paula's story of personal enlightenment and empowerment is a powerful example of how involvement in collaborative research can make a lasting impact on someone's identity and aspirations. The Principal Investigator of the grant, whose prior research used to focus on leadership in large corporations, also recounts how involvement in the CC programme led to a fundamental change in her own aspirations and priorities as an academic but more importantly as a human being:

> 'I don't think I could ever go back to researching in the way I did before the CC programme came along. I have changed immensely as a result of the collaborative work

we've done with our communities over the last three years:
I now speak my mind and stand up for my values without
worrying too much about university politics.'

Legacy as a growing network

The network developed over the last three years has spread at an
exponential rate. The initial networks have deepened and widened
significantly to include academic and community partners in many
parts of the UK (including Newcastle-upon-Tyne, Edinburgh
University and Huddersfield University) as well as across the world
(Canada, Japan, Greece, France, Singapore and Finland). Mapping
the journeys of our artefacts over the last two years demonstrates the
centrality of the non-human actants in enrolling interest and expanding
the network. *The Boat* and the *Tree of Life* travelled to Rotherham in
January 2014 as part of a workshop commemorating the Holocaust.
As a result, strong connections were formed with Sheffield University
and their community partners. The boat and the tree were centrepieces
at a workshop with people with mental health problems held in
Huddersfield in November 2014. Academics from Huddersfield are
now working closely with members of the initial network to develop a
follow-on bid on making mental history come alive through animative
methodologies. The *Tree of Life* installation represented the UK
Connected Community Programme at the Community Academia
Engagement Conference, University of Victoria, Canada, in May
2014. Here we connected with academics and community partners
from the UK, Canada and Singapore. Some of these connections
allowed us to organise a field trip to Canada in June 2015 to work
with communities in London, Ontario and the City of Markham. The
Tree of Life and *Glossopoly* were central in the workshops run in Canada
where participants embraced wholeheartedly both animative and
iterative principles as well as adding a distinct Canadian flavour to our
exercises and techniques. In September 2015, *Glossopoly* and the *Tree
of Life* installation facilitated a number of workshops with communities
in crisis in Athens on another grant held by an academic from the
Open University. *Glossopoly* also returned to Athens in December
2015, forming an element of the Dourgouti Island Hotel Project
(http://www.dourgouti.gr; see also http://comparativeassetmapping.
org/?p=604). Sue Moffat was invited back to Japan by Osaka City
University to work with Osaka's marginalised communities in February
2015 and 2016. Our artistic outputs were showcased at four CC
festivals: London and Edinburgh in 2013, Cardiff in 2014 and various

Staffordshire venues in 2015. As a result of the growing network, we were in a position to launch in March 2015 a new inter-disciplinary community-based research centre at Keele University Community Animation and Social Innovation Centre (CASIC), which brings together over 100 academics and community partners from the UK and 10 other countries (http://www.keele.ac.uk/casic/).

Legacy as novelty and change within repetition

One of the challenges in thinking about legacy is the degree to which activities generate new insights. This has been particularly true of the CC programme, which is addressing issues that have been the focus not only of extensive research, but also of extended lines of practice. In the case of the projects discussed in this chapter, it was also clear that many of the activities could be criticised as producing results that were repetitive of existing understandings. However, it was also clear that many of the individuals were deriving new insights about themselves, others and the issues at stake through these activities. In seeking to address this seeming paradox we have come to draw on the insights of Deleuze, who emphasises the significance of recognising the presence of difference within repetition. A clear illustration of this was a cultural animation workshop held at the Society House in London in 2014, which explored the relationship between the volunteer and the state. Mixed groups of researchers, volunteers, volunteer managers and policy makers from Stoke-on-Trent and London all arrived at a similar conclusion, namely that relationships between the individual and the state were 'paradoxical'. However, in the process of creating this conclusion many participants learnt new things about volunteering and about each other. For example, a senior manager from the Royal National Institute of the Blind (RNIB) talked about their long waiting lists for people wanting to volunteer, yet a group of volunteers from Stoke-on-Trent, 'Mums on a Mission', talked about their struggle to attract people to volunteer for their small organisation. A senior member from an umbrella organisation referred to people on benefits as 'low hanging fruits' that can be picked up and placed in a volunteering jobs without much fuss. A volunteer from Stoke-on-Trent who was in this position disputed this, saying that people on benefits have been commodified and sold on the market by third parties for profit with no consideration for their skills or aspirations. While the verbal exchange between parties had been at times fraught with conflict, when they engaged in cultural animation techniques and started to make things by organising themselves to deliver answers, the hierarchies felt and enacted through the initial dialogue started to melt and the roles began to be reversed, with Stoke-on-Trent volunteers taking the lead in their mixed group.

Conclusions

In documenting the democratic and arts-mediated engagement between academics and practitioners, as enacted in our collaborative research, we also have also illuminated the types of evidence constructed to demonstrate that our research methodologies and resulting artefacts left a legacy. Our distinctive contribution is to highlight the possibilities of performative and creative engagement between different disciplines as well as between theoretical and practical positions. Drawing on the empirical examples and the pluralistic theoretical underpinnings which infuse them (Aguinis, et al 2014; Kieser et al, 2015), we have showed that legacy can be better conceived of as relational, contextual and performative; meaning that we can only define it as it is performed. In arriving at that position, we have analysed the legacy of animative and iterative methodologies beyond the original CC research projects as new audiences across the UK, Canada and Japan engaged, experienced and learnt about our research and considered how they could apply and put it into practice in different settings and with different communities. Based on this, our argument is that if we want legacy definitions that are relevant, useful and, above all, make a real difference, more performative studies are needed to gain insights into the dynamic between academics and community members as they co-produce knowledge.

Guidance for understanding legacy

Do not think that just because you have achieved the same outcome, there has not been any change.

Small objects and artefacts can spark extraordinary change.

The presence of absence is important: always ask who is not in the room and why.

Take responsibility for yourself and the others but be yourself

Play is not only fun but can reveal a great deal about human nature and relationships.

Notes

1   Many thanks to Lindsay Hamilton and Jess Steele for their useful comments and insights into the many topics covered in the chapter.
2   Games of *Glossopoly* were often recorded, with discussions then transcribed and elements incorporated as quotes in new cards for use in later enactments of the game, and cards were also created which required people to produce statements and images to be part of the game.
3   For more see http://www.cocollaborative.org.uk/about-community-organisers.
4   For more see http://localtrust.org.uk/.
5   For more see https://www.keele.ac.uk/greenkeele/.
6   For instance, Thornton et al (2013).

References

Abel, S. (2002). 'Speeding across the rhizome: Deleuze meets Kerouac on the road'. *Modern Fiction Studies* 48: 227-256

Adorno, T.W., with Horkheimer, M. (2002). *Dialectic of Enlightenment.* Trans. Edmund Jephcott. Stanford, CA: Stanford University Press

Aguinis, H., Shapiro, D., Antonacopoulou Gnosis, E. and Cummings, T. (2014). 'Scholarly Impact: A Pluralist Aonceptualization'. *Academy of Management Learning & Education* 13: 623–39

Avenier, M.J. and Parmentier Cajaiba, A. (2012). 'The Dialogical Model: Developing Academic Knowledge for and from Practice'. *European Management Review* 9: 199–212

Barone, T. and Eisner, E. (1997). 'Arts-based Educational Research'. In Jaeger, R. (ed), *Complementary Methods of Educational Research.* New York: Macmillan Publishing, 95–109

Bartunek, J.M. (2007). 'Academic-Practitioner Collaboration Need Not Require Joint or Relevant Research: Toward a Relational Scholarship of Integration'. *Academy of Management Journal* 50: 1323–33

Beech, N., MacIntosh, R. and MacLean, D. (2010). 'Dialogues between Academics and Practitioners: The Role of Generative Dialogic Encounters'. *Organization Studies* 31: 1341–67

Bernstein, R.J. (1992). 'The Resurgence of Pragmatism'. *Social Research: An International Quarterly* 59: 813–40

Bishop, C. (ed) (2006). *Participation (Documents of Contemporary Arts).* Co-published by Whitechapel Gallery and MIT

Callon, M. (1986). 'Some Elements of a Sociology of Translation: Domestication of the Scallops and the Fishermen of St Brieuc Bay'. In Law, J. (ed), *Power, Action and Belief: A New Sociology of Knowledge?.* London, Routledge, 196–223

D'Angour, A. (2013). 'Plato and Play: Taking Education Seriously in Ancient Greece'. *American Journal of Play* 5: 293–307

Denis, J.L. and Lomas J. (2003). 'Convergent Evolution: the Academic and Policy Roots of Collaborative Research'. *Journal of Health Services Research & Policy* 2: 1-6

Dewey, J. (1938) [1991]. 'Logic: Theory of Inquiry'. In Boydston, J.A. (ed), *Later Works 12*. Carbondale and Edwardsville, IL: Southern Illinois University Press

Gauntlett, D. (2007). *Creative Explorations: NEW approaches to Identities and Audiences*. London: Routledge

Gouinlock, J. (1990). 'What Is the Legacy of Instrumentalism? Rorty's Interpretation of Dewey'. *Journal of the History of Philosophy* 28: 251–69

Kelemen, M. and Hamilton, L. (2015). 'The Role of Creative Methods in Redefining the Impact Agenda'. *CASIC Working Paper* No. 1, https://www.keele.ac.uk/casic/workingpaperseries/

Kieser, A., Nicolai, A. and Seidl, D. (2015). 'The Practical Relevance of Management Research: Turning the Debate on Relevance into a Rigorous Scientific Research Program'. *The Academy of Management Annals* 9: 143–233

Latour, B. (2005). *Reassembling the Social: An Introduction to Actor-network-theory*. Oxford: Oxford University Press

Lorino, P., Tricard, B. and Clot, Y. (2011). 'Research Methods for Non-representational Approaches to Organizational Complexity: The Dialogical Mediated Inquiry'. *Organization Studies* 32: 769–801

MacIntosh, R., Beech, N., Sims, D. and Antonacopoulou, E. (2012). 'Management Practising and Knowing: Dialogues of Theory and Practice'. *Management Learning* 43: 373–83

Mason, K., Kjellberg, H. and Hagberg, J. (2015). 'Exploring the Performativity of Marketing: Theories, Practices and Devices'. *Journal of Marketing Management* 31: 1–15

Mouffe, C. (2007). 'Artistic Research and Agonistic Spaces'. *Art and Research* 1: 1–5

Nicolini, D. (2009). 'Zooming In and Out: Studying Practices by Switching Lenses and Trailing Connections'. *Organization Studies* 30: 1391–418

Rehg, W. and Bohman, J. (2001). *Pluralism and the Pragmatic Turn: The Transformation of Critical Theory*. Cambridge, MA: MIT Press

Reynolds, P. (1984). 'Cultural Animation: "Just plain folks" building culture – rather than just consuming it', Context Institute blog post at http://www.context.org/iclib/ic05/reynolds/

Shani, A.B., Adler, N., Mohrman, S.A., Pasmore, W.A. and Stymne, B. (eds) (2008). *Handbook of Collaborative Management Research*. Thousand Oaks, CA: SAGE

Srivastava, P. and Hopwood, N. (2009). 'A Practical Iterative Framework for Qualitative Data Analysis'. *International Journal of Qualitative Methods* 8: 76–84

Thornton, G. et al (2013). *Post-Games Evaluation: Meta-Evaluation of the Impacts and Legacy of the London 2012 Olympic Games and Paralympic Games*. Department of Culture, Media and Sport

Van de Ven, A.H. and Johnson, P.E. (2006). 'Knowledge for Theory and Practice'. *Academy of Management Review* 31: 802–21

Watson, T. (2011). 'Ethnography, Reality, and Truth: The Vital Need for Studies of "How Things Work" in Organizations and Management'. *Journal of Management Studies* 48: 202–173

What is the role of artists in interdisciplinary collaborative projects with universities and communities?

*Kate Pahl, Hugh Escott, Helen Graham, Kimberley Marwood,
Steve Pool and Amanda Ravetz[1]*

Introduction

In this chapter we provide a way of thinking about the impact of artists working collaboratively in order to co-produce ideas with a range of people, including people working in universities. The drive to make art with communities in order to effect change and support community activism has had a long history both in the UK and globally (Kester, 2005; Bishop, 2012). As projects have become more interdisciplinary and collaborative, contemporary artists have been increasingly visible working with academics from a variety of disciplines, including Social Science, Pure Science, and the Arts and Humanities. Artists work within contexts such as schools and hospitals, and when doing so, can challenge conventional practices. This includes 'artist in residence' programmes, where artists respond to place, site and people. In the 1960s Barbara Steveni, John Latham and others initiated the radical and influential 'Artists Placement Group', based in the UK but with European links, which situated artists within unfamiliar spaces including factories, places of work and businesses (Slater, 2000). They argued that coming from the 'outside', an artist might unsettle or question ways of doing things in a setting, create a space for a different kind of practice to take shape, or open up new pathways for thinking. Other partnerships, for example between artists and teachers, created new configurations of practice, enabling them to work together in new and unexpected ways.[2] Often artists' approaches will be different from established norms, creating an unexpected experience for all collaborators. For example, in a school, an artist might suggest stretching time to work on children's messy play longer, while teachers are more likely to remain within the timetable structure. Artists' interventions can change the way people do things that might not have been considered previously. In a hospital, aesthetic considerations suggested by an artist can change how light and space are deployed in a waiting room, altering how people feel in the space.[3] On a council estate, sculpture provides a focal point, or a one-off event might create a new configuration of how space is used and appreciated by those who live there. While the impact of artists working in such contexts may be recognised, what happens in the fine detail of these encounters is not always clear.

How are these relationships put together? Who calls the shots? How do ideas trickle down through the process of doing the projects? Do artists have a say on the outcome, outputs or thinking through ideas, or are they primarily used as public facilitators or to disseminate academic ideas? How do these collaborations work in practice? Is there something about what artists know that contributes to projects in ways that are distinctive and can be acknowledged? Work by Coessens, Crispin and Douglas (2009) has articulated the need to recognise and validate artistic knowledge. This form of knowledge creation, they argue, is insufficiently valued outside the world of fine art. Often provisional, emergent, tacit, embodied, located in practice and experiential models of knowing, this mode of inquiry has been distinctively explored in a range of literature within artistic research (for example Carter, 2004; Barrett and Bolt, 2007) but the value of this has rarely been articulated in other domains. It can easily remain hidden within the context of a project that needs to be delivered via academics' traditional outputs within funding constraints.

Projects in focus in this chapter

In order to study the legacy of artists working with Connected Communities (CC) projects, we put three projects under the spotlight. These were:

1. 'The Time of the Clock and The Time of the Encounter' (http://www. timeofencounter.org)

This was a project that explored the role of time using artistic ways of knowing and included artists as co-investigators.

2. 'Ways of Knowing' (https://waysofknowingresearch.wordpress.com). This project explored ways in which people could make knowledge together using a number of methodologies, including artistic methodologies.
3. 'Writing in the Home and in the Street'. This project paired artists with academics to explore everyday writing practices.

In addition we surveyed artists and academics within a number of other CC projects following a survey of all of the project abstracts. This gave a dataset of nine in-depth studies of how CC project teams had worked with artists.

Below, we give examples that trace the process of looking at what artists contribute. We approached the topic both empirically, using social scientific methods, but also experientially. We present our findings in a way that can be recognised as conventional 'research' but that also draws on artistic research as a mode of inquiry. Our methodology was experiential, heuristic and exploratory, but with an empirical dimension that brought in other voices and experiences from the field of practice.

Artists working on interdisciplinary collaborative projects: a short history

Artists draw on a history of practice that can sometimes be invisible to collaborators who are unaware of that history. Our research demonstrated that artists do not come to their research free of previous professional experience or disciplinary histories. Understanding how these approaches draw on different and often conflicting traditions and particular domains of practice, such as education, health or community contexts, is fundamental to grasping what informs artists' encounters with academic projects. Since we cannot cover all the different situations in which artists have worked, we focus below on two examples as a way of providing a brief context for our research in this field.

Artists' practices are often located within specific contexts, such as arts–based methods in education, and community settings; inevitably, these intersections raise considerable debate about the purpose of art in such settings, often focusing on the quality of the art or the social role of the artist. Bishop (2012) brings a sceptical view to the idea of the artist as *liberator* in relation to a history of artists working with communities to create new spaces for performances and thereby instigating change. Kester (2005; 2011) disagrees for the most part, foregrounding the quality of conversations and dialogue enabled by artists and looking at how they can affect criticality and social change. Alongside what is sometimes referred to as the 'social turn' associated with the 1990s and early 2000s, run older traditions, drawing on Marxist cultural theory of the 1960s and 1970s of community arts practitioners, working in the highly politicised histories of community arts organisations such as Welfare State International and the early community arts movement. Festival culture, hack culture and direct action such as the Occupy movement also provide creative hubs of resistance that draw on artistic transgressive traditions and inform the way some artists are now working within communities. These come together to form new configurations of practice beyond the gallery setting or the 'art market' (see Slater, Ravetz and Lee, 2013). These are conceptualised in different ways, for example as 'critical public art practice' or 'socially engaged art practice'.

The field of art practice has different manifestations, from the concept of an 'artist in residence' perhaps responding to a site, to practices where artists are employed short term to provide workshops within a site or location with a specific output. Artists' socially engaged practice in different public contexts reflects both the protean and changeable nature of their careers (Bridgstock, 2007; Slater, et al 2013) but also the contemporary interest in the interface of art with, for example, politics, community contexts and the everyday. In this research, we were able to surface and identify some of the artistic genealogies on which socially engaged practices are built. However, we found that the socio-political contexts of artists' employment have also intersected with these genealogies.

We were aware that many artists working in CC projects had a history of working in large-scale government-funded programmes such as the Creative Partnerships programme that ran under the Labour government in the UK (2002–2010) and that that initiative was able to provide artists with the opportunity to work collaboratively with schools to shape curriculum work in innovative ways. Research that came out of the Creative Partnerships programme had looked at the impact of artists on educational attainment; rarer however, were studies interested in whether and how artists' practices had impacted on teachers' ways of knowing and approaches within education (See Galton, 2010). Uncovering traces of these practices seemed an urgent task to us in thinking about the role artists took on such projects.

Key resources for thinking about legacy

We made sense of artists' legacies through developing an understanding of artists' histories of practice, including interventions such as the Artists' Placement Group, as well as a recognition of situated practice where taken-for-granted ways of working, such as those involving time and space, were shifted to account for different ways of knowing.

Below, we provide some key texts that both trace the genealogies of artistic practice within communities (for example Bishop, 2012) but also offer a way in which it is possible to understand artistic forms of knowledge production (for example Coessens et al, 2009). Anthropologists such as Tim Ingold have contributed to this through their work connecting different ways of knowing together (Ingold, 2013).

Bishop, C. (2012). *Artificial Hells: Participatory Art and the Politics of Spectatorship*. London: Verso

Coessens, K. Crispin, D. and Douglas, A. (2009). *The Artistic Turn: A Manifesto*. Ghent: The Orpheus Institute

Fisher, E. and Fortnum, R. (2012). *On Not Knowing: How Artists Think*. London: Black Dog Publishing

Ingold, T. (2013.) *Making: Anthropology, Archaeology, Art and Architecture*. London: Routledge

Kester, G.H. (2005). *Conversation Pieces: Community and Communication in Contemporary Art*. Oakland, CA: University of California Press

Our methodologies

Methodologies can have a distracting effect of 'producing reality' (Law, 2004), and they can be seen as 'rigorous' or 'messy' according to the lens that is used to look at them. We were sceptical of the idea that one method would produce the answers; instead, we adopted a mixed methods approach, which we used to explore our question from different angles. Here, we outline our three main methods. These were:

1. an *historical* understanding of the history of artists' practices through a literature review;
2. an *empirical* investigation through discourse analysis of the CC project summaries, followed by a selection of case studies which resulted in a series of interviews with artists, academics and community partners;

3. an *experiential* mode of inquiry that included revisiting existing projects and exploring, in detail, the processes and practices artists engaged with on those projects, 'from the inside out', so to speak.

Below we outline these approaches in more detail.

Historical understanding

Our initial proposition when we began our inquiry was that an historical understanding of the histories and traditions of art practices is often absent within the understandings of academics who have only encountered 'art' through the medium of public or commercial art galleries, or as one of many practical resources to draw on for community engagement. This, we believed, could lead to disenfranchisement of artists' capacity to contribute directly to the research process. Some artists working in the projects that we explored were particularly vulnerable to being disenfranchised, as they came into projects that had been set up by very diverse groups of academics together with community partners who had a specific understanding and set of expectations around the artists' role. There were also misunderstandings about the histories that artists brought with them to work on projects. This complexity is expressed thus by an artist/academic, working on a large CC project:

> **Artist/academic:** So many people who are working with me on [name of project] have a tradition of working with really great community based artists, engagement based artists, but [they] won't necessarily have any understanding of practice as research, let alone some of the situational site specific practice which can look and feel like a participatory project, but it's different, [and] those differences are important.

One of our first tasks was to identify specific traditions or histories that were particularly important for artists when working with academics on CC projects. These included:

- community arts
- arts in health
- participatory arts
- site-specific arts
- art outside the gallery

- relational aesthetics
- dialogical aesthetics
- socially engaged arts practice
- critical pedagogy of the arts

These histories impacted on ways of knowing and the production of work within the projects in ways that the academics were sometimes unaware of. Yet many of these ways of working are common within contemporary artistic practice. We realised that there needed to be a way in which the project participants' understanding of art within projects could be shifted, to include some of these discourses and practices. While some artists, external partners and academics recognised these issues, sometimes artists' epistemologies remained hidden within projects.

Empirical understanding

In order to delve more deeply into these concerns, we carried out a number of interviews with artists and academics. This involved the selection of nine case studies in which artists had featured strongly within the Arts and Humanities Research Council's CC programme. This was a process that involved an initial scoping period followed by the selection of case studies to be explored further. The initial stage involved conducting a corpus linguistics–informed search of the abstracts that were placed online that were used to describe the CC projects.[4]An overview of all these project abstracts identified some specific areas where artists were involved in changing outcomes and the research focus. When we delved closer into this, either through in-depth interviews or analysis of particular projects, we found that this occurred either through conceptual and practical interventions or by working closely with community members or organisations. Through this process we identified that artists were introducing different perspectives and interacting with academics in ways that were not necessarily understood or explicitly discussed. In each case study, we interviewed artists and academics, sometimes together, sometimes separately, and then coded the resulting data through the data analysis programme, Nvivo. This produced themes and ideas which we could work with.

Experiential mode of enquiry

We conducted a 'close-up' analysis of particular projects and practices where a strong sense of artists' involvement had been identified. These close-up studies would 'slow down the action', allowing us to look more closely at the processes and practices of the artists involved on the projects. Sometimes this might involve a new action; at other times a retrospective, reflective analysis. Our inquiry focused in on particular artistic practices that might be useful to explore and explicate in more detail. These were:

1. drawing as community forming –'Time of the Clock, Time of the Encounter'
2. workshops – 'Ways of Knowing'
3. studio as method – developing a way of working together

These came out of insights that emerged partly from the revisiting of particular collaborative interdisciplinary projects, in this case, 'The Time of the Clock and the Time of the Encounter' and 'Ways of Knowing'.[5] These approaches were able to surface particular artistic ways of knowing and to explore and stretch the possibilities of taken-for-granted practices such as running a workshop or drawing a line, or working collaboratively. Linked to this, what we came to call the 'studio method' was proposed as a way of working together (see later).

Taken together, these methods gave us a platform to create an inquiry that probed more deeply into what artists did in collaborative interdisciplinary projects. We were aware of the competing claims of disciplines, of the funding regimes and of the need to retain an anchoring within the academic research, but by being selective in our lens, some new insights could emerge to illuminate practice more generally. These have implications for interdisciplinary projects that are collaborative, situated and community oriented and constructed.

Emerging findings: what did artists change?

So, what did artists do to change the way CC projects evolved? A key characteristic of these projects was interdisciplinary working. We recognised that part of the conundrum of the projects we studied was that they had no specific locus or disciplinary context, but often straddled disciplines in unfamiliar ways. Barthes (1977: 155) talks about the 'creation of a new object' in interdisciplinary research, which resonated with our findings. Below we draw on this idea to present our framing of the ways in which artists have worked on Connected Communities projects.

Through our analysis of the interviews, we identified three different but interconnected modes of approach that partners took to collaborating with artists:

- New object: points at which collaboration, methodology or arts practice considerations point towards *the creation or consideration of a new object* of study. This often meant unsettling or disorientating standard academic practices. This could mean new emerging findings or lenses which came out of this collaboration.
- Conceptual: artists being involved in the *conceptualisation of the project* or research – this could involve writing the bid and constructing the theoretical or methodological lens for the project.
- Instrumental: 'artists being used in a specific manner to deliver' – we do not necessarily see this as a negative quality, but rather the concept of artists as useful, delivering a *shared goal*, was one we encountered frequently.

The processes of integration and collaboration between academics and artists involved both a *widening of outcomes* as well as a diversity of outputs. In the following extract from a conversation between an artist and an academic the complexity of the processes of working together and the diversity of outcomes are highlighted:

> **Artist:** For me it's a collaboration – you make a pool in the middle where you bring your practice you bring your thinking and you bring your skills and knowledge and hope that they are complementary and they create something in the middle so it's not about me interpreting that the science – it's about 'ooh what can we get out of this' and so the ideas should and the creativity should come from everyone involved it's just that maybe I can think of ways to visualise it in a different way …

While the collaboration was highlighted as a 'pool' it was also acknowledged by the artist that she brought specific skills to the project. In many of the projects we studied, the experience of working with an artist was to re-orient and change how things were understood. In some instances, this ended up creating a new conceptual framework for the project. For example, on the 'Language as Talisman' CC project[6] the artist was able to reshape how the academic team conceptualised language in the everyday:

> **Artist:** And what we were really discovering there was that your words are invisible when they come out of your mouth and yet they create your world. And it was just fascinating because it was really about showing people that this was your creative force – your voice – it creates everything – your interactions with people, it creates physical things, it creates how people feel about you, it creates emotional and physical things. And yet it is invisible.

In some cases the artist also had an impact on changing how the research environment worked, and also contributed to the delivery of the project in a fundamental way, both instrumental but also creating a new object. Here, for example, an academic acknowledges how the arts has changed how things have happened in projects:

> **Academic:** I must say that the arts has a massive role because it is the whole de-clinicising the environment and it will open up conversations not even just with patients and the person running the session but they go off and they have a conversation with their family their doctors and they may develop a different dynamic with those people having done something more creative.

While the artist here is seen as having quite an instrumental role in developing a more personal relationship with patients, the academic also acknowledged how this then changed the way doctors worked with the patients in a more fundamental way.

As we went through the interviews it was clear that outcomes and outputs were widened through artists' interventions but also that academics were no longer in control of all the ideas. Artists were building relationships, as described above, as well as opening out possibilities. There were particular aspects of (artistic) practice that we noticed on CC projects where artists were involved:

> **Artist:** So what we are doing is generating material that then gets used in research but also has a creative output – we could be working with clay or working with people's statements or people's ideas about where things should go ...

Here, the artist was working with academics to generate outputs that both chimed in with academic requirements but then moved into other spaces, 'temporary interventions' that chimed in with the concept of 'art'. This braiding together of outcomes was characteristic of many of the projects that we studied.

Drawing as community forming: 'The Time of the Clock and the Time of the Encounter'

'The Time of the Clock and the Time of Encounter' juxtaposed two qualities of experience of time. Clock time controls/regiments everyday experience whereas the time of encounter is open to serendipity and chance. As part of the original project, Anne Douglas, working as a visual artist with Kathleen Coessens, a pianist and a philosopher, Johan Siebers, explored the interplay between both qualities of time through drawing and related sounding.[7] The new project worked with artists Kate Genever and Anne Douglas together with Amanda Ravetz to revisit that original idea, with a focus on what artists know and do when they work together (Douglas et al, 2014). Drawing was chosen as the mode of enquiry because of its accessibility, and its importance to all three researchers (Douglas et al, 2014). Here, on behalf of the three researchers, Amanda Ravetz describes the process they went through in relation to the bigger project's overarching question of what it is that artists do when they work on such improvisatory, emergent projects with communities and academics:

> 'We were interested in using first hand experience to understand the decisions artists make when drawing. We had each experienced drawing's connective qualities, through materials, to the surrounding world and other people – as well as a certain kind of space or 'flow' that can happen when drawing. The experiment was set up to allow us to become immersed in drawing while also distilling and articulating our experiential knowledge. It was important to stay close to the experience of drawing but also necessary to find ways to communicate this in a research setting. Another aim was to explore the question 'why drawing, now?' (Douglas et al, 2014). We were interested in whether there was something specific about drawing compared to other practices (like cooking, or singing); and if as three researchers drawing on our own together, we

could really shed light on how artists had been working with communities?

The experiment yielded two overlapping responses to these queries. The first took the form of a set of reflections on what could be learnt from drawing together in a small group. The second related this to a bigger question of how we might think about community.

We reflected that drawing together had been about trying to open out and hold open a space, through these graphic activities, that allowed us to avoid chasing goals or worrying if something looked like art or not. Instead it was about allowing something unplanned and unexpected to happen.

This seemed to mean valuing what was here and now. It involved being able to grow something from small beginnings, rather than trying to match our experience against anything beyond itself.

It was also about seeing what came to the surface – really trying to notice what was happening in any given moment. For example there were times when our activity together seemed harmonious, and other more wobbly moments when one or more of us felt disengaged or uncertain. Noticing this highlighted the possibility offered by an activity like drawing to be responsive to the pressure points within our shared experiences.

We talked about improvising. We were trying not to follow a blueprint, but respond to things as they unfolded. However, like musical improvisers we realised we were still using a framework of what we knew in a way that helped us to hold open a space of goallessness – something later articulated by Johan Siebers who became our fourth collaborator when he annotated a resulting piece of our reflective writing (Douglas et al, 2014)

It was also important to try and go beyond happenstance to develop a more refined activity of drawing, as a way of trying to reach what might then eventually become a new kind of experience and understanding.

While we were unsure whether these and other qualities were specific to drawing, we felt that they resonated with ideas in visual art about not knowing (Fisher and Fortnum, 2012). Drawing was a way to put aside goals, and as artistic researchers, to demonstrate how research can take the form of creative making.

To the question 'why drawing, now?' in the context of how artists work with communities, we reflected that drawing reveals something about the very idea of community – how it is imagined within participatory art practice and how it might be imagined otherwise (Douglas et al, 2014: 120). Drawing seemed able to put us in touch with a sense of becoming, rather than with something pre-formed. It challenged the idea that what artists should be doing when they work in communities is proposing new forms of access, techniques, conviviality, or modes of data elicitation. We proposed that the 'community credentials' of our experiment of three (later four, when joined by Siebers) could not to be judged on quantity but quality – the qualities of drawing, its immanence, its hovering between determined and indeterminate states of being (Douglas et al, 2014: 128) and the relationship between these and experiences and constitution of community. Rather than drawing encouraging participation, participation might be considered integral to drawing – a social practice that is not manufactured but given (Nancy, 2013: 35). Drawing was not a way of manufacturing community – the more people the better – but of becoming attuned to community as our human condition (Nancy, 1991).'

Workshops: 'Ways of Knowing'

One of the other projects we explored experientially was called 'Ways of Knowing: Exploring the different registers, values and subjectivities of collaborative research'. This project brought different people together – artists, designers, community facilitators, academics, activists – to reflect on workshop methods the team had all used to do collaborative research in previous projects. The effect of moving through the variety of different workshop forms – from making and craft to a consensus workshop and a Socratic Dialogue – made visible how the form of collaboration, how is it staged, both enables and constrains what can be known (Graham et al, 2014; Graham et al, 2015).

As part of a process of revisiting we looked back at the workshops as a particular mode of collaboration. Steve Pool, Tessa Holland and Katie Hill – who all offered arts-based workshops as part of 'Ways of Knowing' – reflected on how research and their artistic, design or making practice intersected. Tessa has described the workshop process as a '"transubstantiation" from concept to representation' using materials, space and movement. The team writes here: "We explored how workshop methods produce a *disorientation*, both in the sense of being slightly lost and off your usual path and in the sense that what was being experienced could not be entirely translated into language-based theoretical frameworks for sense making." As the word 'disorientation' implies, it is not only intellectual, it is embodied. At times, though the workshops focused on creative practice, social conventions of academic and professional spaces were broken down and something less polite and more edgy emerged. This led to a discussion of the role artists can play in unsettling and disrupting. One way of theorising this is as 'dissensus', a term developed by political theorist Chantal Mouffe:

> According to the agonistic approach, critical art is art that foments dissensus, that makes visible what the dominant consensus tends to obscure and obliterate. It is constituted by a manifold of artistic practices aiming at giving a voice to all those who are silenced within the framework of the existing hegemony (Mouffe, 2007).

Mouffe here repurposes for an art audience her long-standing argument about the need for agonism – the value of disagreement – in radical democracy. There is, of course, something attractive about Mouffe's argument that art helps generate dissensus. Yet the experience of the 'Ways of Knowing' project would lead us to caution against any assumption that the first of Mouffe's points here automatically leads to the second. We might also suggest that the disorientation we have discussed is primarily *felt* and not always easy to translate into the linguistic frame of 'voice' Mouffe deploys. Rather we might suggest that one way of thinking about legacy of artists' unsettling and disorientating *exceeds* and cannot be resettled and boxed up too quickly. It can, however, set you off with a new, or adjusted, orientation.

The studio approach: developing ways of working together

Within our endeavours, we were also looking at how artists work, and what their 'work' was. This 'work' is itself socially situated (Willatts, 2012). Artist and Co-investigator Steve Pool proposed the idea of 'studio' to articulate how we could work together as a group, drawing on his experience of previous projects. This idea was complicated in that our group contained people who were primarily academics, and also people who were primarily artists. In making the group work, there had to be a kind of meshing of practice.

Many of the collaborative projects we studied involved groups of people with different perspectives and experiences working together to produce new knowledge. Experience on a number of these projects encouraged a group of participants to reflect deeply on where and how these relationships worked well and where deep-seated behaviours and value systems conflicted with people's abilities to work together. The idea of a studio approach grew from a collection of observations and the struggle to find a word that describes something that we could see when it emerged yet found it difficult to describe in the abstract.

We look to the roots of the word studio, a place of study rather than any of its physical manifestations. Our conception of the studio is spatial, a set of interrelationships between people, place, power and knowledge.

The studio identified the following points, which we felt help us to clarify an approach to working together.

1. The studio is a conceptual space where groups form and grow things.
2. It emerges from something we recognise as working already.
3. It involves a group of people who operate beyond the structures of the university.
4. It transcends individual projects.
5. It recognises different types of expertise – all participants can emerge as 'experts'.
6. It is acknowledged, however, that people in universities do know something.
7. It is not fixed. It is adaptable and responsive to particular situations.
8. It cannot contain everything. Its contents are assembled for a shared purpose.
9. It draws on the methods of arts practice but is not a place to produce art.
10. It is not a physical space, a digital environment or a structured set of meetings.
11. It can operate through any of these but is at root an approach and not an institution.

Our studio focused on exploring the role of artists within CC projects. We describe this central object of study as a *through line*: a theatre term used as a way for actors to understand what their character is doing not just within a specific scene but also for them to strive to understand the through line of the play which linked the parts together and pushed the character forward through the story. In many research projects, including those using grounded or inductive methods, this driving force focuses on a research question or hypothesis. Within our studio approach we explore emergent spaces, constructing openings for new collectives and ideas to emerge. We suggest that the complexity of the groups that come together to take part in CC research requires the construction of a space that can hold difference, permeate boundaries and be robust enough to collapse and reform.

Conclusion

So, what did we conclude regarding the contribution artists made to CC projects? These particular approaches to working collaboratively were particularly noticeable from the interviews that we conducted and can be translated into some key points:

Think about the creation of knowledge as process. We thought a lot about how knowledge emerges, and ways in which knowledge can be constructed collaboratively. While this process sometimes appeared to be opaque to some of the academics we interviewed, artists were able to highlight how 'other' forms of knowledge construction, outside academia, were just as important as knowledge built on citation trails and articles. Recognising the value of experiential knowledge was also an aid to creating more horizontal, equitable structures when working across disciplines, in community settings, with a wide variety of partners. Sometimes a feeling of disorientation helped in this process. Not necessarily having a plan, or being in control was vital to surface these different kinds of knowledge creation, as a film maker articulated here:

> **Film maker:** So [name of academic] was very shocked at the prospect of not having a plan, but it worked out really well ... I work quite often without a plan – there's only so much you can plan something that is documentary style ... but that was really successful because he had all of the knowledge – the archaeological knowledge that people were actually interested in ... so the combination of our skills and our practices made for quite a successful piece in the end ...

Here, this film maker acknowledged the process as something that was collaborative. It was not that is was unstructured. Rather the film maker imagines structures differently – as being already within the people involved (their existing knowledge; their abilities to respond to the social moment). This more emergent approach to structure allows important things to emerge.

Accept difference as productive and keep the space open. In many of our modes of enquiry, the task involved opening a space (collaborative drawing, workshops, studio) and keeping it open, in order to observe, experience and reflect on what happened. The nature of space and time constructions in these contexts also had an important bearing on what happened. Many events that academics organise tend to be in buildings that are institutionally constructed, and the forms of their presentations determined by pre-existing structures such as the academic paper and the PowerPoint. Questioning those institutionalised practices was a consequence of the work that artists contributed, and instead more collaborative forms of presentation, such as community-curated blogs, publications, participatory films and open-ended events, were acknowledged as important within projects. In Mouffe's term a certain consensus of knowledge forms needed to be disrupted and openly contested. These formats also enabled divergent voices to be heard, and people who did not necessarily draw on traditional academic forms to be included:

> **Academic:** Yes I mean it's very collaborative all of this – I mean there was a lot of autonomy by many of the artists – at the same time it was integrated together and so there was a lot of work involved in trying to make that happen – one of the things that we did when we did the website was to focus on places for all in different senses – questioning whether everybody did feel that in [name of place] there was a place for them and in that sense the diversity was important but also the sense that people whose stories of place weren't necessarily listened to or weren't necessarily valued ...

This academic described how a website created by artists enabled people's voices to be heard and 'people whose stories weren't necessarily listened to' were able to contribute in different kinds of ways.

Abandon control and acknowledge 'not knowing' as part of coming up with new ideas. This seemed important as projects often were initiated by academics, but as they progressed became collaborations that stretched beyond this. Artists often were more comfortable with the idea of creating ideas and jointly not knowing and they were sometimes able to construct a space that enabled academics to do the same, as this artist described, in conversation with an academic:

> **Artist:** My practice I think is about the idea of being outside of myself, I'm like the captain of a ship with the idea so it actually helps to have the idea and the role and I think things can bounce off it, doesn't limit it, it expands it and helps it ...

> **Academic**: for this particular project it wasn't to explore a pre-existing idea – it was to be experimental and new ... it was a very improvised process.

The artist here was deliberately working with the idea of 'being outside of myself' while the academic acknowledges the effect of this, which was the construction of an improvised process that the artist was constructing deliberately to expand what is possible within a project.

Artists can have a vision or 'ego' that can be useful in shaking up a project. The particular identity of the artist and their way of working was often recognised by academics as something that was uniquely shaping the project, and a part of the practice of the artist. Here an artist talks about this vision:

> **Artist:** For me as an artist I'm interested in collaborative processes – working with other practitioners. That could have a form where you suggest a venue, or suggest a word, for me in my collaborative outcomes it is very important for there to be an end and a beginning. [describing the project] I then looked at it, and I had this really weird idea it was ... and I came to the meeting with that idea ...

Here the artist does come with an idea, and this idea is described as 'weird'. The idea of the artist creating a provocation or intervention in a space was also something we noticed did happen on collaborative projects such as festivals or dissemination events. Artists were able to support academics to plan unusual, one-off, often process-led events, together with sustained interventions with communities that were themselves innovative, unusual and a bit different.

In summary, artists worked in a number of ways to pluralise research, acknowledge lived experience and work with uncertainty and emergent practice. We were exploring the legacy that artists left on CC projects and how they influenced practice. Legacy implies both something material and some kind of traceable ancestry. Yet a common theme in the interview and research experiments we conducted was that one of the implications of artists' involvement in CC projects has been to shift and complicate the relationship between research and dissemination – or process and product – and increase repertoires of what knowing might be and how it might happen. We sum up here the legacies the project has traced in three ways:

- *What*: pluralising what is recognised as research and knowing
- *Who*: fully recognising and using the social and lived nature of collaboration
- *How*: working through, and enabling in others, a certain orientation to the world, one that can cope with uncertainty and is attentive to what is emerging

What: pluralising what is recognised as research and knowing

The legacy of artists' involvement in CC projects is embedded and difficult to isolate within the projects. While we have drawn out specific quotes, the experience of being involved in projects was messy, complicated and can only be partially articulated or rationalised in ways that are distinct from the interactions themselves. We suggest that artists can play a role in unsettling knowledge production processes. They bring different forms of knowing and these forms do not claim to be replicable or transferable. We found a constant sense of *excess*, that is, things happened beyond the projects' limits both in terms of time and space. Outputs were differently positioned within the project and normative forms of dissemination such as the academic article were less salient within the projects.

Who: fully recognising and using the social and lived nature of collaboration

The value of much of this work could be found in the small details of situated human interaction and not the broader theoretical, political or ideological forms of knowledge production. Artists were able to locate projects within the 'everyday' and articulate the value of small actions that could shape wider, more important pieces of insight. Sometimes this could also be in the form of a provocation that altered how people saw things.

How: working through, and enabling in others, a certain orientation to the world, one that can cope with uncertainty and is attentive to what is emerging

Subtle shifts in the atmosphere or layout could then alter what happened in that space. Within lived experience, this is often a process that artists notice and value. We are interested in the potential of this approach for collaborative, interdisciplinary projects across universities, communities and artists and, as we have argued, suggest there are implications for collaborative inquiry in a wider range of contexts. Our project was able to trace the legacies of artists' interventions in ways that recognised experiences, values and ways of knowing that sometimes go unrecognised. We would like to see these ways of knowing become more acknowledged within the wider world of policy, practice and university knowledge structures.

Guidance for understanding the legacy of artists' practices in collaborative research

Think about the creation of knowledge as process.

Accept difference as productive and keep the space open.

Abandon control and acknowledge 'not knowing' as part of coming up with new ideas.

Artists can have a vision or 'ego' that can be useful in shaking up a project.

Notes

[1] We would like to thank Castlefield Gallery, Manchester and AN the Artists Information Company, for their involvement in this project.

[2] See resources for artists and teachers here: http://www.capeuk.org/capeuk-resources/tapp-series.html.

[3] See for example this project: http://designingfordignity.co.uk/Project-Results.

[4] http://www.ahrc.ac.uk/research/fundedthemesandprogrammes/crosscouncilprogrammes/connectedcommunities/.

[5] These were AHRC Connected Communities funded projects. 'Ways of Knowing' explored divergent conceptual frameworks for how knowledge was generated. See http://waysofknowing.leeds.ac.uk/. The 'Time of the Clock brought together artists, community organisations and academics in order to investigate the difference between lived time and clock time. Their blog is here: http://www.timeofencounter.org/.

[6] 'Language as Talisman' was an AHRC Connected Communities funded project that worked with a number of youth and community groups together with schools to explore everyday language and literacies. See: http://languageastalisman.group.shef.ac.uk.

[7] http://ontheedgeresearch.org/sounding-drawing/.

References

Barrett, E. and Bolt, B. (2007). *Practice as Research*. Chippenham: UK I.B. Tauris and CoBarthes, R. (1977). 'From Work to Text'. In *Image – Music – Text*. London: Fontana

Bishop, C. (2012) *Artificial Hells: Participatory Art and the Politics of Spectatorship*. London: Verso

Bridgstock R. (2007). '"Success in the Protean Career": A Predictive Study of Professional Artists and Tertiary Arts Graduates.' PhD thesis, Centre for Learning Innovation, Faculty of Education, Queensland University of Technology, Australia. Available online: http://eprints. qut.edu.au/16575/ [12/10/2012]

Carter, P. (2004). *Material Thinking*. Melbourne: Melbourne University PressCoessens, K. Crispin, D. and Douglas, A. (2009). *The Artistic Turn: A Manifesto*. Ghent: The Orpheus Institute

Douglas, A. Ravetz, A. and Genever, K. with Siebers J. (2014). 'Why Drawing Now'. *Journal of Arts and Communities* 6(2-3) ISSN: 17571936

Fisher, E. and Fortnum, R. (2012). *On Not Knowing: How Artists Think*. London: Black Dog Publishing

Galton, M. (2010). 'Going With the Flow or Back to Normal? The Impact of Creative Practitioners in Schools and Classrooms'. *Research Papers in Education*, 25, 355–375

Graham, H., Banks, S., Bastian, M., Durose, C., Hill, K., Holland, T., McNulty, A., Moore, N., Pahl, K., Pool, S. and Siebers, J. (2014). *Ways of Knowing: Exploring the Different Registers, Values and Subjectivities of Collaborative Research*. Report. Available at: http://waysofknowing. leeds.ac.uk/

Graham H.C., Hill K., Holland T. and Pool S. (2015). 'When the Workshop Is Working: The Role of Artists in Collaborative Research with Young People and Communities'. *Qualitative Research Journal* 15(4): 404–15 DOI: 10.1108/QRJ-06-2015-0043, Repository URL: http:// eprints.whiterose.ac.uk/91439/

Kester, G.H. (2005). *Conversation Pieces: Community and Communication in Contemporary Art*. Oakland, CA: University of California Press, 1

Kester, G.H. (2011). *The One and The Many: Contemporary Collaborative Art in a Global Context*. Durham, NC: Duke University Press

Law, J. (2004). *After Method: Mess in Social Science Research*. London: Taylor and Francis

Mouffe, C. (2007). 'Artistic Activism and Agonistic Spaces'. *Art and Research: A Journal of Ideas, Contexts and Methods* 1(2). Available at: http://www.artandresearch.org.uk/v1n2/mouffe.html

Nancy, J. (1991). *The Inoperative Community* (ed. Peter Connor and trans. Peter Connor, Lisa Garbus, Michael Holland and Simona Sahey), Minneapolis, MN: University of Minnesota Press

Nancy, J. (2013). *The Pleasure in Drawing* (trans. Phillip Armstrong), New York: Fordham University Press

Slater, A., Ravetz, A. and Lee, K. (2013). *Analysing Artists' Continual Professional Development (CPD) in Greater Manchester: Towards an Integrated Approach for Talent Development*. Manchester: Castlefield Gallery publications

Slater, H. (2000). 'The Art of Gove: The Artists Placement Group 1966–1989'. *Variant* 2(11) Summer: 23–6

Willatts, S. (2012). *Artwork as Social Model: A Manual of Questions and Propositions*. Research Group for Artists Publications. Yorkshire Artspace. Distributed by Cornerhouse Publications, Manchester

SEVEN

Material legacies: shaping things and places through heritage

*Jo Vergunst, Elizabeth Curtis, Oliver Davis, Robert Johnston,
Helen Graham and Colin Shepherd*

Introduction: why do materials matter?

Historic research, by its very nature, questions old narratives and develops new ones. Material goods, taken out of circulation perhaps for decades, centuries or millennia, will re-enter society, receive new roles and have effects wildly different from those anticipated by their makers. The site of a former house or castle, once rediscovered, provides the impetus for a range of experiences that may change the worldview of a person or community. In heritage – by which we mean the process of being involved with the past – communities make links between past, present and future through encountering materials in different forms. Heritage thus provides a particularly good field for exploring how 'the material' matters in collaborative research.

On one level, we need to recognise that all life is of course material and that it happens within places and landscapes. Archaeologist Ian Hodder describes the 'entanglement' of humans and things, which are forever making and being made by each other. He writes: 'humans get caught in a double bind in relation to things since they both rely on things (dependence) and have to reproduce things they have made (dependency)' (Hodder, 2012: 112). We make things, and so we have to go on making things. That these human-thing interdependent relations happen in places, and that such places matter, is also fundamental (Casey, 1996). Places are the very grounds in which life, including social and cultural life, happens. When we consider materials in the legacies of collaborative research, we need to acknowledge the constant interaction between people, things and places.

In the particular cultural world of the professional heritage sector and parts of academic heritage studies, however, the 'material' world is frequently divided from the non-material with reference to the 'tangible' and 'intangible'. The recognition by UNESCO in 2003 that heritage could take the intangible forms of performance, ritual, voice and movement was a shift from a preservationist discourse focused on historic sites and objects. The way was opened towards valuing contemporary cultural practices and performances along with the means by which they persist through time. While this is clearly important, the problem is that materiality (that is the quality of being material) becomes associated with just the monumental and the iconic (Smith, 2006). From here emerges what Smith calls the 'authorised' version of heritage of professional museums and tourist sites in opposition to the seemingly more personal scale of intangible cultural heritage. So there is a 'politics' of heritage, in which heritage professionals are empowered to define and act as the stewards of heritage, preserving it 'forever' for a generic 'public'. When materiality is linked narrowly to the desire to preserve for posterity and 'keep things safe', limits to those who can use, touch or adapt the designated thing may appear (Hetherington, 2003).

Key resources for thinking about legacy

This chapter uses theories of materials, place and heritage. Materials and places need to be thought of as open rather than closed off, and therefore heritage should be amenable to change and reinterpretation. Collaborative research happens through material encounters.

Auclair, E. and Fairclough, G. (eds) (2015). *Theory and Practice in Heritage and Sustainability. Between Past and Future*. London: Routledge

Coole, D. and Frost, S. (eds) (2010). *New Materialisms. Ontology, Agency and Politics*. Durham, NC and London: Duke University Press

Hodder, I. (2012). *Entangled: An Archaeology of the Relationships Between Humans and Things*. London: Wiley

Smith, L. (2006). *Uses of Heritage*. London: RoutledgeWaterton, E. and Watson, S. (eds) (2013). *Heritage and Community Engagement. Collaboration or Contestation?* London: Routledge

---

Exploring the material legacies of heritage research

We argue in this chapter that the sense of time and the constituencies of heritage as a universal, continuous public may be subverted by the realities of communities, power and multivocality. Rather than drawing a dividing line between apparently non-material research outcomes (for example knowledge, values) and material ones (things such as artworks or archaeological finds, or places remade through research), we seek to explore the mutual shaping of material and non-material processes. Places, landscapes and things come into being through means which are neither exclusively performative nor exclusively material, but both performative and material. 'Heritage' from this perspective acts not by way of a passive handing down of traditions but by the continual re-creation of cultural forms, as generations mix and novices learn alongside skilled practitioners (Ingold, 2000). Perhaps the most interesting theme is how the process of collaborative research in heritage specifically entails the emergence and negotiation of knowledge through materials. This approach does not retreat to a post-modern relativism in which all heritage is equal, but it reveals the actual sites and conditions of the production of knowledge about the past, and thereby opens wider the possibility of alternative voices.

So, while the non-material is important and perhaps undervalued in more positivist research discourses, collaborative research does more than just attend to the intangible aspects of social life often implied by the rhetoric of co-production. It engages with materials in interesting ways, creating material assets and outcomes, affecting existing things and places, and wrestling with the particular problems that materials throw up for research. How, for example, do processes of material discovery, creativity, ownership and curation work in collaborative research? Narratives of material/non-material entanglement continually emerge from heritage projects, and research in other disciplines too. Such projects are working with and through materials as well as through non-material processes, and the qualities of the materials (as things, objects, places, landscapes, and so on) are central to the progress and legacies of the research.

To this end, we will present a series of narratives from the heritage research we have been involved with. They are written from within the projects but they draw on diverse voices and perspectives, and they are also informed by a process of joint evaluation and reflection. This included shared meetings, project and site visits, and working together on the meaning and value of legacies in the context of heritage research with communities. In some cases (Caerau, in Wales, Bennachie in Scotland and York in England), we are dealing with collaborative research as 'mutual learning' (Introduction to this book), in which communities and universities are working together in a multifaceted way over a long time period. In others, such as the Sheffield projects (a series of heritage projects based in the City of Sheffield, UK), the collaboration has – so far – been of a shorter duration and yet is doing much to 'correct the record' (Introduction to this book) of silences and gaps in heritage research. What emerges is a set of diverse practices, and diverse entanglements with materials, that value open-endedness and wide participation in the research process. At the end of the chapter, we discuss common themes and touch again on the politics of materials in this kind of research.

Projects in focus in this chapter

Caerau and Ely Rediscovering Heritage Project: this project was based in Wales, UK. A collaboration between Cardiff University, schools, residents and community group Action in Caerau and Ely, with the aims of raising awareness of heritage and challenging marginalisation. Co-production is based on mutual learning and long-term partnership between the university and community.

Bennachie Landscapes Project: this project was based in Scotland, UK. A collaboration between the University of Aberdeen, community group the Bailies of Bennachie, schools and local people, with the aim of exploring landscape history through research. Co-production is based on mutual learning and long-term partnership between the university and community.

Researching Community Heritage: this project was based in the north of England, UK. The University of Sheffield offered support to local community groups in undertaking heritage research in archaeology, oral history and archival research. Co-production is based on communities taking the lead and learning skills including how to access resources from the university.

York: Living With History: this project was based in the historical city of York, in the north of England, UK. This was part of the 'How Should Decisions About Heritage Be Made?' project (see Chapter four). The aim was to experiment with participative approaches focused on action and argument, in the context of a place known as a heritage city.

A question of things and places (Oliver Davis)

The Caerau and Ely Rediscovering (CAER) Heritage Project, based in Cardiff, Wales, is not a straightforward community archaeology project. It has from the beginning embraced co-production principles and sought to create new communities of practice through the process of multi-disciplinary research. However, while the project aspires to full co-production, and involves and values the contributions of community members in the research process, project activities are currently largely developed by the academic team and the group Action in Caerau and Ely. In this sense CAER is best thought of as a middle-way collaborative project which attempts to amalgamate top-down and bottom-up approaches (Ancarno et al, 2015: 128).

Among the wide-ranging suite of co-production activities, it is the physical experience of archaeological research, particularly excavation, which has often been the most effective for addressing the project's social objectives of inclusion and participation. Excavations have centred on Caerau Hillfort, a large prehistoric Iron Age settlement that has seen little previous archaeological attention and research. The hillfort is today surrounded by the housing estates of Caerau and Ely in west Cardiff, Wales, which face significant economic and social issues, not least high unemployment and poor educational attainment. At issue here is how the things that are found become part of relationships of identity, power and place among people in the present, as much as they inform on the past.

Archaeological excavation, including that at Caerau, culminates in the production of a material assemblage that includes the intangible – the 'story' of the site – and the tangible – an often considerable collection of written records, artefacts and ecofacts. The curation of this material assemblage – 'preservation by record' – takes on particular importance, not least because the process of excavation itself is inherently destructive (once excavated, the site cannot be put back as it was). Yet this raises issues about the material assemblage, such as statutory obligations, legal requirements, ownership, storage, access and interpretation.

Everything on the Caerau hilltop is legally the property of the landowner, and moreover the site and its finds are an emplaced part of the biography of the hill and local community. Yet, as a condition for granting consent for the excavation, Cadw (the Welsh government's historic environment service) insisted that the material should ultimately reside with the National Museum of Wales, which could curate it in the long term. Under current heritage legislation this is a responsible position. However the required removal of material assets, from a community which has very few, reinforces opinions of marginalisation and disenfranchisement by local people.

Such contradictions can be complex to address. It was necessary to obtain a signed contract from the landowner in order that the material could be donated to the National Museum. Initially he was reluctant – this was material, after all, he associated with his land, the place where he lived and farmed – although pragmatically he realised that the benefit of the excavation to the community would not be realised without this condition. There were broader concerns among the community, too, that the material would simply be taken away and never seen again. We have been careful not to do this. Considerable thought was given to involving local communities in every stage of the archaeological process, from survey and excavation through to finds analysis and interpretation. Although the artefacts are sometimes stored at the university for periods of time, they are all brought to the local community to be worked on, which has included a range of adult learners' courses analysing the finds. However, the ultimate destination for the finds is far from resolved. Legally they are now the property of the National Museum, but the desire for some of them at least to remain in the locality in which they were found is strong and must be recognised.

The discovery of things is almost always the most engaging aspect of the excavations. It is very noticeable that almost all volunteers treat archaeological material with the utmost respect – even those artefacts (such as endless Roman pottery sherds) which professional archaeologists may regard as relatively unimportant. This is undoubtedly linked to a sense of ownership – this is *their* history – but also the shock at being trusted to be involved in such work that they consider being the realm of professionals. Perhaps the very physical act of being part of excavation and the very act of discovery strengthen the relationship between things, place and identity and enhance the values assigned to particular objects. This was exemplified during the 2014 excavations when one volunteer was less interested in the fragment of a 6,000-year-old Neolithic polished stone axe than he was in a fragment of coconut shell he had discovered in a spoil heap. The shell had brought back childhood memories from the 1960s when fairs had been held on the hill every Whitsun, and he remembered winning goldfish from coconut shies. Such personal accounts are often impossible to recover from archaeology alone. They highlight the affective relationships of things and places, which we need, perhaps, to better account for not just in our stories of the past, but in the curation and management of the present, too.

At once landscape and thing (Jo Vergunst)

The hill of Bennachie is a prominent landmark about 20 miles north-west of Aberdeen in the Aberdeenshire countryside in Scotland. There, a community group called the Bailies of Bennachie have since 1973 been looking after the hill, protecting it from unwanted development and working to ensure public access to the hill and public interest in its history. While the presence of multi-period archaeological remains has long been known about, in 2010 the Bailies began a co-ordinated effort to research the natural and cultural landscape of the hill in the form of the 'Bennachie Landscapes Project', which was given an initial shape by our co-author and independent archaeologist Colin Shepherd. In 2011 the University of Aberdeen secured funding through Connected Communities (CC) to work with the Bailies, with a specific focus on the 19th-century crofting colony that existed on its eastern slopes. While the Bailies had been involved in surveying the colony in the late 2000s, the CC funding enabled an upgrade of the archaeological research at the hill, along with archival and oral historical work that were also premised on notions of co-production.

As at the Caerau Hillfort described above, the process of archaeological field research has been very engaging for local participants. Indeed, it is the specific form of engagement with the landscape that has been so revealing. With a focus on low-tech, easily accessible forms of fieldwork (such as offset surveys and shovel test pitting, which require little more than measuring tapes, sieves and shovels) along with excavation and finds analysis, much of the work has been about the collective rethinking of relationships with the landscape both in the past and today. The croft houses and dykes discovered during the work are made of stone quarried from the hill, and we can imagine the quarries deepening into the hillside as the houses and dykes rise up from it. Now the walls have tumbled back into the land again and participants are faced with the task of distinguishing the worked blocks of granite from the natural. Each is 'landscape' and 'thing', which counters the modern concepts of landscape as scenery and material culture as commodity.

As we dug test pits, participants reflected on the depth and richness of the topsoil, which is testament to the work of the crofters to improve it. The 'finds' in it, pottery that is often richly coloured and decorated, made us think of the crofters not as marginalised hill dwellers scraping a meagre living, but as thinking about the future, and working on the land for the future. The narratives told by the community and university participants at a subsequent exhibition shared these new understandings of the links between the things, the landscapes and the people. Participants are enabled to think themselves about new futures for the land, through research on the futures of the past.

A newspaper journalist came to a post-excavation day at the Bennachie Centre, at the foot of the hill, in order to write a story for the local newspaper. We were all carefully labelling the washed pot sherds and categorising into groups of transfer ware, sponge ware, white ware, and so on, and we trying out some reconstructions too. The journalist asked one of us: "Are you an archaeologist?" "No," was the reply, "I'm an enthusiast." On one level, the lack of professional identity in the community participant jarred with her manifest archaeological expertise in dealing with the pot sherds in front of her. But perhaps the declaration of enthusiasm for the task at hand is the more fundamental point, and one that might serve as a more useful grounding for collaborative heritage research. It is fundamentally from such enthusiasm that the power to take part in heritage develops in communities, and not merely to be its passive recipients and consumers.

Long-term landscapes of research (Colin Shepherd)

In between accumulations of intangible heritage and codified datasets, there are fuzzy co-productive spaces. Further parts of the Bennachie Landscapes Project, introduced above, can be explored in this regard, where longer time frames can permit a more nuanced analysis of co-production than those of shorter durations.

Keig Primary School in Aberdeenshire in Scotland has been attempting to understand the cultural and ecological development of their parish. This has included working alongside myself in the role of community archaeologist for two hours every week of the school year since 2010. A hitherto unknown mill site and an 18th-century building are being excavated and these form the grounds within which social and ecological change are discussed with the pupils.

Interesting temporal cycles enter the research. At Keig, Scotland, the work unfolds alongside the school terms, but a longer cycle involves pupils progressing through the year groups. Periodically, the fundamentals of the purposes of the project need to be rehearsed to the new, younger pupils. Co-production proceeds by means of discovery of the local landscape, becoming a formative aspect of experiential development. During discussions, Keig teachers have often remarked that it is likely to be many years hence that the personal effects of the landscape study will manifest themselves in the life choices and behaviour of the pupils. The understanding of how cultural and material landscapes are made will, the teachers feel, impact on them increasingly as they progress through their lives and encounter new environments. The legacies from this co-productive process – understood here as the ways in which the lives of the young people are being affected by the research – are unending and certainly defy quantification.

The work at Keig, and that described below at Druminnor, both in Scotland, have both been supported by local landowners who also wish to discover more about the landscapes within which their families have lived for generations. Parents and other local inhabitants are helped in understanding more about the places.

Results from the Keig project are frequently communicated at social events hosted at the school hall, which also doubles up as the local community hall. In a radical move, school work is research informing a local community about its cultural heritage. The usual educational rationale, in which older people teach younger members of the community, has been subverted.

To take a second example, the Bennachie Landscapes fieldwork group have been involved in excavations at nearby Druminnor Castle since 2012. Again, the long time frame permits cohesion among participants rarely felt within the confines of short projects. Having minimal expenses, the research unfolds at a rate commensurate with extracting the maximum information from the site. As at Keig, the research develops its own cyclical pattern based on the seasons of the year. Many participants have been around from the start, some attend more than others, and some have left and others join. Young people engage through the Young Archaeologists' Club or the University of Aberdeen, or the Duke of Edinburgh Award Scheme for example. A school trip from Keig school presented an opportunity to stretch the pupils' observational skills and to demonstrate 'time in action' by means of the stratigraphies visible in the sides of the Druminnor trenches. For all participants and despite the changing personnel, cohesion is provided by experiencing the work itself.

So, what conclusions concerning material legacies may be gleaned from these ongoing projects? Within the groups, individuals develop roles particular to their interests and talents. All participants are drawn closer together by the passage of time and through sharing in the experience. In terms of academic research, both projects are discovering, recording and disseminating ever more detailed understandings of their landscapes. But, it is within the arenas of the intangible that further effects are hidden.

No model can replicate the effects set in train by such research. When this research involves co-production processes engaging with broader communities, the effects are even harder to follow. At Druminnor, the intangible history of medieval baronial feuding that lay behind the constant historical need for renewal at the castle is materially present within the archaeological record of those rebuilding works and in the scattered remains of the material culture of its inhabitants. This history is rehearsed as a matter of course in the local traditions of the inhabitants of the former lordships of Huntly and Forbes in Aberdeenshire. Within this co-productive 'fuzzy space', contemporary participants pool life experiences and synthesise the material legacy with received tradition to produce a revised, contemporary historical narrative.

A key point, however, is that Keig and Druminnor projects both exist because of the access permitted by the owners of the land. Such access to heritage is a fundamental necessity for the subsequent regeneration of heritage as culture. The interplay of communities with their heritage initiates new cultural experiences. For the children at Keig and the community diggers at Druminnor, material legacies from the past are doorways to cultural experiences of the future. But, without access to that heritage (in these instances, their landscapes), such experiences would be impossible. Cultural development, in these particular geographical areas, would take alternative trajectories in which heritage would be less privileged. Sadly, in Scottish law all historic finds, no matter how insignificant, are the property of the Crown (unlike in England and Wales, although similar circumstances can arise as described at Caerau above). Legally, it is not possible for the finds discovered in these co-productive projects to automatically reside within the communities to which they pertain.

A story and a place (Robert Johnston)

Marcus Hurcombe, a youth worker in Rawmarsh, Rotherham, in the north of England, leads a group of young children along a suburban pavement. They stop by a woodland, the start of their journey into Rawmarsh's Viking past: "There were bears and there were wolves, very dangerous animals, you have to be really quiet. Also ogres, tree spirits, demons and monsters, not to mention marauders from other tribes of Vikings. So, carefully, come down here …"Marcus's introduction to the children's walk is imaginative and theatrical (https://portalstothepast.wordpress.com/film/). It is not directly evidenced by the landscape history or archaeology of Rawmarsh. I might say 'the story is not the place': there were no ogres, demons, monsters, nor were there marauding tribes of Vikings – at least not that we can prove. And yet as contemporary myth making, this story has much in common with early medieval cultural landscapes (Overing and Osborne, 1994). It is given power and resonance by its performance at the threshold of an urban 'wild place'. How intrinsic are places to stories about the past? During community heritage research projects in and around Sheffield, we have explored how the stories that we tell about places are the means through which we bring those places into being. Importantly, the stories we found are partisan, contestable, partial and fragmentary, often leaving open their endings in ways that encourage further participation.

In Sheffield, a city in the north of England, a long-established group called Heeley History Workshop researched past social life: sports clubs, excursions and so on. Heeley's boundaries are well defined and form the geographic limits of the group's enquiries. Members of the group meet weekly, bringing documents, objects, oral history and personal memories, and debate and assemble their history of the place. Heeley's past is re-inhabited through the creation and telling of stories. The knowledge of Heeley is extremely fine grained (and passionately contested – down to the detail of who lived next to whom), yet is not easily mapped in a cartographic sense. A University of Sheffield researcher, Gilles Marciniak (2012), asked the group to produce sketch maps showing the heritage that mattered to them in Heeley. Almost all the maps were fairly perfunctory. This revealed not a gap between perception and reality, but instead that the stories of the past were rooted in precise but unmappable spaces.

By comparison, young people researching with Roundabout youth housing charity in Sheffield carried very different connections with the place they studied. The research centred on a Georgian building that is now a hostel for homeless young people, many of whom are transient and some not from the region. The history of the building was researched through the local archives and the architecture of similar buildings in Sheffield. Excursions also offered some vivid moments: visiting a former 19th-century asylum, one described the electric shock treatment he imagined went on inside and joked, 'I can see into the past'. As with the marauding Vikings of Rawmarsh, imagination of the past is catalysed by places. A further session worked on a scrapbook of residents' personal stories to go alongside the building research, and as with the archives, the potential for personal histories had most resonance. The building is less a historical artefact than a means through which the historical and personal can be connected. Tangible and intangible are not helpful categories as they separate what are intrinsically experienced together.

The 'Midhope at War' project was situated in a rural, moorland landscape north of Sheffield. Led by Woodhead Mountain Rescue Team, participants studied Second World War tank training ranges and the troops who were billeted in nearby camps and villages. Remains of the ranges can still be found, including the shells of unexploded ordnance that are occasionally revealed from the peat and heather. Like Heeley, the participants knew their landscape intimately. Unlike Heeley, they researched it on the ground and on foot: following the metalled roads prepared for tanks, shining a torch into an underground troop shelter, searching for a rusted mobile target. Despite this material heritage, the Midhope team prioritised collecting oral histories and studying archival documents. The material places were there, knowable and known, but the stories were missing, and oral histories – the memories of elderly people in the village – were most vulnerable. Yet still, the team returned to the landscape as a means of anchoring the stories in the past. Material legacies in the forms of onsite interpretation panels and a guided walk were made.

In a lecture entitled 'The Sense of Place', poet Seamus Heaney grappled with the tension between places as intrinsic to everyday experience and places as literary constructs:

> I think there are two ways in which place is known and cherished, two ways which may be complementary but which are just as likely to be antipathetic. One is lived, illiterate and unconscious, the other is learned, literate and conscious ... both are likely to co-exist in a conscious and unconscious tension (Heaney, 1980: 131).

Heaney raises a difficulty with experiences of place: there is a divergence between the richness to our intrinsic, lived experience of the world, and the constrained ways we write about and represent that experience. Furthermore, the lived and the literary are contingent on one another: if our experiences of places are superficial or limited, then our literate understandings will also be impoverished.

If we modify Heaney's observation to distinguish between a lived and an 'academic' reading of places (and perhaps also between a narrative and a material expression), then a strength of all these projects is that the lived and the academic, the narrative and the material, were not consciously separated. In Rawmarsh, the imagined and the factual were equal. At Heeley 'talk of heritage was talk of life' that was founded in places. At Midhope, walking through the landscape and recounting stories were inseparable. What they reveal is that the stories we tell about places are intimately connected with their material history and qualities, although not in straightforward or perhaps predictable ways. Storying places allows for political, partisan and personal readings of places and things. This a formative experience for an archaeologist whose disciplined approach is to uncover the material layers of the landscape – academic and professional specialisms are usually based in a logic of separating in order to categorise. I have become more open to the bricolage of stories that make up the heritage of places, and to encourage the blurring of the technical and precise with the narrative, open and performative. Community heritage projects may lack the separations that are more critical to academic enquiry, but by performing the reverse move, of connection, they seem particularly able to open up new stories and new places.

Material concerns in heritage decision making (Helen Graham and the Heritage Decisions project team)

One of the first insights of the 'How should decisions about heritage be made?' project team as we gathered together at Bede's World museum in Jarrow, north-east England in March 2013 was about the material qualities of heritage. Aiming to collaboratively design our own research project, we noted that thinking of heritage as finite and non-renewable – as *material* in specific ways – was a potential block to greater direct participation in decision making by non-professionals. We noted that prioritising material preservation usually entails professional stewardship and certain kinds of bureaucratic and institutional structures and practices, such as museums, or practices of listing and scheduling: the preservation of material has tended towards specific modes of elite governance. Yet, a new politics of heritage – one which makes room for active participation by a wide range of people – requires not a simple preference of the intangible over the tangible but a more active assessment of their relationship.

An exploration of the politics of materiality within heritage practices of storytelling and memory took place through the 'York: Living with History' strand of the project. In the UK, so-called blue plaques, and plaques of various other kinds, have since the 19th century been a recognisable icon of urban heritage memorialisation. Commemorating who was born in a certain house or where a specific event took place, they make material what would otherwise be intangible within the cityscape. Their own tangible and intangible qualities suggest permanence, as they require planning permission and therefore have a legal status and are made of durable materials and firmly attached to buildings. In terms of decision making, the blue plaques in England are associated with Historic England (previously English Heritage) the organisation responsible for designating and regulating 'heritage'.

To explore the decision-making process – and to draw attention to the question of what is and what is not commemorated in York – we ran two Do-It-Yourself heritage days, one using cardboard versions of blue plaques and another for LGBT History month using rainbow plaques. At both events the material qualities of the cardboard plaques were crucial. The plaques were made ourselves. They were cut out, written on and prepared with double-sided sticky tape. The ritual of the event meant us going out into the streets and ceremoniously sticking the plaque on to brick or stone, with the person whose plaque it was saying a few words. Yet these very specific forms of materiality, scissors, sticky tape, surfaces on which the tape can be safely stuck (to not cause damage) were also, of course, a play on the other forms of materiality the plaques *almost* could be mistaken for. Whereas the official plaques were made to last, ours were not. While the official plaques go through legal permission processes and are secured pretty much permanently to buildings, ours were done without permission and can be very easily removed.

For those involved, the transience of the plaques meant different things. For some it was a damning indictment of histories untold by official channels. For others, the transience worked to question more the false hope of any form of heritage preservation. One of the outcomes of the DIY plaques has been digital records and blogs, but also the social connection between people who participated. The cardboard plaques commemorated above all the desire to create a living and adaptive use of heritage in the present, which would draw into being the city in which we want to live.

Synthesis: the legacies of materials and material legacies

Being in touch with materials and things

The narratives presented here describe the significance of direct contact with the materials and things that become 'heritage' for the communities involved in research. The point is not just that field archaeology is simply popular or enjoyable for members of the public, which is noted by Simpson and Williams (2008). Tactile contact with things, through digs and forms of other heritage research, can enable a distinctive imagination of the past. It is a past made tangible, that really happened, and that is in a way made 'present' as the existence of the thing continues into today's world. The process happens variably, as shown by the different reactions at Caerau to a Neolithic find and one from the 1960s. But it is not simply that the age of an object makes it more or less distant from us. We have seen the significance of storytelling and interpretation, in which the development of a story is a key output of research, and it is the narrative afforded by the things themselves that makes them important. A potsherd found at Bennachie may be understood as part of a plate used by the actual inhabitants of a croft house, and not merely as a marker of a particular cultural style.

The legacies of things in collaborative heritage research may be less about an absolute historical value than their relational value – a value based in the relations between past and present that are created by the things that are found and handled. Such 'things' may seem to be a far cry from 'objects' discovered and preserved within the stricter realm of professional heritage practice (Smith, 2006), and yet the transfers between these realms are pivot points. Things found by a community project *may* also be caught up in professional practice with all that that entails, but communities can still be involved with them if the right set of structures and the will to make it so are present. There is no necessary 'natural' or right way of organising these matters, and there should be more discussion of how they could be in the future. For the moment, our finding is that the moments in which community participants literally 'have their hands on things' are very important for creating narratives of the past. Successful collaborative heritage projects expand the opportunities for encounters with material culture, and enable these legacies of materials to happen.

The material qualities of places and landscapes in collaborative heritage research

The process of narrating and storytelling is also very much present in the qualities of places and landscapes in our examples. The potential for connections between place and narrative are well attested in anthropology among other disciplines (for example Cruikshank, 1998), but our finding is that the research process itself can enable stories in places to have a 'life' – to be found, told, heard, recorded – in novel ways. Community heritage research enables narratives of places to be created by and for their inhabitants, often much more effectively than professional or academic practice can manage. Enabling people to tell a story about their places, and thus themselves, has often been a key part of the research process. Communities, through the practice of research, have been spending time in 'their' places and landscapes and thereby coming to be a part of them more knowledgeably and more richly. We need to explicitly recognise and value how research itself can be the means by which the narration of place, landscape and community happens.

The material qualities of the places are implicated deeply in the stories about them, although again this happens in different ways. At Caerau, Wales, the hill of the Iron Age fort is still very much present in the landscape, providing a counterpoint to the suburban streets that have become politically and socially removed from centres of power. Learning about the hillfort opens the possibility of understanding the landscape as powerful and influential. Developing an alternative to the preservationist forms of heritage in the city of York also meant creating a sense of place that valued the subaltern and transient in the urban fabric, together with a more inclusive participation in creating narratives about it. In these cases and many others we have come across, the 'heritage' of place created or discovered through research is certainly material and yet combines aspects of the tangible and intangible at every turn. However, the long-term projects at Keig and Druminnor near Bennachie, and also the work at Caerau, give us pause because of the importance of relations with existing landowners. These are reminders that places in the present are often owned by powerful private individuals or organisations with whom negotiations over access need to take place. Heritage situated in places is rarely 'open', and yet research on the pasts of place and landscape can also open on to questions of ownership and use of such resources in the present too.

Material creations as a means of doing collaborative research

Materials, things and landscapes are not merely the objects of research – studied as heritage – but can also be the subjects of research, or in other words the means by which research is carried out and an aspect of its legacy in themselves. Things have been made by research projects, and places and landscapes remade or otherwise influenced, and so material creations have value in both the process and results of research. At the same time, legacies of research that take material form (which we might describe specifically as material legacies) pose challenges to those involved in the research, and the way these play out in the context of heritage research is also distinctive.

Many heritage projects produce material outputs from their research. Examples of things made include the likes of exhibition panels and interpretation boards, but also art works, temporary displays, publications of many sorts and other kinds of material culture.

In different ways, these material legacies have given a tangibility to successful research processes and a feeling of achievement for participants. At Bennachie, producing exhibition banners gave the impetus to community and university participants to decide on the historical narratives that were felt to be most significant, but also made them reflect on collective participation in the work. The 'York: Living With History' research brings out the possibilities of working creatively with materials in heritage on several levels. The temporary commemorative plaques made by this group both challenged the supposed 'permanency' of heritage (Smith, 2006), and opened up the process of who is authorised to make decisions about the award of heritage status. They also drew attention to a variety of alternative sites and stories of heritage. Working with distinctive material outputs can allow community heritage projects to reflect back on the nature of what is created as heritage, rather than just considering materials as the objects of research. This in turn leads on to a critical appreciation of the political structures that control heritage and how it is valued.

There is a contrast between this interest in material outputs and the requirement that community groups funded through the UK-based Heritage Lottery Fund's 'All Our Stories' programme provide a 'digital archive' of their projects. For many, this involved submitting photographs of their work in progress to the HistoryPin website. In our research we found a number of groups who saw this more as an awkward condition of funding rather than an opportunity to secure another kind of legacy for their work. However, this question of archiving brought up issues about the longer-term storage, use or curation of material legacies too. While a digital photo can be stored and accessed relatively straightforwardly (notwithstanding concerns about changes in technology causing compatibility problems) once a material 'asset' is created, who should it belong to, and who should be responsible for it? These questions may be particularly pertinent where groups come together for the purposes of a research project but do not necessarily have a longer-term structure. At the same time, material outcomes like a publication or exhibition can provide the impetus for a group to stick together with a goal in mind, and then continue on to further work.

Conclusion: the politics of materials in collaborative research

Where academic literature and professional practice have frequently juxtaposed 'tangible' and 'intangible' heritage, the reality for much collaborative research is more akin to Hodder's notion of an entanglement of people, materials and values. It therefore follows that concerns with the legacies of materials (materials 'from the past') and material legacies (materials created within present research) are by no means neutral, in the sense of merely academic. Contestation over meaning and interpretation, ownership and accessibility, and preservation and use, are often the very stuff of a heritage research project. Where the research involves communities or collaborative co-production, these questions take on particular import.

This leads us to reflect on the nature of collaborative heritage research itself. Community participation in the research process can work against what Smith describes as the authorised heritage discourse of the professional heritage industry. Smith argues that in the professional heritage industry, the materiality of heritage, or the way in which it is equated with discrete sites, objects, buildings and so on, is equated with 'boundedness' in a way that limits awareness of broader values and ideologies (Smith, 2006: 31). She goes on to identify forms of 'subaltern or dissenting' heritage discourses in which alternative values of heritage are performed, often within community settings (Smith, 2006: 35). This kind of politics plays out through materials as much as it does through the intangible.

In all of this, we see the importance of research as a process of exploring and creating heritage that can lead to community empowerment in material as well as non-material forms. While the cumulative impact and legacies of this work are hard to judge because many projects operate on an intentionally local scale, heritage research certainly plays into broader agendas discussed in this book. We also have seen the power of connecting community groups with each other in developing new perspectives, confidence and critical mass that can counter mainstream organisations. Heritage projects, moreover, exemplify how research is not the sole province of a university but can be a successful community-led activity, too. And in considering co-production, where university and community-based researchers work together, we can go further still towards decentralising and sharing expertise in research and power in defining the narratives of heritage.

Guidance for other researchers of legacy

- Consider the material things that have been encountered during the research. How have people come together, or been pulled apart, by them?
- Consider the places of research too. How have they been influenced by the research?
- Consider what has been made by the research. How could material legacies be created, curated, stored or shared?
- Find ways of telling stories that encompass the entanglements of people, things and places.
- Find ways of recognising the material qualities of politics and ethics in collaborative research. Access to and knowledge about things and places is important.

References

Ancarno, C., Davis, O. and Wyatt, D. (2015). 'Forging Communities: The CAER Heritage Project and the Dynamics of Co-production'. In O'Brien, D. and Matthews, P. (eds), *After Urban Regeneration: Communities, Policy and Place*. Bristol: Policy Press, 113–30

Casey, E. (1996). 'How to Get from Space to Place in a Fairly Short Stretch of Time: Phenomenological Prelegomena'. In Feld, S. and Baso, K. (eds), *Senses of Place*. Santa Fe, NM: School of American Research Press, 13–52

Cruikshank, J. (1998). *The Social Life of Stories. Narrative and Knowledge in the Yukon Territory*. Lincoln, NE: University of Nebraska Press

Heaney, S. (1980). *Preoccupations: Selected Prose 1968–1978*. London: Faber and Faber

Hetherington, K. (2003). 'Accountability and Disposal: Visual Impairment and the Museum'. *Museum and Society* 1(2): 104–15

Hodder, I (2012). *Entangled: An Archaeology of the Relationships Between Humans and Things*. London: Wiley

Ingold, T. (2000). *The Perception of the Environment*. London: Routledge

Marciniak, G. (2012). *The Impact of Heritage Involvement on Landscape Perception*. MA Dissertation, University of Sheffield

Overing, G. and Osborne, M. (1994). *Landscape of Desire: Partial Stories of the Medieval Scandinavian World*. Minneapolis, MN: University of Minnesota Press

Simpson, F. and Williams, H. (2008). 'Evaluating community archaeology in the UK'. *Public Archaeology* 7(2): 69–90

Smith, L. (2006). *Uses of Heritage*. London: Routledge

EIGHT

Translation across borders: connecting the academic and policy communities

Steve Connelly, Dave Vanderhoven, Catherine Durose, Peter Matthews, Liz Richardson and Robert Rutherfoord

Introduction

In this chapter we look at the legacy of a set of Connected Communities (CC) projects which made connections between the 'research community' of academics and the 'policy community' of civil servants based at the Department for Communities and Local Government (DCLG), UK. They had the potential to leave behind something which might have significant effects at a national scale, – 'impact' in the current policy jargon. We make a distinction here between 'legacy' in a very broad, everyday sense of 'anything handed down by … a predecessor' (OED, online edition) and 'impact' with its specific policy meaning of 'an effect on, change or benefit to the economy, society, culture, public policy or services, health, the environment or quality of life, beyond academia' (HEFCE, 2015). Colloquially, the 'impact agenda' refers to the increasingly insistent pressures on the academy to achieve demonstrable impact; in this sense it is an external pressure which may reinforce or conflict with academics' own commitments to achieving social change through their research.

The three interdisciplinary projects created 'policy briefs' for the DCLG, the UK government department responsible for localism, local government, housing, planning and related functions in England. As a central government policy-making body, DCLG is continually in search of robust, research-based evidence to support its work. The policy briefs were to be short and accessible reviews of research relevant to policy on localism. In particular they were intended to identify novel insights from the Arts and Humanities in order to broaden the range of ideas available to policy makers.

Projects in focus in this chapter

The legacy explored here is that of three CC projects, commissioned to create 'policy briefs' to inform policy making in DCLG. Their topics, agreed between the Arts and Humanities Research Council (AHRC) and DCLG, were local representation, co-production of local services, and accountability in the context of decentralisation and fiscal austerity. In this chapter we refer to these as 'the representation brief', 'the co-production brief' and 'the accountability brief'.

The principal written outputs were Connelly et al, 2013 (representation), Durose et al, 2013 (co-production), and Richardson and Durose, 2013 (accountability). The latter two project teams overlapped in membership, while the representation brief project was entirely separate.

The project through which this legacy was explored was called Translation across Borders.

An immediate, though unforeseen, legacy was the Translation across Borders (TaB) project, on which this chapter is based. Intrigued by the fate of the policy briefs and curious to explore whether these very different projects had left any legacy within DCLG, members of the research teams came together with civil servants who had been the 'audience' for the briefs, and co-produced a new project. Starting with a narrow focus on the direct legacies of the policy briefs, this swiftly developed into a broader investigation of what happens at and on either side of the knowledge creation/policy border. It involved an action research element, to test ways of overcoming the long-acknowledged frustrations of both academics and policy makers over the utility of academic research (see, for example, Weiss, 1975).

In the legacy project we used a humanities-inspired conception of 'translation' as a way into the complexities of academic and policy practice. Although widely used as a metaphor, a return to the disciplinary roots enabled us to see the border as the site of active, strategic work being done by academics and civil servants to reformulate research 'texts' and move ideas into policy making. Engagement with the discipline of translation studies prompted us to pay attention to the *practices* of translators, to the normative *contexts* in which they work, and to the *material* aspects of their communication across borders. It also encouraged a symmetrical approach, looking at practices on both sides of the border, paying attention to perspectives from the domains of the 'producers' as well as 'consumers' of academic knowledge.

Key resources for thinking about legacy

Our thinking about legacy in terms of how academic research must be 'translated' in order to have influence within government policy was informed by two distinct disciplines. First, conceptualising policy making as essentially a meaning-making process is at the core of *interpretive policy analysis*. Key resources here are:

Hajer, M. and Wagenaar, H. (eds.) (2003). *Deliberative Policy Analysis: Understanding Governance in the Network Society.* Cambridge: Cambridge University Press
Yanow, D. (2000). *Conducting Interpretive Policy Analysis.* New York: SAGE

Secondly, a wide range of *translation studies* scholarship informed our approach, in particular Schaffner's work on translation as purposeful action. Her work and others' can be accessed through:

Baker, M. and Saldanha, G. (2012). *Routledge Encyclopedia of Translation Studies.* London and New York: Routledge
Munday, J. (2012). *Introducing Translation Studies: Theories and Applications.* London: Routledge

At the intersection of these disciplines, the idea of translation as a fruitful metaphor in policy studies is set out in:

Freeman, R. (2009). 'What Is "Translation"?' *Evidence & Policy* 5(4): 429–47

and explored as a new theory of policy making in:

Clarke, J., Bainton, D., Lendvai, N. and Stubbs, P. (2015). *Making Policy Move: Towards a Politics of Translation and Assemblage.* Bristol: Policy Press

In the next section we set out our approach to the key concepts of legacy and translation. We then use our experience from TaB to describe the legacies of the three policy brief projects; suggest how different approaches to co-production and interdisciplinarity affected their influence on the policy audience; and identify the broader legacies which set the stage for TaB. We conclude that close collaboration in translating academic research both enhances its impact and is potentially self-reinforcing: in the same way as when academics work with other kinds of communities, significant legacies of co-production with policy communities are trusting relationships and changed values and practices, the effects of which may reach back from the borderland deep into both the civil service and the academy.

Approaching legacy: from 'impact' to 'translation'

From the outset the 'impact agenda' influenced all the projects. The policy briefs were explicitly intended to create impact by introducing new ideas into the policy-making process. TaB aimed at a different, broader kind of impact: through investigating the legacy of the briefs, its purpose was to increase the usefulness and impact of Arts and Humanities research within policy making. Thus, as the editors suggest in this book's Introduction, evaluating the policy briefs' legacy became a site of 'collaborative and generative research'.

This investigation was based on our conviction that policy making should be seen as an intrinsically interpretive activity (Yanow, 2000). We are therefore concerned with how meanings move between people, places and policy fields, and are transformed and re-created as they move. The notion of 'translation' is therefore central. While the concept is increasingly mobilised in policy studies (Freeman, 2009) this is principally as a metaphor in reconceptualisations of policy making itself (see, for example, Clarke et al, 2015). Our interest is rather in *the movement of meaning* (embedded in data, evidence, ideas, arguments and so on (Weiss, 1991)), across the borders between academic and policy domains which are widely recognised as having their own cultures and languages. This concern with border crossing suggested that taking 'translation' rather literally might be a fruitful approach for understanding what happens to academic research as it passes from academia into policy, and through this explaining its observed lack of influence.

Translation studies, like all disciplines, is a heterogeneous, dynamic, complex and contested field. We abstracted from it a few key ideas for our current purpose. Fundamental is conceptualising translating as a *socio-cultural act* (Munday, 2012), and thus as:

- *purposeful* action oriented to achieving strategic as well as communicative *functions* – and so shifting attention away from the translated texts to the active translator (Reiss, 1977/1989; Nord, 1997; Schaffner, 1997);
- *situated* action, taking place in contexts structured by *norms* which are both about translation itself (for example what is 'good' and 'bad') (Freeman, 2009) and which constitute the broader institutions of

economic sanctions and rewards and status within which translators work (Lefevere, 1992);

- *communicative* action, which therefore always comprises three *dimensions* beyond its cognitive content: its design; the substance which bears the content; and the processes through which it is produced and distributed (Kress, 2010).

These three aspects point to different aspects of possible 'legacy' which we explore here: translating academic research may achieve particular *functions* and influence the *normative context*, and such achievement will in part depend on – and in turn shape – choices made across the different *communicative dimensions*.

Studying legacy

The focus on interpretation and practices led us to using a mix of qualitative and ethnographic research methods. We interviewed 11 civil servants in analyst and policy teams within DCLG, and most of the academics who were involved in the three policy briefs (11 in all, including four of this chapter's authors). Vanderhoven spent three separate weeks based in DCLG observing and interviewing, and we ran four workshops: one solely with civil servants, two with academics and the project teams, and one with a mixed academic/civil servant group. We also introduced elements of action research, like Kelemen et al (Chapter Five in this book), being inspired by the pragmatist principle that understanding action in a complex environment requires actively prompting change, not merely reporting practices. So an important part of the project became the iterative development of a range of 'tools' in collaboration with professional artists, to catalyse diagnosis and challenges to barriers to translation. Like many 'legacy' researchers, we also had performative intentions: to create as well as investigate legacy. This partly stemmed from a shared normative agenda to effect change, but was also a pragmatic necessity: the civil servants' condition for cooperation was that the research should test ways of overcoming the barriers and not merely lead to better understanding.

Close collaboration at each stage was also absolutely essential. Academics needed access to civil servants over an extended period and in work settings, which would have been impossible without their support and ongoing involvement in project design and management. Further, we wanted to challenge the academic bias of most research in this field (Oliver et al, 2014) and probe the context for translation on both sides of the border. Rutherfoord, the civil service member

177

of the project team and a social research analyst working on localism in DCLG, interviewed academics, co-designed and co-facilitated workshops and was continuously involved in project design and analysis. This level of co-production was enabled by pre-existing trust, in itself a legacy of contacts between the academic researchers and DCLG pre-dating the policy brief projects.

Superficially the legacy project's team was not particularly interdisciplinary, all self-identifying as social scientists and based in university departments and the central government ministry whose academic affiliations would naturally be public administration, housing and planning. Closer examination, though, reveals a wider range of disciplinary backgrounds, including philosophy, history and social anthropology, and varied experience in community development and action research, as well as in qualitative and quantitative research. Ultimately the project team's interdisciplinarity appeared to have little relevance, however. What wove us together was the shared desire to improve academics' and civil servants' understandings and practices: this common normative position was the precondition for the collaboration which enabled innovative research.

The 'policy brief' projects and their legacies

Here we set out TaB's findings: an outline of the legacies of the CC policy briefs drawn up for DCLG. We look first at the obvious legacies they left behind, and consider how co-production and interdisciplinarity affected these. We then turn to a richer understanding of their legacy as the effects of 'translatorial action' (Schaffner, 1997) in terms of functions fulfilled and influence on norms, and the relationships of these to the dimensions of communication.

The three policy brief projects: co-produced and interdisciplinary?

As noted above, the point of the policy briefs was to introduce new ideas into the policy-making process, and in particular draw on Arts and Humanities thinking which might be less familiar to civil servants than ideas from Social Science. The remit was broad, with a focus on helping DCLG reconceptualise issues, rather than provide solutions to immediate policy problems. Alongside interdisciplinarity in approach and team membership, an element of co-production with (unspecified) communities was also required (as with all CC projects).

All three projects (based in different universities) worked with a range of external partners to explore their topics, and so to co-produce the understandings which then fed into the policy briefs. In particular, all strove to represent to central government some of the ground-level experiences of citizen activists, voluntary sector organisations, and officers and politicians in local government. Although none involved DCLG as 'co-researchers' (Martin, 2010), Durose and Richardson worked more closely with the civil servants to produce something that spoke directly to policy questions in the accountability and co-production briefs (Durose et al, 2013; Richardson and Durose, 2013). In contrast, guided by a desire to avoid too instrumental a use of Arts and Humanities in the representation brief, the University of Sheffield team stayed away from DCLG, apart from at the mandated project presentations; contact was otherwise limited to sending project outputs, with little or no dialogue or attempt at interpretation.

Across their respective topics the teams rose to the challenge of being innovative, for example bringing new ideas from Ostrom (1993; 1996) on co-production; a reworking of Arnstein's familiar 'ladder of citizen participation' (Arnstein, 1969) to address accountability; and insights from Hall (1997) and Kress (2010) to expand conceptualisations of 'representation' beyond the political. Underpinning these was a common normative theme: not only did the academics wish to see changed understandings, but they shared a substantive goal of a more participatory local governance. Aiming for this involved surprising the civil servants and challenging their preconceptions, for which different strategies were chosen. Reflecting their positive approach to co-production with DCLG, Durose and Richardson tried to work as 'critical friends'; in contrast the University of Sheffield team gave much less thought to the immediate users and uses of the representation brief, focusing instead on 'disrupting' accepted and traditional perspectives in order to effect change.

These common aims and strategic differences were manifested in the range of different project outputs and the ways they were communicated. Even though the DCLG project lead had requested reports in a standard '1:4:20' format (that is, a one-page summary, a four-page summary, and no more than 20 pages of detail) the outputs were immensely varied, as the academics deliberately translated the 'findings' from their desk and field studies into different forms in order to maximise their effectiveness.

The 1:4:20 format was ignored. The principal output from the co-production brief project (Durose et al, 2013) consists of a 'slide pack' of 39 PowerPoint slides, deliberately modelled on a format used in DCLG's internal communications and which the authors were informed was gaining in popularity. The slides are useful at different levels: from their complete content, through the core messages communicated by viewing only the slides' titles, to individual slides which can be extracted and used for different purposes. The most conventional output from the accountability brief project was a '7:56' format report (Richardson and Durose, 2013) comprising text, bullet points in the summary, and tables which translated academic 'grand theory' into descriptions of how decentralised governance models were experienced in practice. Rather different from these more obviously 'policy-friendly formats', the team also produced a series of non-traditional outputs, including an interactive self-assessment 'quiz' for local practitioners, which they took care to introduce to DCLG. In contrast the representation brief team's outputs mixed the stereotypically academic with consciously innovative artistic formats, but without the same attention to communicating their intent. Connelly et al (2013) is 33 pages of relatively dense academic language with no summary. DCLG were also sent a DVD comprising videos of various acts of representation, including a shadow puppet performance to convey young people's concerns in a city in northern England, without additional interpretation or explanation. An interim report and associated presentation opened with a poetic exhortation to 'tell all the truth but tell it slant' (Dickinson, 1998).

Different trade-offs were being made here. The representation brief team paid less explicit heed to the impact agenda, and so to direct policy relevance, and prioritised academic, and especially artistic, freedom. This was not necessarily a loss: it seems plausible that if they had worked more closely with DCLG they would have been less able to develop innovative ideas. However, in terms of leaving a legacy within DCLG, content which was deliberately unsettling was inevitably going to be hard to communicate. Where Durose and Richardson skilfully used design and communication strategy to get their message across, the representation brief team strove to destabilise expectations about these as well as about content, and consequently failed to have any significant effect. As a senior analyst in DCLG put it, "Poems I'm not sure about … it comes down to getting across really clear, really simple messages."

Legacies as changes in knowledge

Given this difference in approach to their main audience, it is not surprising that only the accountability and co-production briefs left a visible legacy, in any straightforward sense of the transfer of their 'findings' to DCLG. But for all the innovation and richness of the projects there was rather little to be seen. Our (perhaps naive) expectation was that through the legacy project we would be able to trace within DCLG at least the core ideas from the briefs, and possibly even the material forms in which they were carried as they were reworked through a series of translations. However, while we know that individual tables and slides from the accountability and co-production outputs have been reproduced and used within DCLG, and promoted outside DCLG by civil servants, identifying and following the trace further at national government level was more difficult than expected.

Less naively, this should not be a surprise, given that much scholarship shows that linear 'research impact' is unusual. So we need to look to the broader legacy of the projects, and consider what translation might leave behind as well as 'translated texts'. As noted above the translation studies discipline points towards seeing these in terms of achieved purposes and functions, changed practices (in particular communication modes), and changes in the norms which provide the context for translation.

First though, we note some of the complexities inherent in the production of translated texts. When texts are produced by academics for government audiences – without co-production – their translations of their own findings are almost necessarily based in incomplete understanding of the dynamism and complexity of the civil service world. The usefulness of a research communication is conditional not just on its form, but also on the timeliness and relevance and acceptability of its message. Academics are therefore usually second-guessing, and as one told us, "Our second-guesses about what we thought you [the DCLG analysts] thought that they [the DCLG policy teams] needed were a long way from the reality." However, the representation and use of academics' research-derived knowledge is rarely confined to single 'texts'. So as well as the explicit outputs we can see the ideas developed within the policy briefs being internalised by the researchers, and then reintroduced into the policy-making process over time and in different places. In particular, driven by their concern with localism, Durose and Richardson have introduced their ideas directly to local practitioners to substantial effect.[1]

On the civil service side we see a complexity which contributes to the lack of apparent use of research. *If* the analysts – whose official task is to provide policy teams with 'the best research evidence and thinking from the social sciences' (Civil Service, undated) – can access the ideas in incoming academic material, their key judgement is always whether research is useful. If so, it will be used selectively, often merged with material from other research, and deployed across different time scales: some ideas may be used immediately and others 'banked' for later, depending on political and policy rhythms and trends. In doing this work the analysts are – and see themselves as – translators, creating from academic source texts material which is useful, accessible and acceptable for 'their' policy teams.

In the conclusions we return to the implications of the above for co-production. Here we turn to legacies beyond the translated texts, starting with the functions fulfilled by the briefs.

Their primary ostensible function was met, as DCLG seemed pleased with the outputs and the new ideas they contained. There may well be symbolic *and* practical aspects to this: whatever the utility of the content, it was useful for both DCLG and AHRC to demonstrate engagement over policy research. That the Richardson and Durose teams' ideas about neighbourhood accountability, co-production and peer learning are being used is evidence of fairly direct effects, which fulfils the academics' personal objectives. More diffuse and long-term conceptual change is impossible to assess.

The projects served other functions for the academic researchers. The theorising which took place has contributed to individuals' personal intellectual projects, now being manifested in peer-reviewed, academic outputs only tangentially related to the policy briefs themselves. In this, of course, they also address the academics' need to publish: as with non-academic impact the scholarly and instrumental goals are intertwined.

Legacies as changed relationships

Many of the academics shared a strategic goal of developing and maintaining links with DCLG. This was also true of the organisations – the overall project was developed through consultation between DCLG and AHRC, and reflects the desire of both to create stronger links between researchers and policy, going beyond the limits of the three policy brief projects themselves. During the projects this contributed both to a sense of competition between the teams, and to tensions within some teams over the relative importance of satisfying the civil servants. Finally, though, relationships *were* strengthened and are part of the legacy in both academic and civil service domains.

A concrete aspect of this was the rapid development of the legacy project (TaB), which brought together members of all the policy brief teams and the DCLG analyst closest to them in a project that was more co-produced and collaborative than the initial projects. Indeed, we identified co-production in the legacy project as a solution to the problems of translation we experienced in the first three policy briefs projects. In this way, it was more successful than the briefs in influencing policy and academic practice, reflecting the insights reached through much closer co-production. The ties developed through the briefs and TaB have also led to other opportunities for research to affect policy, with Durose's and Richardson's appointment as pro bono advisors to DCLG's Delivering Differently in Neighbourhoods initiative, influence from Pahl's CC research into the design of DCLG's Women's Empowerment Fund, as well as the extension of the legacy project into a programme to enhance CC's overall policy impact. Reinforcing Matthews et al's findings from the Valuing Different Perspectives project (Chapter Two in this book), the general point here is that the relationships between researchers and communities, and between projects and other community activity, make attempts to associate legacy with specific projects quite problematic. Effects emerge from complex and always evolving webs of activity.

These effects included changes in communicative practices between academics and civil servants – in particular their mutual willingness to engage in open dialogue – which are attributable in part to the policy brief projects. These were manifested in the very different approach taken in the legacy project. The academics – particularly the representation brief team – had learned through experience how difficult it was to achieve visible policy 'impact', and the importance of co-production. That they needed this lesson (given that they already 'knew' these things in theory) shows the striking dominance of the linear research impact model embedded in the policy brief call, and of the surrounding norms about possible relationships between academy and civil service. Reflection on this was one factor which created, or perhaps revealed, a willingness to act differently in order to be more effective. Crucially, though, this also rested on the development of familiarity and trust: in particular the civil servants' confidence that their professional commitment to political neutrality would not be compromised by the academics.

These changes are manifested in the cooperation of civil servants in the design and implementation of the legacy project. Such co-production in design and analysis, the presence of an embedded researcher within DCLG, and the action research approach (let alone a civil servant interviewing academics!) is unusual in UK central government. Another salient change is in the shared interest in employing professional artists in creating 'tools' such as cartoon academic archetypes and a set of cards for diagnosing communication problems. It can also be seen in the continuous reflective engagement between academics and civil servants in meetings, informal conversations, shared meals, reflective blogs and so on. All of these were unthinkable prior to the policy briefs.

Predictably, though, the projects' impact on the 'hard' structures (such as staff performance measures or work load allocations) of civil service or universities was unobservable and probably nil. Even though the innovative content of the briefs has institutional implications for how DCLG interacts with local communities, the project process provided few opportunities to promote institutional change, as opposed to encouraging learning. Again in contrast, the legacy project's co-productive approach has led to discussion and experiments about institutional change, at the borders if not in the core structures.

While co-production is clearly essential to achieve such institutional changes, interdisciplinarity's role seems less important. The contributing factors here are assumptions and attitudes and practices: interdisciplinarity might be more significant in terms of changing ideas. The role of the artists in TaB is the outstanding exception, however. Learning the hard way that academic reports, on their own, are often not a useful means of communicating with government analysts left us at a loss, given our core communicative skills as academics. We therefore turned to community-oriented artists with the skills of using design and performance to engage and communicate and evoke change. This leaves a major question unanswered: how can and should we communicate such a project's findings? A report seems self-contradictory, and yet expected by the civil service – the internal innovative logic of the project clashes here with entrenched norms of research communication.

Co-producing policy-relevant research – some final thoughts

To recap: the policy brief projects left behind a range of material legacies, in the form of reports in a range of styles, a DVD, an interactive governance quiz and so on, through which the academic teams attempted to convey their translations of their research to the DCLG civil servants working on localism. More than that, they embodied new ideas which the academics hoped would change ways of thinking within DCLG, and were the product of processes intended to lead to further engagement across the academic/policy border. As detailed above, in these aims they were varyingly successful; perhaps most in developing and strengthening relationships which led on to other things, and in particular in changing expectations and norms around joint working, which enabled the close collaboration on TaB.

Presented like that it seems straightforward, but we need to re-emphasise that these outcomes, and this analysis, are parts of continuing processes. They are impossible to completely disentangle – for example to attribute 'impact' – and need to be seen as developmental, iterative and reflexive pragmatic engagements between researchers and the policy community, who are collaboratively producing new understandings and praxis. As a study of legacy, our project had both the virtues and the limitations of depth and focus, in looking at the activities of a small number of academics working with civil servants from a single directorate of a single government department. The details of the legacy and the processes are of course unique, and the norms which govern translation probably differ significantly between academic groups and across government. However, it seems likely that both the analysis and the kinds of processes we uncovered through using the lens of translation are more general in their relevance. In these concluding paragraphs we put forward some thoughts about the relevance of co-production and interdisciplinarity to the creation of policy-relevant knowledge as a final legacy both from the policy briefs and TaB.

A clear conclusion is – unsurprisingly – the value of co-production, in particular as a route to fostering mutual understanding across the academic/civil service border. One striking finding from TaB was the extent of mutual ignorance and reciprocal stereotyping, which is at least part of the story of why academic knowledge has less purchase than it might in the policy world. With relatively few exceptions, academics and civil servants have little experience or understanding of the complexity and pressures within the others' world, and consequently work with often inaccurate assumptions about how and why people behave as they do. So as individuals we variously found ourselves surprised by such things as the enormous importance to some academics of the impact agenda (as manifested in the UK government's Research Excellence Framework[2]), by academics' overtly expressed politics, by the rapidity of staff transfer and promotions within the civil service, and by the Arts and Humanities backgrounds of many civil servants. Even brief exposure started to change these assumptions, yet for many academics working in isolation from the policy world this is not easy to achieve. The chances of producing the 'right' knowledge, and translating it into a meaningful form at a useful time, are extremely small without some detailed knowledge of a policy field and its inhabitants. This is particularly so given the extreme and dynamic variation between ministries, policy fields and individual civil servants in terms of acceptable forms of knowledge and communication, functions to be met, and appetite for academic research. Within TaB we showed how co-production, in the strong sense of co-designing and co-implementing research, addressed this need for understanding in two interconnected ways. Cognitively it increased mutual knowledge of the other domain, though arguably no outsider can ever fully grasp the dynamism and complexity of either the academy or the civil service. But perhaps more important is the affective and relational impact of co-production – the building of knowledge of 'the others' as people and the creation of mutual trust.

While it seemed that co-production was crucial for effective research for government, interdisciplinarity was not. The latter was imposed on the projects on the putative grounds that it leads to useful innovation. While the academics involved were largely motivated by the possibility of achieving change through introducing new ideas to policy makers, academic interdisciplinarity did not seem central and relevant to this. It was a secondary, pragmatic condition which had to be met in order to pursue the common intellectual and political agenda of promoting more participative ways of working with communities. Interdisciplinarity in conceptual terms was important, but at a larger scale. Academics and civil servants shared the goal of introducing new ideas in order to broaden DCLG's disciplinary horizons, in particular to be more receptive to ideas from the Arts and Humanities – but broadening the range of ideas drawn on by the civil service does not entail that any individual project needs to be interdisciplinary. However, ideas are not the only ingredient within a project, and our experience researching legacy points to the value for co-production of a mix of *skills* and *approaches to communication* – in particular in art and design – which go beyond those stereotypically held by social scientists. Finally, interpersonal skills are vital, and these are clearly not tied to disciplinary affiliation.

This last point seems very generally relevant, and so brings us to the legacy of the policy briefs, as investigated by TaB, for any projects working towards co-production research with policy makers. Recognising the importance of translation seems essential, and so also considering who acts as translators. Academics are not necessarily alone in translating their work for policy makers – for instance in the UK the existence of the analytical professions (primarily social researchers, economists and statisticians) within the civil service is crucial, and apparently little known in academia. Given their official role as evidence providers *within* government such people are often receptive to knowledge produced by academics and may be keen to develop trusting relationships with researchers. For this translation to be possible, however, research must have visible use, or at least potential use, and so needs to be accessible – if its meaning is so obscure that it cannot be 'translated' by an analyst then it will not enter the system. So all involved, but particularly perhaps academic researchers, need to attend to the communicative aspects of their work. This means paying attention not just to content but also design and materiality, and how people communicate with each other across the academic/ policy border – here we can see clear potential for more arts practice to enhance communication. Further, learning about each other's domain is vital, and so therefore is creating opportunities for learning. Here co-production potentially has a major role, but also other forms of engagement with an experiential element such as internships and work shadowing.

Running through this chapter is the importance of dialogue and collaboration to co-produce translations of academic research, in order to increase mutual understanding and to develop trust and reshape norms of acceptable communicative practices. As with other social endeavours such approaches are risky and potentially conflictual, but also provide sites for resolution and progress unattainable without such engagement. Our experience is that for sustained legacy and impact the relational changes are paramount and emergent, as they arise from collaboration in unpredictable ways. When successful, such relationships create a virtuous spiral, reinforcing and expanding the possibilities for further innovative working across the academic/policy border, and so for enhancing the legacy of research projects which aim to influence government policy.

Guidance for understanding and creating legacy

The legacy of academics working with policy makers can be both the immediate impact of research and in changed *relationships* and *understanding* of policy makers and academics – paying attention to the latter should pay dividends in achieving the former.

Academic research has to be *translated* before it is useful to policy makers. Co-producing translations is a better approach than guessing at what the government might want.

Communicating with government means paying attention not just to content but also to the design and materiality and practice of communications. Arts practice can be important here, as long as it remains committed to enhancing communication.

Academics and policy makers work in very different, highly pressured worlds. Unhelpful stereotypes abound, so co-production requires mutual learning, respect and empathy, and recognising the motivations, incentives and constraints imposed by the contexts in which people work.

Creating relationships based on dialogue and trust lies at the heart of successful co-production; these take time and care to develop and nurture.

Notes

[1] The multiple sites at which 'policy' is made and knowledge potentially used introduces further complexity. While the impact of the policy briefs at local level is clearly important, in this chapter – as in the project – we are concerned with academics' influence on the central government policy makers responsible for localism.

[2] See www.ref.ac.uk for detail.

References

Arnstein, S. (1969). 'A Ladder of Citizen Participation'. *Journal of the American Institute of Planners* 35(4): 216–25

Civil Service (undated). 'About the Government Social Research Service'. Civil Service, London. http://webarchive.nationalarchives. gov.uk/20150922160821/http://www.civilservice.gov.uk/networks/ gsr/about-the-government-social-research-service

Clarke, J., Bainton, D., Lendvai, N. and Stubbs, P. (2015). *Making Policy Move: Towards a Politics of Translation and Assemblage*. Bristol: Policy Press

Connelly, S., Dabinett, G., Muirhead, S., Pahl, K. and Vanderhoven, D. (2013). *Making Meaning Differently: Community Governance in the Context of Decentralisation*. Sheffield: University of Sheffield

Dickinson, E. (1998). 'Tell All the Truth But Tell It Slant'. In Franklin, R.W. (ed), *The Poems of Emily Dickinson: Reading Edition*. Cambridge, MA: The Belknap Press of Harvard University Press

Durose, C., Mangan, C., Needham, C., Rees, J. and Hilton, M. (2013). *Transforming Local Public Services through Co-production*. Birmingham: University of Birmingham

Freeman, R. (2009). 'What Is "Translation"?' *Evidence & Policy* 5(4): 429–47

Hall, S. (1997). 'The Work of Representation'. In *Representation: Cultural Representations and Signifying Practices*. London: SAGE, 13–74

HEFCE (2015). *Policy Guide: REF Impact*. London: HEFCE, http:// www.hefce.ac.uk/rsrch/REFimpact/

Kress, G. (2010). *Multimodality: A Social Semiotic Approach to Contemporary Communication*. London: RoutledgeLefevere, A. (1992). *Translation, Rewriting, and the Manipulation of Literary Fame*. London: Routledge

Martin, S. (2010). 'Co-production of Social Research: Strategies for Engaged Scholarship'. *Public Money & Management* 30(4): 211–18

Munday, J. (2012). *Introducing Translation Studies: Theories and Applications*, 3rd edn. London: Routledge

Nord, C. (1997). *Translating as a Purposeful Activity: Functionalist Approaches Explained*. Manchester: St. Jerome

Oliver, K., Innvar, S., Lorenc, T., Woodman, J. and Thomas, J. (2014). 'A Systematic Review of Barriers to and Facilitators of the Use of Evidence by Policymakers'. *BMC Health Services Research* 14(2): 1–12

Ostrom, E. (1993). 'A Communitarian Approach to Local Governance'. *National Civic Review* 82(3): 227–33

Ostrom, E. (1996). 'Crossing the Great Divide: Co-production, Synergy, and Development'. *World Development* 24(6): 1073–087

Reiss, K. (1977/1989). 'Text types, Translation Types and Translation Assessment'. In Chesterman, A. (ed), *Readings in Translation Theory*. Helsinki: Finn Lectura, 105–15

Richardson, L. and Durose, C. (2013). *Who Is Accountable in Localism? Findings from Theory and Practice*. Manchester/Birmingham: Universities of Manchester and Birmingham

Schaffner, C. (1997). 'Action (Theory of "Translatorial Action")'. In Baker, M. and Saldanha, G. (eds), *Routledge Encyclopedia of Translation Studies*. London: Routledge, 3–5

Weiss, C. (1991). 'Policy Research: Data, Ideas or Argument'. In Wagner, P., Weiss, C., Wittrock, B. and Wollmann, H. (eds), *Social Sciences and Modern States*. Cambridge: Cambridge University Press, 307–32

Weiss, C.H. (1975). 'Evaluation Research in the Political Context'. In Struening, E.L. and Guttentag, M. (eds), *Handbook of Evaluation Research Vol 1*. London: SAGE, 13–25

Yanow, D. (2000). *Conducting Interpretive Policy Analysis*. New York: SAGE

NINE

Culturally mapping legacies of collaborative heritage projects

Karen Smyth, Andrew Power and Rik Martin

Introduction

In this chapter we explore how cultural mapping can act as a means to understand the legacy of collaborative heritage research. We reveal the difficulties inherent in capturing this story, including resolving the tensions between organising structures and the practices of chance and serendipity that shape the experiences of people in their heritage work. This gets to the heart of what happens to knowledge and our understanding of practices when we try to capture, share and translate specificities from our research collaboratively. Here we suggest how the visual and discursive aspects of cultural mapping can offer a means to accommodate such tensions. Using data from community groups and focusing on the collaborative role of a community partner in designing and evaluating this research, we introduce our mapping toolkit (available at www.heritagediy.co.uk) as a legacy output. We trace some of the actual stories from the heritage groups and show how they draw attention to legacies of conducting community-based heritage projects. The underpinning research involved in producing this legacy output highlights the attention we need to pay to multiple voices, narratives and types of impact that are important in people's lives.

The heart of our chapter is concerned with the question of why and how we should tell the story of community-based heritage research projects. Why might stories need to be captured? Might it be for new community groups to learn lessons to succeed in future projects; for strategic thinking about policy initiatives in relation to participatory research; or for researchers and funding bodies in relation to collaborative practices? These questions draw attention to what legacy capturing is all about for community-based heritage projects: that it is not simply the nature of the heritage itself, the outputs created, or quantifying the number or nature of people involved that is important; it is about the qualitative impact that such storytelling can have on *how* we understand, share and practise processes involved in collaborative heritage projects. Once the content of the legacy narrative is identified, this leads onto a related question of how we can best articulate the legacy. What is the best way to represent the stories and their various twists and turns? Can, and should, those twists and turns be organised into some kind of structure; or will this diminish features of emergence and serendipity that may be at the heart of volunteer–led community projects?

Within heritage studies, particularly in the last few decades, benefits of community projects have been established as contributions towards individual and social well-being (Dodd et al, 2002), community cohesiveness and regeneration through a sense of belonging to place (Tuan, 2008), and economic benefits of raising the profiles of distinctive local identities (Davit, 2009). But rather than focusing only on social and policy outcomes, our emphasis shifts attention to what happens when those involved are encouraged to reflect on how they tell and share their story of participating in such research. Our focus is on how to identify, represent and share the myriad of voices involved in such projects, including community groups (which are not always cohesive), the heritage industry, academics and social action charities. Can such a collected mix of experiential stories be understood as collaborative in any sense? In collecting these voices, how can the form of the story we create affect future practices, and help to disseminate further the knowledge gained about legacies of community-based heritage research to date? Our conclusion, we propose, is that discursive and visual cultural mappings of these stories aid in identifying, articulating and sharing legacies of participating in community-based heritage projects.

Projects in focus in this chapter

Our legacy research team consisted of a group of academic and community collaborators who tried to work out how to tell the story of community-based heritage projects. We explored the legacies in mapping the stories of 21 selected heritage groups who worked with the Universities of East Anglia (UEA) and Cambridge in an 'All our Stories' UK national programme. This programme was the first ever collaboration between the Heritage Lottery Fund (HLF) public body, which supports local voluntry community groups and the Arts and Humanities Research Council (AHRC), which funds academic research. Combined, our two chosen universities had worked with a total of 73 community groups. Some of these groups were well established, running multiple projects, while others had come together for the first time in response to the funding call. Some had narrowly defined projects (for example, the history of the village's telephone box) while others were wide-ranging (for example, examining medieval and early modern letters of a whole county region). Some had half a dozen members, others had several hundred. The groups we selected for our legacy research represented the diversity of membership, reach and vision of the original cohort.

How to tell the story: inherent tensions

Later we give examples of how we attempted to bring this tapestry of experiences together into a fruitful dialogue while acknowledging inherent tensions and questions about structure and provisionality. After all, some community groups are sometimes led by one leading star; others have steering groups. Some already exist and have project ideas before they source funding while others come together for the first time in response to a funding call. Some only use the skills within their group; others actively seek to learn new skills and buy in expertise. Underpinning this analysis, then, are two related questions: to what extent is the traditional historic social–materialist account of the world, as advocated by Marx and others, in play, where large structures shape and frame our reality? And to what extent do emergent theories around hazard, chance, novelty, chaos and unpredictability provide a different or overlapping account of these processes? Such an approach promises to reveal much concerning the specific cultural topography to which particular community actions and motivations often uniquely belong.

At the heart of this tension about representation lies a debate concerning anthologies (organised collections) and miscellanies (random collections). The tension lies when seeking principles of what unites collaborative practices, especially when there are frequent dissimilarities between the stories from different groups (of, for example, whether aims need to be established at the start and adhered to or whether they are best kept flexible, or whether expertise is best drawn from within the project group or bought in as expert consultants, or whether telling your story by hard copy leaflets and booklets or by interactive websites is the best option). What becomes the principle on which to interpret the practices, on what to edit and what to include? By looking outside the heritage field into the literary world of medieval manuscripts, an interesting model emerges that sees contents of large, hybrid collections as a net of captured stories that have disruptions, connections, translations and sometimes emerging organic organising principles all at once. This mobile and all-encompassing model argues that dissimilarities of stories is an organising principle in itself, and opens up opportunities for a healthy multitude of interpretations. See, for example, the analysis of a French lyric companion in Nichols (1996: 83–121); Lerer's study of a Chaucerian compilation (1993: 60); also, Boffey and Thompson (1989: 279–315). In these terms, there needs to be a focus on not just the content and links across the content that we capture from the stories of those involved in heritage projects, but a focus on how to represent: a discursive cultural mapping exercise is required.

Co-production: a novel group of storytellers

Community-based heritage groups typically do not collaborate with groups from other parishes or communities. Concomitantly, most experiences are temporary, with no lasting legacy created for future generations beyond physical outputs (no passing on of skills or insights). One of the most frequent and forcefully made feedback responses to the 'All our Stories' training sessions had been how such groups relished the opportunity to exchange experiences, insights and tips with one another. Throughout our legacy project, therefore, we not only interviewed the groups on their own, but also held focus groups and feedback days, with built-in networking times.

In addition, our participants included the Principal Investigators (PIs), research assistants and Early Career Researchers from UK universities; namely Andrew Power (Geography, Southampton), and from UEA Karen Smyth, Rebecca Pinner (Literature), Jon Gregory, Sarah Spooner (History), Julie Bounford (Health Sciences), Ruth Selwyn-Crome (Community Engagement), and Stephen Laycock (Computers), and the co-operation of Carenza Lewis (PI of the University of Cambridge 'All our Stories' programme). Our team also included a funded community co-investigator, Rik Martin (Community Action Norfolk). We are also grateful for the participation of Karen Brookfield (HLF), heritage professionals and other local actors such as media consultants and technology experts.

We used our combined expertise in conjunction with research that has identified cross-disciplinary cultural taxonomies, such as the studies by Szostak (2003), Yi-Fu tuan (1974) and Relph (1976), for capturing the wide varieties of group characteristics, the routes they took, pragmatic innovations in their processes, materials used and their relationships with space. Understanding the underpinning taxonomies within storytelling is important as taxonomy is a question of definition, of choice, of perspective and of stress. Our narrative identity here is that of 'cultural taxonomies', where links between idiosyncratic and shared values, attitudes and actions are examined. A cross-disciplinary approach means we have taken into account social, political, economic, material, creative, aesthetic and health characteristics of these values, attitudes and actions. (These routes are illustrated in the data collection section later.)

The tone, pace and rhythm of a story also affect whether we remember it or not, how we understand and respond to it. How it is told can depend on what is included, how it is edited, how well it is structured, and how easy it is to follow. For example, is it full of description or action? Are protagonists central or do minor characters play key roles? Within heritage research practices, being alert to the discourses and structures used by participants can reveal the underlying motivations and successful ingredients in sustaining local communities in their cultivation of heritage research.

For instance, the HLF's evaluation of the 'All our Stories' national programme was undertaken by ICF GHK external consultants. (They are a firm who explore international research and evaluate public social, economic and environmental policy issues to help organisations in the UK reduce costs and maximise benefits. Details available at: [http://www.icfi.com/regions/europe/united-kingdom]. Their report on the HLF programme identified three outcomes as lasting legacies of the co-production model:

- the building and extending of community resources through the creation of new partnerships;
- increased understanding of local community networks;
- increased skills base of volunteers, through oral history training, sound recording and photography skills, which enabled participants to carry out further community heritage projects and share the findings more widely. [http://www.hlf.org.uk/all-our-stories-evaluation]

These outcomes clearly affect individuals and communities. Building resources creates outputs; increasing understanding of networks provides lasting potential for impact in the form of community cohesiveness; and enhancing individuals' skills has individual knowledge enhancement and well-being and community spirit as positive outcomes. But does everyone understand legacy as a collective of outputs, impact and outcomes, or does each project have its own story? Our study enabled us to disentangle these different threads, and map out the different drivers behind the legacies of the community heritage projects.

A key driver in our project was Community Action Norfolk (CAN), which acted as a co-investigator. CAN (formerly the Norfolk Rural Community Council) is the leading organisation for engagement with the voluntary, community and social enterprise (VCSE) sector in the county of Norfolk. We work closely with VCSE organisations and other partners to build the positive relationships needed to collaboratively develop strategy, policy, research and services. We provide practical support to VCSE organisations, and aim to be their first port of call for support to achieve their goals from helping to find funding and running an organisation, to engaging the community and strategic planning. CAN played a vital collaborative role in the engagement with the 'All our Stories' groups and in the co-design of evaluative models with the university. This community intermediary ensured key elements of our discourse and governing structures were scrutinised in our gathering of stories. For instance, what is a community in the first place and how do we maintain, build and connect new communities, and where does place fit within that structure? How much would a project progress if the community were left to its own devices, and how much is it influenced by partnerships with universities or other professional organisations, and by the funding opportunities? In these terms, 'preserving stories' becomes the process of understanding how communities work when undertaking heritage research.

As shown below, recording these structures and telling their story formed the agenda of our 'Preserving Place: A Cultural Mapping exercise' 2014–15 project. These acts of recording aim to reveal how the structural, anthologising processes *and* the serendipitous, miscellaneous nature of community-based research narratives can shape the dynamics and outcomes of heritage research. Mapping the main roads and the side twists and turns was our next step.

The impact of combining mapping and storytelling for heritage research

A mapping exercise will, on the one hand, provide a clarification; on the other hand, there is the complexity, the personality and the embodiment that you get of stories that need to be encapsulated. This is where stories and maps need to combine. The geographer Doreen Massey describes place as a collection of 'stories-so-far':

One way of seeing 'places' is as on the surface of maps: Samarkand is *there*, the United States of America is *here*. But to escape from an imagination of space as surface is to abandon also that view of place. If space is rather a simultaneity of stories-so-far, then places are collections of those stories, articulations within the wider power-geometries of space. Their character will be a product of these intersections within that wider setting, and of what is made of them. And, too, of the non-meetings-up, the disconnections and the relations not established, the exclusions. All this contributes to the specificity of place (Massey, 2005: 130).

The ongoing advances in digital humanities concerning the visualisation of concepts through maps offer, we suggest, new ways of thinking about and exploring stories of heritage. A comprehensive survey of the vast array of visualisation methods to make data blend with its connections, context and relationships is McCandless (2009). A more recent survey of visualisation techniques in representing, remediating and analysing research processes was conducted by Palm and Murphy (2014), with anthropological, genealogical, historical, archaeological, literary, sociological, museological, geographic and linguistic applications explored as well as traditional infoviz and dataviz. As Greg Young elucidates, 'mapping makes culture more visible so that it can be utilised in new ways – exchanged, linked and further developed' (Young, 2003: 11). Mapping is meant here in a diagrammatic sense: displaying information spatially to reveal complex relationships in a recognisable way. It is a model of mapping with which we are all familiar. If once a map seemed only about getting from A to B, now new technologies allow all of us to make maps to make sense of the seemingly mundane (for example, where to get the nearest exotic cup of coffee) to the controversial (for example, a map that exaggerates, for effect, the impact of global warming on sea levels). The influence of new technologies have given us dramatic new perceptions of the world(s) we inhabit.

But there is also a historical continuity in the story of mapping place and the legacies of how we inhabit that space. In the earliest known Western map, the 13th-century *Hereford Mundi* map (see Hereford Trust, undated), the world is interpreted in spiritual as well as geographical terms. Superimposed onto the continents are drawings of the history of humankind and the marvels of the natural world, acting as a visualisation of belief. (Around 500 drawings include 420 cities and towns, 15 biblical events, 33 plants, animals, birds and strange creatures, 32 images of the peoples of the world and 8 pictures from classical mythology.) *Mappae mundi* are not so much a delineation of formulated space, but rather they act as symbolic documentation of imaginative perceptions by connecting the world with spiritual journeys. What stories, then, might a mapping of 21st-century heritage practices embody? How does representing stories of past movements by heritage groups provide a lasting legacy, provide a means of future navigation in this field? What is the impact of abstracting while also capturing the serendipitous nature of heritage practice?

Benefits and obstacles in cultural mapping

Our legacy project aims to save duplication of effort among various heritage community groups, telling the story-so-far, while accommodating the potential for new discoveries. How to achieve this lies in a practice known as cultural mapping:

> If one were to ask what is cultural mapping we would firstly have to say that it involves mapping the culture of who or what you are – be it a tribe, an organisation, community group, school association, business or an individual to find your unique strengths and assets. Culture can in this sense be defined as your intellectual property, your special way of being or doing, the purpose of your existence, the business you are in, or the special story that you have to tell, such as your reason for doing what you do. It is a process that has a purpose, and through the use of a proven system cultural mapping icons can be harnessed and directed to create sustainable futures ... Cultural mapping allows us to see where we've been and where we are in order to find our way forward, just as any mapping process might. The difference is the objects of cultural mapping are not topographical features, but tangibles like assets and resources and intangibles like identity, relationships and possibilities (Cultural Mapping Toolkit, 2010).

Thus, in our project we explored how to interpret the process of cultural mapping in terms of a cartographical metaphor, which extends beyond its ostensible geographic implications into central Arts and Humanities concerns. While we were concerned to locate selection, use and legacies of preserving heritage, we framed our account in terms of mobility rather than stasis. It is about stories of past movements by community groups and narratives about future navigation. Using this model of cultural mapping allowed us to imagine community work in terms of dialogue, fluidity and disturbances, over the location. Cultural mapping, in these terms, belongs to a model of culture that prioritises traffic and transition. The anthropologist James Clifford expresses the benefit of such a model: 'constructed and disputed historicities, sites of displacement, interference, and interaction, come more sharply into view' (Clifford, 1997: 25).

Disruptive voices (displacements, interference and dead ends) in this storytelling project certainly exist. Mapping, of any sort, raises questions about the main plots of representation. Community groups are heterogeneous, some with excellent documentation and organisation, others relying on ad hoc memory recollections. Lack of categorisation creates difficulty in mapping trends, concerning types of engagement, partnerships and even in reference to discourse (for example, some groups did not view that they generated 'data' but that they did create 'material'). Even the purpose of the mapping raises questions, as to whether the visualisation is to be a snapshot of activities, a planning tool or an analytical framework. But approaching from various disciplines and experiences of community engagement, and allowing disparate community voices a central role in the design process, raises questions surrounding how our legacy research team understand strategic priorities. The lack of visibility, ambiguity, and how relationships are identified and profiled are all potential barriers to mapping. Meanwhile, data gathering and analysis can result in proformas that are limiting, failing to capture the non-linear, dynamic and temporal implications so necessary to maps.

In considering this array of different options for our cultural mapping exercise, bringing the model of anthologies and miscellanies into this field offered a new way to interpret cultural mapping as a cartographical metaphor for heritage research. The literary critic Derek Pearsall observes that medieval 'anthologies, though they often have or are given an air of serendipity, inevitably have a character, a self-conscious unity, an ideological slant'." (Pearsall, 2005: 19). He also explains how 18th- and 19th-century novels 'incorporated passages in their novels suitable for extraction ... the modern idea that a novel like *Clarissa* has to be read through from beginning to end would probably have surprised its author. The morality, for the modern reader, has been transferred from the content to the act of reading (Pearsall, 2005: 21). Pearsall may be talking about the composition and structure of manuscripts and books, but it also serves as a descriptor for mapping mechanisms.

Key resources for thinking about legacy

Cultural Mapping Toolkit (2010). Partnership of Legacies Now and Creative City Network of Canada: http://www.creativecity.ca/database/files/library/cultural_mapping_toolkit.pdf

Evans, G. and Foorde, J. (2008). 'Cultural Mapping and Sustainable Communities: Planning for the Arts Revisited'. *Cultural Trends* 17: 65–89

Massey, D. (2005). 'The Elusiveness of Place'. In *For Space*. London: Sage Publications

McCandless, D. (2009). *Information is Beautiful*. London: Harper Collins

UNESCO (2006). 'Cultural Resource Management and Methodologies for Cultural Mapping Workshop Proceedings', *Tools for Safeguarding Culture*, Bangkok: UNESCO: http://www.unescobkk.org/culture/diversity/culturalmapping/cultural-mapping-at-unesco-bangkok/cultural-mapping-workshop-lahore-pakistan/

The need for qualitative conversations in exploring legacies

Methods used

A mixed methodology was designed involving quantitative questionnaires and in-depth qualitative interviews. (Redacted versions of these datasets are available at our legacy project website: www.heritagediy.co.uk.) This provided a rich data set for our project, including detailed information on the histories, processes and everyday experiences of the heritage groups. It was co-produced with a community partner, an interdisciplinary group of university researchers and community engagement experts. Interactive digital visualisations were embedded which liberated the multiple voices and narratives for our cultural mapping exercise.

Stage 1: questionnaires to capture data for mapping

Initially, our cross-disciplinary project team compiled a questionnaire, consisting of tick box, scalar and free text response modes. The questionnaire was centred on investigating the everyday, often mundane activities and processes of the heritage groups (how ideas developed, who was involved what roles were needed, how funding applications were made, what methods were used to interpret the research, what outputs were created and where they ended up). The questionnaire and summary analysis can be accessed online at our project website: www.heritagediy.co.uk.

Stage 2: analysis of data

At the start, this work was relatively straightforward: the 'All our Stories' groups had clear aims and objectives and were all successful in delivering what they set out to do (many exceeded their targets). Heritage had been preserved in many forms and there were many tales to share about what had worked well and how difficulties had been negotiated in their production. Many tales were to be found in, for example, books outlining histories of local communities, archives containing materials gathered, travelling exhibitions, websites and Facebook pages dedicated to passing on information, artistic representations in paintings, murals and animated films. See the 'how to tell your story' part of our legacy project website: [http://www.heritagediy.co.uk/pgStory.html?name=gBubble_6]. Although not all of the outputs, both digital and physical, had found a permanent home, they were at least accessible. Nevertheless, it was clear that we could map their production histories, forms and current locations.

Stage 3: conversations about process not product

However, questionnaires are self-limiting to the directed questions and to the limited response modes available. Throughout the early conversations with members of the community groups (whom we involved in the analysis of the questionnaire feedback through focus groups), a clear difference in emphasis emerged when they were encouraged to freely tell their stories: group members did not talk about the legacy in terms of artefacts and outputs. Instead, they talked about the impact of the physical legacy on the community and on the people involved in researching and developing the project. For instance, the reactions of people seeing the information, the efforts of the group to bring it to life, the camaraderie, the nature of volunteering, the aspirations (or lack of them) for future projects and how the activity they had just completed was enjoyable or difficult or exasperating, were all reported. In short, the members of the community groups talked about the process not the product, and the people not the things. It quickly emerged from our study that there was more to this mapping than simply understanding the choices of what to study and where to put everything when you were done.

Stage 4: emergent legacies

What emerged from these conversations as important legacies was how acts of preserving heritage are ultimately underscored by both conviviality of causes and the political landscape. These two factors shape the contexts for volunteering, the issue of social and emotional capital, and reports of serendipity concerning why people are in a particular place at a particular time. For a study of place-based autobiographies of volunteers, see Milligan, Kearns and Richard (2011). Meanwhile, places are sites of significance in shaping people's paths of community activity.

Stage 5: interviews

Tracing these paths is foregrounding cultural mapping at the heart of our toolkit: these paths will foreground how and *where* people become connected with, and forge connections among, local groups and how they use narratives to make sense of their involvement. Thus we identified the need to create interviews to examine the *localness* of narratives that people use to make sense of their lives (that is, they are used to define who we are and what we do) and to explore the deeply anchored links between identity and place.

In order to understand the legacies of these projects:

1 You need to understand the legacies of these projects for those involved.
2. The best way of getting at this is by listening to the stories they are telling about their lives.

A small sample of the tangible and intangible routes we discussed in the interviews included influences on aspirations, motivations, reciprocity (sense of sharing commonsense of history), values and goals. Also included were the skills base of groups, influences on perceptions and on voice, relating to language, register, age, and audience anticipation, and these influences on choices in creative forms and expressions, from written forms to exhibition, display and performance modes. Non-human factors also became important routes in the stories told, such as topography, climate, transport infrastructures, built environments, population density and rhythms of place, be they quiet, busy, loud, day or night. Other aspects included considerations of social structure and institutional politics of groups and of the bodies they interacted with (from funding bodies to archival repositories), including precedent, decision-making hierarchies, budgets and protocols. Thus, the Social Science model of querying organisation, behaviour and attitudes became our anthologising structure.

Stage 6: analysis of the interviews

The transcripts were qualitatively analysed by the project team but also through the quantitative software package of Nvivo. This software provided a word/phrase frequency report, ensuring one legacy that we identified was the empirical lexicon of the communities when telling their story (for example, 'archives' was not a word employed but 'records' were frequently mentioned, 'people' for 'audience', and so on). All key words in our heritage toolkit derive from this quantitative analysis of the focus-group discussions, thus making it a more 'co-produced' output.

One legacy of telling, listening to and sharing the stories is the emergence of an empirical lexicon that belongs to collaborative heritage research projects.

Alongside the computational approach to the data generated by cultural heritage research practices we also adopted a humanistic approach which incorporated 'user' feedback. UNESCO (*Tools for Safeguarding*, 2006) outlines the need for such a humanist approach, especially in consideration of intangible cultural heritage because it is 'transmitted from generation to generation, is constantly recreated by communities and groups in response to their environment, their interaction with nature and their history, and provides them with a sense of identity and continuity, thus promoting respect for cultural diversity and human creativity'.

Intangible cultural heritage is defined by UNESCO (*Tools for Safeguarding*, 2006) as 'the practices, representations, expressions, knowledge, skills – as well as the instruments, objects, artefacts and cultural spaces associated therewith – that communities, groups and, in some cases, individuals recognize as part of their cultural heritage'.

Reflections on the disruptions and emergence of the legacies in the capturing process of these stories

The pragmatic change in emphasis between the questionnaire and interviews, as influenced by the community groups' participation, was to prioritise practical discussion around the processes, around the 'how to' aspects of the project. Discussions focused on the fluidities and disruptions in management, funding, training, volunteers, archiving, marketing, partnerships, location of projects and access to resources, and decision processes and obstacles faced in developing outputs, but also in terms of lasting social and cultural legacies for participants as much as for heritage.

During one such workshop, a roundtable discussion by more than 12 project participants was recorded. During the discussion, the groups were asked to discuss the legacy that their project had left. The first thing to note is the inability to differentiate legacy as something handed down to others and outcomes (see Table 9.1).

The second feature noted was a commonly shared narrative structure concerning when known and implicit legacies arose across the groups. These are identified in Table 9.2.

The legacies identified above outline how important it is to capture conversations and dialogues, scrapbooks of the project lives, rather than solely relying on quantifiable word frequency analysis. This need to recognise a model that does not simply employ quantifiable data to construct and provide direct evidence of a qualitative impact narrative speaks to the current research impact agenda prevalent in academia (see, for instance, Rochester, 2013).

Table 9.1: Outcomes or legacies?

Tangible	16 mentions of tangible legacies (books, websites, static displays, etc).
Intangible	53 mentions of intangible legacies – greater awareness of the groups, more volunteers, unwilling to apply for future funding, looking for future funding, ideas for a new project, offers to speak in other villages, asked to provide advice to other groups, sense of achievement, greater confidence among the group, improved knowledge on the subject by others, fun of doing it, new skills, skills gaps identified.

Table 9.2: Narrative structure for recounting legacy

Identified at the start of a project
Hard outcomes – books, museum, database, websiteSoft outcomes – working group, promotion, greater awareness Increased volunteering
Identified during a project – these may be positive and negative legacies
Willingness to continue/unwillingness to continue as a group Better understanding of own group
Not predicted or known at time of project
Knock on effect on other – involvement of CAN on wider agenda Funders more/less willing to fund in future Ideas for next project formed Willingness/unwillingness to apply for future funding

Visualising legacies: heritage DIY mapping toolkit

Part of our story-maps of contemporary heritage research practices, then, should appear and be used as an anthology of extracts, each extract being seen as only one part of a more miscellaneous collection and route. Our toolkit (www.heritagediy.co.uk) appears as a visual map, to help users navigate their way through the various stories, insights, tips and experiences shared in the stories we heard during our legacy project. Why a map? Mind maps offer a pluralising function, allowing for multiple entrance points (see Figures 9.1 and 9.2).

The moral is in the multiple parts and ruptures, rather than in the act of progressive reading. One group might already know what their motivations are and have a management and volunteer team ready, but are unsure of all the 'getting started' steps. Meanwhile, another group might need specific advice on research methods, while another may seek inspiration on new and relevant ways to share their story. While we have one entry screen as shown overleaf in Figure 9.1, each option (bubble) on this screen takes users to other maps, but each map offers interconnections between them all.

On the website, colour coding is used to cluster different vignettes or chapters in the process together. A user exploring the range of issues that need to be considered at the start of a project, the 'Why do this?' stage, can explore the options all clustered in the same colour (in this instance red). When the other red bubbles are clicked (about passion, making friends, incomers' desire to belong, desires to connect with and protect local identity, family activity, desire to learn and share skills) they each in turn become the central focus with all related bubbles appearing, many of which will be red but other related areas in other colours will also appear.

Figure 9.1: Mind map of heritage toolkit

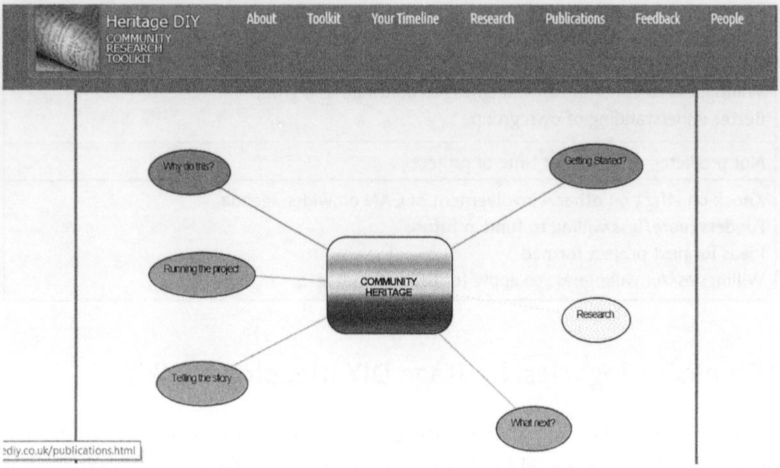

The text in Figure 9.1 appears with explanations, insights, tips and quotes from others who have shared their valuable and difficult experiences, the actions they took and benefits they noted. But the user can return to the first screen by selecting the 'community heritage' bubble in the bottom right at any stage. This enabled participants to highlight that while any one stage of the project was engaged, other parts of the process also needed to be considered. Thinking about protecting the local identity, which is part of the red cluster, but also has interconnections with another stage, and hence the related yellow bubbles, allows consideration of the yellow cluster, for example how to use archives, and all the copyright, budget and skills implications that go with that will be important. Management issues need to be considered in tandem, hence the cluster of the processes of recruiting and retaining volunteers will be important, as will skills training and therefore the budget, and so on. The map we used provided a dynamic interface for project planning rather than a linear one.

The user determines the route that they take. That such an interrelated storytelling platform and multi-directional offer is a beneficial legacy of sharing collaborative heritage research processes is demonstrated by the variety in format, starting points, departures and interconnections in the tailor-made timelines that community groups have created when using this toolkit. For example, two rather similar and well-established community groups, each with diverse and detailed projects,

Figure 9.2: Mind map 'Why do this'?

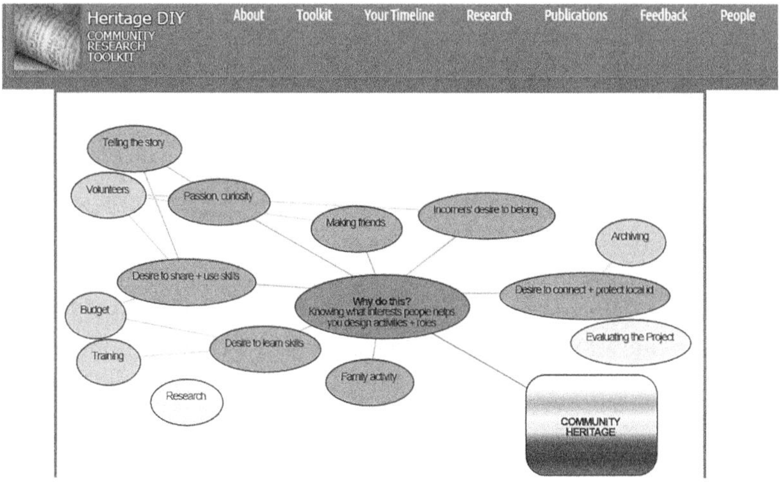

and a similar number of participants and demographic of audience, produced different, but context-specific organising structures for their future projects from the abstracting mapping template. One group produced a core timeline with tangential clusters, whereas the other group produced multiple timelines, with relational crosses. Different stories require different genre structures: context specificity, flexibility of translating guidelines and blurring horizons between producer and user are the organising principles of the toolkit.

But the mapping tool is not only about visualising a timeline for a project, for it also acts as an asset map. Asset maps with their thickening description have something to offer in a cultural mapping project, as they enable the tangible and intangible legacies to be highlighted, and the idea of future exploitation to be incorporated in the story-so-far. For that reason, in this mapping work, we have built-in 'quotes' and 'insight' commentaries from numerous groups when the various text boxes (or bubbles) are clicked, with 'how to' advice, tips on navigating pitfalls, and advice on useful resources. For example, in the 'getting started' route of our map, when 'who is involved' is clicked a detailed description of roles and possible participants is offered, with guidance on facets such as the desirable skills needed in a leader or steering group. But explanations are not the only narrative provided, hearing the 'quotes', the various voices, of those who have experienced this journey offers a thickened level of description:

- "I think you need somebody that actually leads it, who's got the enthusiasm and the ideas that they can instil it into the rest of the group."
- "But what you don't want is somebody who puts people off, which is quite a difficult trick. Sometimes if you are really enthusiastic others tend to think, 'well you, you go away and do it then.'"
- "You need people who can be organised, committed and with a basic set of skills relevant to the project."
- "With a steering group leadership is equally shared. We all have different expertise, one is a computer genius, one a journalist and writer, one an artist and another a teacher. Anything to do with the community, the person who lives there does that. Anything to do with formal partnerships with institutions like the schools, university and Record Office, then the teacher and journalist do that. We have our own areas where we've historically been knowledgeable. Use the strengths and skills at your disposal."

The option to go into a deeper level of narrative through the map's multiple entrance points prevents the map from being solely an abstracting function, and allows for different options to be presented. As the example above shows, one voice calls for a single leader while another for a steering group where leadership is shared equally.

In addition, if full-version stories rather than episodes are preferred, these are available through the case studies tab, which appears on every screen. Users have the option whether they wish to read these as 'miscellanies' from beginning to end, as four different versions of conducting community heritage research practices, or if they wish to be guided by an 'anthologising' structure, where the colour coding of the screen's topic is highlighted in the case study depending on which screen is used to enter the case study. For example, if you only wish to read 'how the story is told' in any of the case studies, entering via the yellow entrance point takes you to highlighted yellow passages in the case study.

The need for multiple navigation means through these routes, hierarchies and thickening description again only emerged during the user-testing phase of the project. Feedback from community groups revealed that while some visual thinkers warmly responded to the mind-mapping model, that others preferred a text-based approach. We have therefore devised our toolkit to have the option to switch modes at all times; the user can choose to navigate through a text-based presentation rather than the mind map.

Guidance for understanding legacy

Thus, our evaluation of community-based heritage research projects has produced a legacy output: a heritage toolkit for communities, which shares insights, lessons learnt, tips and stories from across a wide cross-section. The aim is that this may help in the sharing of knowledge across geographical boundaries and generational shifts. This legacy focuses on the dynamic processes and impacts of those processes on individuals and communities' knowledge, understanding of resources, processes and aims to enhance collaborative networks. The toolkit is about the transits in doing community-based heritage research, the journeying rather than the destination.

But the process of capturing and organising the stories for this cultural mapping visualisation has a number of wider legacy guidelines, offering ideas and ways of working that can be of benefit to other collaborative projects:

- Participatory research characterises the cultural mapping process. Some examples below of statements from public members of the 'All our Stories' community groups about being involved in our legacy research show the benefits of having a collaborative group of storytellers directing the research design, questions and evaluations: "This sharing of experiences has been about bringing communities together, encouraging us to talk within our group and to neighbouring ones, we feel involved in something that might have a longer life, gives us more reasons to do what we do, we certainly feel engaged in a 'next' stage."
  - One way to circumvent the temporary life-span of volunteer projects is to keep the process going, helping them understand that their activities relate to a wider audience in the community-based heritage research field, and in turn one's definition of community expands.
  "Hearing all the great work of others, and thinking about how we could help other people doing what we do, we've learnt so much, like what partners to work with, specific groups, charities, tips, which we really need, on working with schools, and how to go about thinking and doing new things like animations, films, and so on."
  - A legacy of mapping the various routes people take in doing heritage research is that those involved in sharing their stories gain reflective skills by becoming aware of their knowledge

enhancement, resulting in networks of sharing and mentoring opening.

"Until we talked with your team and these other history groups about all the ins and outs I never really thought about it. We just did it. I never realised just how much energy we use and how many skills we all have. It gives me hope that retirement is going to keep me very busy!"

– A well-being benefit from storytelling emerges, as increasing self-confidence and a desire to continue in social participation.

"We like to think we are organised, but it is all pot luck. Just who has what skills and what interests. But I don't feel, after these talks, that that's a bad or worrying thing. This heritage research is as much about what we can give as it is about what we can learn, right?"

– A legacy of culturally mapping the collaborative processes involved is identifying the intangible legacies of community participation.

"What have I got out of this reflection process? It always takes longer than you think. Seriously, it does! And there're buzzwords when it comes to funding applications, but if you understand them they'll actually help you do your project. We need to talk more to others, yay, it might give us ideas for short-cuts or how to reach more people. Yes, that's it. Talking is good. And because we're just a small local voluntary group we never have any forum for that. Except here. But we do have ideas we can share. The toolkit is going to be great, something to keep us engaged and we can add to in years to come."

– Participatory research practices are key to identifying the impact legacies on people. Part of legacy research must be about creating new forums for participation in reflection and evaluation, so that a diversity of voices are given a chance for expression.

• Another benefit of wider application from our project is the reinforcement that the need for funding bodies to permit room for emergent and pragmatic research design and application is clearly reinforced by this case study. Research into current practices in community projects also supports the argument for crowd-sourcing pragmatic project aims and objectives (Moshenska and Dhanjal, 2012). This emergent kind of practice is not new; that sense of experiential risk-taking scholarship takes us back to older aspirations when higher education aspired to be a 'public good in its own terms, valuable both for the student and the wider society … concerned with the development and transmission of knowledge and culture' (Skeates, 2012).

- The idea of multiple narratives that interrelate rather than compete as a way of describing impact highlights a legacy lexicon that may be used by others: for example, capturing stories, structure and provisionality, miscellanies and anthologies, abstractions and thickening descriptions, individual and communal, quantitative and qualitative, emergent and designed, translations and disruptions, risk-taking, participatory, impact-led and connected communities.
- The miscellaneous nature of voices coexisting within the collaborative field of community-based heritage research is one of the hallmarks of this legacy narrative. Representing the explorations in the impact of collaborative heritage projects on people relates and contributes to advances in digital humanities, specifically in relation to data visualisations and also with digital narratives in the literature field, for example, JR Carpenter's work on plural voices in poetry [http://luckysoap.com/webprojects.html].
- Cultural mapping is an enriching and emerging practice in heritage research. Championed by UNESCO as a means for bringing tangible and intangible assets of communities together, within legacy research it can act as a means to allow the diversity, tensions and hybridity of community research processes to be heard, expressed and shared.

Guidance for other researchers of legacy

1. Think about the language you use to tell the story of your research. Legacy narratives are discursive processes as much as abstracting ones; focusing on how the story is told is part of the legacy as the form affects meaning.

2. Consider what structures you use to organise your story and their effects. For these selection and organising principles influence what is preserved and shared from these experiences.

3. Explore what opportunities there are for emergent notions of disruptions, fluidity and transition in your research. The dead ends and crossroads allow for multiple narratives and voices to be heard, as well as 'stories-so-far' to offer alternative routes and potential new routes to be assimilated.

4. In co-production projects, embrace tensions in terms of aims, discourses and practices used by different participants, as they illuminate the challenges about power and politics of legacy.

5. Adopt best practices of user-generated studies to be found in the field of digital humanities (moving away from the jug-and-mug model of research and then impact added on), as they offer a powerful co-production model for researchers of legacy when creating outputs, outcomes and evaluations.

References

Boffey, J. and Thompson, J. (1989). 'Anthologies and Miscellanies'. In Griffiths, J. and Pearsall, D. (eds), *Book Producing and Publishing in Britain 1375–1476*. Cambridge: Cambridge University Press.

Cultural Mapping Toolkit (2010). Partnership of Legacies Now and Creative City Network of Canada. http://www.creativecity.ca/database/files/library/cultural_mapping_toolkit.pdf

Davit, E. and Henholt, K. (2009). 'Economic Impact of Cultural Heritage – Research and Perspectives'. *Journal of Cultural Heritage* 10: 1–8

Dodd, J., O'Riaian, H., Hooper-Greenhill, E. and Sandell, S. (2002). *A Catalyst for Change: the Open Museum*. Leicester: Research Centre for Museums and Galleries, http://hdl.handle.net/2381/24

Graeme, E. and Foorde, J. (2008). 'Cultural Mapping and Sustainable Communities: Planning for the Arts Revisited'. *Cultural Trends* 17: 65–89

Hereford Trust (undated) 'Explore the Mappi Mundi'. http://www.themappamundi.co.uk/

Heritage Lottery Fund (2015). 'All our Stories Evaluation'. http://www.hlf.org.uk/all-our-stories-evaluation

Lerer, S. (1993). *Chaucer and his Readers*. Princeton, NJ: Princeton University Press

Massey D. (2005). *For Space*. London: SAGE

McCandless, D. (2009) *Information is Beautiful*. London: Harper Collins

Milligan, C., Kearns, R. and Richard, K. (2011). 'Unpacking Stored and Storied Knowledge: Elicited Biographies of Activism in Mental Health'. *Health and Place* 17: 7–16.

Moshenska, G. and Dhanjal, S. (2012). *Community Archaeology: Theory, Methods and Practice*. Oxford: Oxbow Books

Nichols, S. (1996). '"Art" and "Nature": Looking for Medieval Principles of Order in Occitan Chansonnier N (Morgan 819)'. In Nichols, S.G. and Wenzel, S. (eds), *The Whole Book: Cultural Perspectives on the Medieval Miscellany*. Kalamzoo, MI: University of Michigan Press

Palm, F. and Murphy, O. (2014). 'Information Visualisation' project, NeDiMAH. http://www.nedimah.eu/workgroups/information-visualisation

Pearsall, D. (2005). 'The Whole Book: Late Medieval English Manuscript Miscellanies and their Modern Interpreters'. In Kelly, S. and Thompson, J.J. (eds), *Imagining the Book, Medieval Texts and Cultures of Northern Europe.* Turnhout: Brepols

Relph, E. (1976). *Place and Placelessness.* London, Pion

Rochester, C. (2013). *Rediscovering Voluntary Action: The Beat of a Different Drum.* Basingstoke: Palgrave Macmillan

Skeates, R., McDavid, C. and Carman, R. (2012). *The Oxford Handbook of Public Archaeology.* Oxford: Oxford University Press

Szostak, A. (2003). *Schema For Unifying Human Science: Interdisciplinary Perspectives on Culture.* Selinsgrove, PA: Susquehanna University Press.

UNESCO (2003). Text of the Convention for the Safeguarding of the Intangible Cultural Heritage.

UNESCO (2006). 'Cultural Resource Management and Methodologies for Cultural Mapping Workshop Proceedings', in *Tools for Safeguarding Culture,* Bangkok. http://www.unescobkk.org/culture/diversity/culturalmapping/cultural-mapping-at-unesco-bangkok/cultural-mapping-workshop-lahore-pakistan/

Yi-Fu Tuan (1974). *Topophilia: A Study of Environmental Perception, Attitudes, and Values.* New York: Columbia University Press

Young, G. (2003). *Cultural Mapping in the Global World,* Keynote speech to ASEAN Cultural Ministers' Conference

Pillay, S. and Shepherd, J. (2012). *Information Visualization for ...* NeDiMAH, http://www.nedimah.eu/reports/information-visualization.

Pickard, D. (2007). *The Winter Book: Jute, Machinery, English Mills and ...* Mineral use and their Meaning. Proceedings, In: Kelly, S. and Thompson, H. (eds.) *Knowledge and the Making of Literacy Cultures of Writing in Europe*. Amsterdam, Hoyal.

Riddle, E. (2011). *Personal Experiences*. London, Vint.

Romanstein, C. (2014). *Partnering Cultural Heritage.* Vol. 1, 278. Berlin. Biblioteca Universitaria, Biblioteca, Ragusa, M., ...

Thomas, R., McDonald, S. and Lukman, R. (2012). *The Oxford Handbook of Public Scholarship*. Oxford, Oxford University Press.

Scott, H. A. (2004). *Scholarship and Information in a Revolutionary Response to Value Scholarship*. ... Southampton, University Press.

UNESCO. (2003). *Text of the Convention for the Safeguarding of the Intangible Cultural Heritage*.

UNESCO (2016). *Cultural Resource Management and the ...* for Cultural Information. Proceedings... and for Safeguarding ... Statistics. http://www.uis.unesco.org/...

http://collaborative/cultural/mapping/... ... ... mapping, workshop, ...

Wilson, F. (2010). *The Social Life of Information and Formation ...* trends, and Polices. New York, Columbia University Press.

Venturi, G. (2015). *Cultural Engagement and Social Well-Being ...* Issue, 28. *Cultural Mapping, 35* of services.

SECTION 2

Understanding collaborative research practices: a lexicon

Kate Pahl and Keri Facer

Collaborative interdisciplinary research processes, as we have seen in the preceding chapters, necessarily unsettle assumptions about expertise and about what counts as a valuable 'research outcome'. What we have found is that part of the challenge of evaluating these sorts of projects is the development of a language to talk about how project teams held open spaces for new possibilities to form and new ideas to emerge in ways that then could transmute and cross boundaries. This way of working is very different from linear models of research that have clear lines of causality and in which research 'ideas' are associated with particular individuals in the form of intellectual property. Instead, these ways of conducting research are enmeshed, entangled and complex, and are associated with divergent outcomes as well as sometimes-difficult experiences and contrasting clusters of ideas.

This complexity, however, is not a reason to think we need to start from scratch as we seek to find a language for talking about and evaluating this sort of work. Rather, it is an injunction to seek out the existing theoretical and methodological resources we might already have at hand to help us make sense of these process-based, contingent and emergent ways of working. Such problems have, after all, been explored before in other contexts.

A lexicon for making sense of collaborative, interdisciplinary research

It is very easy, when confronted with such highly diverse and locally situated forms of research practice, to throw up your hands and say that any attempt to develop a language to understand and make sense of such work is unachievable and will necessarily over-simplify. And indeed, it would be folly to attempt to produce a standardised one-size-fits-all framework against which such projects could be assessed. If we do not attempt to find a way of describing and articulating the key features of this research, however, we risk allowing it to be assessed and valued by measures which are patently inadequate. Moreover, without some way of talking about its common characteristics we lose the opportunity to find common ground on which we can discuss what constitutes high-quality practice, and so develop and improve how we work.

To that end, we propose a lexicon to describe the distinctive features of this research. This lexicon should not be mistaken for a new 'evaluative framework' for collaborative research. Indeed we are clear that a new 'strong theory' clearly stating a single set of features to look for in collaborative research would be an intellectual and practical misstep. Instead, we need to find ways to educate our attention to the situated and shifting qualities of this sort of work, to help us tease out how it is happening in particular contexts and for particular purposes and how it might be enhanced in these settings. We are looking in (after Sedgwick's) terms, for a 'weak theory' that offers a welcoming context for emergent ideas and practices (Gibson-Graham, 2008). This is why we propose a lexicon; it offers a vocabulary that can be used to articulate the realities of this sort of work, which can evolve and develop over time. It embodies a set of concepts that can be 'worked with', in the same way that language can be worked with, to foreground and pay attention to different aspects of these collaborative projects. It provides a foundation for asking questions about what constitutes 'quality' in this sort of work; as well as the flexibility to enable this language to be used differently according to the different situations at hand.

The following eight terms are the foundations for the lexicon we propose:

- *Productive Divergence*: divergent and sometimes disorienting ways of knowing and doing things together is a core characteristic of much of this sort of research (for example as described in Chapter Six on what artists do when they work with partners to do research together.)
- *Materiality*: a *material* engagement with texts, objects or things in general was also common to many of these approaches, so that instead of ideas moving invisibly across sites, their movement could be traced within objects and things. Collaborative research, as Vergunst et al point out in Chapter Seven, is materially situated; it is often also felt and experienced.
- *Messiness*: a characteristics of these kinds of research projects, in that things don't always go to plan, and often things look uncertain and vague in process (Cook, 2009).

- *Complexity*: openness and divergence require an attention to *complexity*, and the entangled ways in which meaning gets made and constructed within projects. Clear lines of causality can be less obvious when many different kinds of knowledge and stakeholders are involved.
- *Praxis*: many of the chapters stressed the importance of *praxis* (for example Chapters Two and Five) – the value of knowledge being produced in and through action rather than as disentangled theoretical knowledge. Many of the projects stressed that collaborations were inherently useful in ways that might not always be articulated back to the academic field.
- *Translation*: the work often requires attention to process of *translation* and border crossing, as knowledge and understanding is transformed through its move from place to place and person to person.
- *Stories*: were often the site of exchange, dialogue and reflection and the connections between objects and stories provided rich sites for exploration, as Chapter Four showed, as well as the more historically located work of Smyth et al (Chapter Nine).
- *Embodied Learning*: legacies were often personally transformative and involved the development of new capabilities as Chapter Three highlighted. Such projects led to *embodied learning* that could not be dis-articulated from the people involved in the project.

Theoretical and methodological resources for working with the lexicon

The aim of the lexicon is to signpost areas of particular and distinctive interest if we are trying to make sense of the legacies of these sorts of projects. A lexicon alone, however, is insufficient – simply naming these characteristics offers little insight into how we might then begin to use them to evaluate what is going on. The question we need to ask then, is: what resources do we have available to help us deepen our understanding of these terms, and to operationalise them in practice in order to interrogate what is going on in collaborative and interdisciplinary research?

Some of these terms are able to draw on a well-established set of theoretical and methodological resources familiar from the worlds of action research (for example praxis), others encourage us to draw on traditions and resources outside of this field (for example translation, materiality). We introduce these below as they relate to each of our core terms. We make no attempt to suggest that these ideas all make comfortable intellectual bedfellows – complexity theory, for example, poses profound challenges to the humanistic traditions of American Pragmatism. Indeed, perhaps we should not be surprised if the messy, interdisciplinary and multi-sectoral practice of this research requires a theoretical and methodological pluralism for its evaluation.

1. Working with 'productive divergence'

Our first core term is 'productive divergence'. Our search, therefore, is for resources that help us make sense of how projects might be working with difference, whether these are the symbolic resources emerging from projects – such as the idea of learning to 'hear each other's voices' or the idea of the collaborative project as a diamond with multiple facets and multiple refractions (see Chapter Four) – or theoretical resources emerging from the existing literature.

Theoretical resources come from a variety of traditions. Anne Edwards' work on inter-professional collaboration, for example, talks about the development of 'relational expertise' and the capacity for collaborators from multiple disciplines to come to work with each other's questions and concerns (Edwards and Kinti, 2009). Another resource is Chantalle Mouffe's concept of 'agonism', which seeks to develop a theoretical basis for making sense of how to work productively with difference that draws on sources ranging from Gramsci to Ranciere (Mouffe, 2007). Mouffe differentiates the concept of 'agonism' from the concept of 'antagonism', arguing instead for the creation of a frame in which different opinions can be held together and put into play in one space without seeking to reconcile them or determine which is 'right'. Such a position moves beyond the Habermasian concepts of the ideal speech situation, which can so often prove excluding to marginalised groups. Instead, it seeks to create conditions in which difference can be acknowledged, and kept alive, while enabling productive dialogue and action:

> What is really necessary today is to create an agonistic public space, an agonistic type of politics ... I think that what is important is to subvert the consensus that exists in so many areas to re-establish a dynamic of conflictuality. And so, from that point of view, I can see that what you call the 'outsider' could play a role. Personally, I would put it differently, because it is more the person who disagrees, who will have another point of view. It is not necessarily an outsider. It could be somebody from within the community, somebody who has a different point of view, who is not

part of the prevailing consensus. He or she will allow people to see things differently ... There are also some voices within the communities that have been silenced ... I am not necessarily saying that they have not been given the right to speak, but maybe a voice that has not yet emerged, because the whole culture of consensus simply does not allow for people to envisage that things could be different, you see (Mouffe 2007).

These theoretical approaches to working with spaces of dis-sensus are complemented by a range of methodological resources. Tools such as the familiar 'ladder of participation' (Arnstein, 1969) encourage projects to pay attention to the differential power relations in a project. More recently, dialogic co-inquiry methodologies have encouraged a move away from a simple evaluation of projects against a notional ideal hierarchy of practices and instead encourage attention to the ways in which highly diverse forms of knowledge might be simultaneously made visible in projects. Dialogic co-inquiry methods, for example, recognise that 'knowledge' can be hidden if presented in unfamiliar ways and seek to enable recognition of ways of knowing that are rooted both in lived experience and in academic knowledge (Banks et al, 2014). The work of the 'Starting from Values' project (Chapter Three also demonstrates techniques for making visible and holding together diverse and often divergent values in one space. The 'studio' method in the artists' legacy project (Chapter Six) similarly offers a method for exploring and sustaining productive divergence, inviting project participants to work with principles of: knowledge as process, difference as productive, and 'not knowing' as valuable.

2. Working with materiality

The stuff of research, its material qualities, matters in this research. Objects are both the focus of research as well as becoming carriers of different ways of knowing through the creation of joint artefacts and products. At the same time, research happens in place, it happens between people and the institutions, landscape, histories and material cultures of specific situations. Such places shape what research is possible in fundamental ways. Understanding the materiality and the place-based nature of these research processes is therefore central to understanding their legacy.

There is a long and rich history of the theorisation of materials and materiality. We might begin, for example, with Daniel Miller's work on the 'humble life of things' (1987), which articulates how 'things' themselves can direct, influence and affect how collaborative research gets made and remade. The diverse traditions of archaeology provide theoretical and methodological tools for understanding the traces of 'stuff' within landscape, and through which the process of meaning making in relation to landscape is articulated. Actor network theory and science and technology studies also provide another set of resources – from Latour (2005) we can take the idea of things as social actors in the world, providing a traceable element that has to be taken on board when looking at the complex 'mess' of social life (Law, 2004). The theoretical resources of 'new materialism' (Bennett, 2010) encourage attention to the way in which the 'vibrant matter' of the material world itself becomes a conduit for communication and agency. Through this process of entanglement (Ingold, 2011) people, place, things and matter interact, and 'action, then emerges from the interplay of forces connected across the meshwork' (Ingold, 2011: x). More recently, the field of post humanism has signalled ways of understanding emergence and the intra-action of matter and discourse, from the work of scholar Karen Barad (2007). Tracing emergence of ideas across people and things involves a sensory engagement with the world and an attention to the concept of embodiment, and felt and apprehended understandings of evolving matter (Pink, 2009). Another key characteristic of this kind of work, therefore, is the attention it forces onto the radical de-centring of the knowing academic 'subject'.

By paying attention to materials, place and their 'work' within projects, the connectedness of matter and things comes alive. The 'Heritage Legacies' project (this book) provides insights into how this attention to materiality might be operationalised as a method for evaluating and understanding interdiscplinary and collaborative research, making clear how 'materials, things and landscapes are not merely the objects of research ... but can also be the subjects of research, or in other words the means by which research is carried out and an aspect of the legacy of research in themselves' (see Chapter Seven).

In seeking to understand collaborative and interdisciplinary research, this material lens therefore encourages us to pay attention particularly to the role of objects and place in these research practices and the co-emergence of ideas and knowledge between people and materials in specific contexts and settings. Materials focus attention on the co-production of knowledge between humans and objects, and humans and the natural and historical landscape around them. In particular, they encourage attention to the ways in which: objects disturb or shift knowledge structures; material practices and places can create conditions for participants' thoughts and ideas to be credited and supported; object-generated knowledge can lie outside disciplinary structures; objects can enable the rethinking of key concepts; objects can call up hidden stories and surface different kinds of relational activities; objects can become the subject of debate or contestation and call up memory or relationships; objects can flatten hierarchies and provide a lens to understand experience and memory.

3. Working with complexity

In understanding collaborative interdisciplinary projects, we need a language for talking about new models of change, in which there is a recognition that the legacies of these projects might emerge in tangential or unexpected ways. Here, the constellation of theories dealing with 'complexity' are particularly helpful.

Complexity theory invites social actors to consider themselves as part of larger assemblages and interactions in which cause and effect do not operate according to linear dynamics and in which the attainment of stability and integrity of systems is produced less through blueprints and more through self-organising and emergent behaviours (Osberg, 2010; Byrne and Callaghan, 2013). These ways of thinking about the world trouble human-centred and intentional models of change and instead help us become aware of change as being constituted by complex, human and more-than-human systems characterised by dis/equilibrium, unintended consequences driven by feedback loops, and stratified ontologies in which emergent behaviour can lead to new social formations.

Complexity theory recognises the limitations of a simple causal approach as a way of understanding the social world (Byrne and Callaghan, 2013). Context and the nature of the social world comes to the fore within this approach. Complexity theory recognises the role of path dependency – that histories, identities, cultures, shape what happens – but also acknowledges that such seeming 'conditions' of existence can be subject to radical disruption. In this perspective, the social world is understood as messy and fuzzy (Duranti and Goodwin, 1992) and as resistant to simple boundaries within neat 'cases' (Ragin and Becker, 1992).

What this means for the researcher interested in evaluating such research processes in practice is the need to find ways to pay attention to the unexpected, the messy and the entangled nature of research as a social practice. Indeed, this reframing of causality as complex and non-linear opens up space for new forms of optimism about what might come from research projects (consequences may be unexpected and radical) as well as modesty (the capacity to influence change is constrained and unpredictable and dependent on multiple actors). Such work encourages us to pay attention to unintended consequences, the potential for unexpected disruption and the significance of accreted small actions in changing practices that come in time to achieve stability. Methodologically, such a perspective encourages attention to context, to the path dependencies within which projects are operating, to the assemblages which research projects are constituting and are also seeking to disrupt, to the way in which new practices achieve stability. The attention of the researcher seeking to evaluate these projects, then, is drawn to questions of dynamism and the specific articulation of the distinctive project within the wider complex networks of social practices.

4. Working with mess and uncertainty

Collaborative interdisciplinary projects are necessarily characterised by an epistemological and ontological shift away from the confidence of 'knowing' to a more de-centred knowledge creation system that hinges on 'unknowing' (Vasudevan, 2011) and unsettling assumptions. This perspective prioritises chance and mess as characteristics of emergent practice. Here, we echo the question from Smyth et al (Chapter Nine): 'To what extent do emergent theories around hazard, chance, novelty, chaos and unpredictability provide a different or overlapping account of these processes?'

In many of the projects described in the chapters, we found that mess, uncertainty and chaos produced a disorienting effect (See Cook, 2009). In the artists' legacy project, experiential research techniques like 'drawing as community forming' and 'studio' enabled the team to make sense with each other of process as it emerged. Decision making, knowing best, understanding 'what it is we are doing', all these mechanisms for knowledge production that academics are used to controlling, begin to slip away as things emerge from a seemingly messy and chaotic space of practice. To make sense of this emerging knowledge means to begin to explore the realm of the 'not yet' and incoherent (Daniel and Moylan, 1997). Making sense of this kind of intertwined knowledge production and its affordances mean understanding the relationships built up in the process of creating the knowledge. Bashforth et al (Chapter Four) articulated this when they quoted from Paul Carter: 'creative knowledge cannot be abstracted from the loom that produced it. Inseparable from its process, it resembles the art of sending the woof-thread through the warp. A pattern made of holes, its clarity is like air through a basket. Opportunistic, it opens roads' (Carter, 2004: 1).

These theories of knowing or 'unknowing' allow for the unexpected, the 'not yet' and a theory of knowledge in which what is to come is not planned and unpredictable. Holding on to this space, and keeping it open is a key challenge for all involved in this kind of project.

5. Working with praxis

We are not alone in identifying 'praxis' as a core component of any lexicon that might be used to understand collaborative research. Indeed, the process of understanding and articulating the ways in which community-led and engaged research produces both social action and knowledge, and the ways in which action is itself a form of knowing, is the subject of a wide range of theoretical and methodological resources drawing on diverse traditions. These include the emancipatory pedagogic traditions of Freire and the related field of participatory action research (Kindon et al, 2007); the practices of collaborative ethnography, in particular as expounded by Campbell and Lassiter (2015); the traditions of American Pragmatism (see Chapter Five); and the theoretical and methodological work in action research of Eikeland, Greenwood, Brydon-Miller and Fine among others. The fields of feminist and post-colonial studies (see Facer and Enright, 2016) also equally disrupt the separation of 'knowing' and 'acting' that characterises mainstream accounts of the research–world relationship; encouraging a 'bifocal' world view (Fine, 2013) while also often problematising the claims of the knowing human-centred subject that is privileged in Western research traditions.

It is not our aim to restate here the familiar arguments about how best the distinctive nature of praxis knowledge might be evaluated – in sum, the necessity of embedding evaluation within process, the impossibility of disentangling outcomes from practice, the situated, embodied and embedded value of the knowledge that is produced. Techniques for eliciting such knowledge include everything from the 'communities of practice' approach (Hart et al, 2013), to dialogic co-inquiry (Banks et al, 2014), to Carter's (2004) conceptual framing of the relations between everyday and conceptual knowledge as the warp and weft of history (Chapter Four).

Rather, it is our claim that we might need to recognise the highly diverse forms of praxis that are now emerging today, the four dominant models of which we outlined in the introductory chapter to this book. In other words, we want to argue that praxis, the combining of social action and knowledge, now takes many different forms and that evaluation of such processes therefore needs to be alert to the different claims, and in particular the different ways of knowing, with which such research is working. Evaluating such projects, then, requires techniques for surfacing the assumptions about social change that are in play in such projects – from the creation of policy-level impact to the development of grassroots capabilities – and the development of situated and specific proxies to measures the success of such practices. There is, in other words, no single form of praxis and the mode of its evaluation needs to be located and situated in the distinctive aspirations for social change presented by each project.

6. Working with translation

Interdisciplinary and collaborative research explicitly foregrounds the concept of borders and the way that knowledge and expertise might be enabled to move across discursive, material and institutional boundaries. Such concepts require us to engage with theoretical resources from beyond the field of collaborative research.

Connelly et al (Chapter Eight) describe how they turned to translation studies to make sense of the shifts in academic discourse to the world of policy:

> Engagement with the discipline of translation studies prompted us to pay attention to the *practices* of translators, to the normative *contexts* in which they work, and to the *material* aspects of their communication across borders. It also encouraged a symmetrical approach, looking at practices on both sides of the border, paying attention to perspectives from the domains of the 'producers' as well as 'consumers' of academic knowledge.

This perspective works with attention to the spatiality of knowledge, and acknowledges the ways in which knowledge changes as it moves across borders (McFarlane, 2011). It pays attention to the processes of translation as purposeful, situated and communicative (Connelly et al, Chapter Eight).This perspective also encourages attention to the way that knowledge can become sedimented into particular forms of representation such as 'the report' with its executive summary, and the way that it can lose force in some situations when the medium of communication is no longer respected or valued in its new context.

This perspective makes visible the way that 'knowledge exchange' is a process of transformation rather than transfer, a process which is inherently unstable and contested.

Signalling the process of translation if we are seeking to evaluate these projects encourages attention to cultural forms of the modes of knowledge production in these projects. It offers diverse methods for the researcher – from multi-modal analysis that surfaces attention to the forms within which knowledge is produced; to reader-reception studies that focus attention on the way that meaning and texts are produced in situ, by readers as much as by authors. It also, as with the focus on working with materiality above, pays attention to the spatiality and situatedness of legacy within specific contexts and traditions of knowledge.

7. Working with stories

Narrative theory is a way of making sense of the world – a methodology as well as a way of describing how people communicate (Ochs and Capps, 2001; Bruner, 2004; Langellier and Peterson, 2004). Stories are part of the everyday; they come from reservoirs of knowledge that are discursively constructed and relationally understood. Stories can become told by others, and reshaped, to form knowledge structures that are assumed or inherited (Hymes, 1996). Stories were the bedrock of many projects, as people exchanged stories that turned them into the subjects, not objects of research. These storied spaces of practice became alive in material ways, through digs, exhibitions, shared collaborative discussions and theatre productions.

Narrative theories acknowledge that everyone brings their stories and they are told and retold until they become a tale told by others (Hymes, 1996). Stories can produce new knowledge and their qualities mean that they give voice to people who might not always get heard (see www.storyingsheffield.org.uk). Stories open up new ways of seeing things (for example Langellier and Peterson, 2004). The relationship between objects and stories calls up ways of storying and re-storying objects in different ways within narrative told to others (Hurdley, 2006). These form material and immaterial legacies that are passed on within songs and artistic objects as well as told across generations. This dynamic emergent way of looking at research is echoed in Bashforth's chapter:

> Making the research process become the research: we weave the story of our project with the aim of showing how our research emerged through dynamic connections between

know-how generated through practitioner reflections, *dialogue*, characterised by conversations between us as a project team and *conceptual innovation*, in terms of the way this allowed us to think about heritage and decision making differently (Bashforth et al, Chapter Four).

Stories, in this project, as in many projects, became the way in which 'thinking differently' was enabled. The importance of narrative as a mode of inquiry was common to many collaborative interdisciplinary projects. They enabled participants to become research subjects, and to exchange knowledge in ways that then shifted the terms of knowledge production and the ways of knowing that were used within projects. Narrative as a source of information about lived experience and the everyday was a bedrock for many projects and a sustaining methodological approach for producing a more equal research space. Methodologies that stemmed from narrative approaches, such as oral history, storytelling, drama and creative methods were used to elicit ways of knowing that informed and steadied projects, giving accounts of the legacy of the projects that drew on diverse and divergent perspectives.

8. Working with tacit and embodied knowledge

At the heart of the collaborative interdisciplinary research projects we have explored in the preceding chapters is the attempt to work with ways of knowing that are embodied in different ways of being – whether this is the tacit and situated knowledge associated with life experiences or with different disciplinary traditions. Making sense of how projects work with and engender such embodied knowledge is often overlooked in traditional processes of evaluation that seek to deracinate research 'outcomes' from the participants in the process. Indeed, our own attention to 'legacy' is associated with the idea of what people 'leave behind', with the knowledge and practice that survives after the person disappears from the scene. This is despite the long-standing recognition that all forms of research are dependent on embodied networks and communities for their production and dissemination (Nowotny, 2003).

Developing ways of making sense of interdisciplinary collaborative research as a set of embodied practices necessitates, therefore, a different approach. There are a wide range of theoretical resources that might be used here. These include the work in learning theory that recognises 'non-academic' forms of knowledge (for example Hart et al, 2013);

the field of 'practice as research' (Barrett and Bolt, 2007), which works with an ontological understanding of the world as produced through tacit and embodied ways of knowing. Arts practice also offers the concept of 'art as knowing' (Coessens et al, 2009), and of the processes of making art as producing forms of situated knowledge.

What these different perspectives offer is the recognition that sense making is done relationally, in conversation and in context. It recognises the ways in which collaborative research is enmeshed in other voices, frameworks and practices and these cut across the research endeavour in ways that are sometimes invisible. Here, Ingold's (2013) concept of 'learning with' is again useful, as it articulates the process of attentiveness to each other that is a key characteristic of these projects.

Attentiveness to embodied and tacit knowledge, however, is not simply a sensitising process. Rather, it may require more radical ruptures with existing ways of working and modes of knowing; it may require disruption and challenge of dominant accounts of the world and the mobilisation of diverse forms of knowledge production – oral knowledge, musical heritage, embodied and place-based theories of knowing, dwelling and doing. Here traditions of post-colonial thinking, of de-colonising practice and of indigenous knowledge are particularly important. Tuhiwai Smith's work (1999), for example, has been foundational in thinking these ideas but a rich tradition of thinking lies behind the work of indigenous scholars and scholars seeking to challenge hegemonic cultural values to transform learning, scholarship and research (for example Naqvi, 2014; Tuck and Yang, 2014). What counts as important in research terms is then reframed and restructured through this lens. Equally, research methodologies are constructed in which communities work together with universities in more equitable ways.

Conclusion

Understanding interdisciplinary collaborative research requires a different kind of attention to particular practices. Rather than focusing on outcomes and the search for linear lines of cause and effect, this kind of work might produce a highly diverse range of different legacies – embodied, material, relational. It may not produce outcomes in the form of simple solutions, rather, it might produce 'hard answers' that require further questions (Williams, 1985). This is confusing for policy makers who need to have quick and clear research on which to make decisions, as Connelly et al demonstrate in Chapter Eight. However, the weighting of research processes towards complexity, materiality, emergence and divergence, with a focus on lived experience and the telling of stories in the everyday, can only be helpful in opening up the academy to wider ways of knowing.

It is not enough, however, to simply state the value of such research. If we think collaborative research is important, we need to explore how we might enrich, deepen and strengthen these processes, to ask how such work can be improved *in its own terms*, and to develop a wider repertoire of strategies for achieving these goals. To that end, this chapter has developed a lexicon to help conceptualise what is going on in this sort of work, and has begun to map out the significant hinterland of theoretical and methodological resources that might assist in this aspiration. This hinterland suggests that there are a series of productive questions we might ask of interdisciplinary collaborative projects in order to better understand what is going on in these processes, and how they might be enhanced and developed in future. These are as follows:

1. Understanding productive divergence: what are the mechanisms and processes by which diverse ways of knowing are being surfaced and put into dialogue in a project?
2. Understanding materiality: what role is being played by material objects in the creation of knowledge in these processes?
3. Understanding complexity: what practices are being unsettled or consolidated through this research, and through what human and non-human processes?
4. Understanding openness: how do projects keep open the possibility of the unexpected?
5. Understanding praxis: what ways of knowing are projects working with? How do they conceptualise the relationship between knowledge and social action? What situated and specific measures might therefore indicate success for this project?
6. Understanding translation: how is knowledge translated and transformed as it moves between people and contexts in these projects? What role does the medium of communication play in shaping the way that knowledge is produced and interpreted?
7. Understanding narrative: how do the stories told in and about this project support particular identities and relationships in the processes of knowledge production? What genres and roles are invoked in these stories and how do they evolve?
8. Understanding embodied knowledge: how are bodies, practices and tacit knowledge mobilised in these projects? How are embodied ways of knowing and doing – from dance to agriculture – made visible in these projects?

Taken together, such questions provide a new foundation for making sense of, understanding and valuing interdisciplinary and collaborative research that will have implications for funders, for researchers and for those wishing to support such research in future. They offer a mode of evaluation that enables attention to be paid to the way that research processes grow, change and evolve. Putting these into dialogue with the intentional and linear theories of change approach we outlined in the introductory chapter will, we believe, have implications for the way that collaborative research processes are assessed at the outset, funded and evaluated. It is to these implications that we turn in our final chapter.

References

Arnstein, S.R. (1969). 'A Ladder of Citizen Participation'. *Journal of the American Institute of Planners* 35(4): 12–54

Banks, S., Armstrong, A., Booth, M., Brown, G., Carter, K., Clarkson, M., Corner, L., Genus, A., Gilroy, R., Henfrey, T., Hudson, K., Jenner, A., Moss, R., Roddy, D. and Russell, A. (2014). 'Using co-inquiry to study co-inquiry: community-university perspectives on research collaboration'. *Journal of Community Engagement and Scholarship* 7(1): 37–47

Barad, K. (2007). *Meeting the Universe Half Way*. Durham, NC: Duke University Press

Barrett, E. and Bolt. B. (2007). *Practice as Research*. Chippenham: I.B. Tauris and Co

Bennett, J. (2010). *Vibrant Matter*. Durham, NC: Duke University Press

Bruner, J. (2004). 'Life as Narrative'. *Social Research* 71(3) 691–711

Byrne, D. and Callaghan, G. (2013). *Complexity Theory and the Social Sciences: The State of the Art*. Abingdon: Routledge

Campbell, E. and Lassiter L.E. (2015). *Doing Ethnography Today: Theoretical Issues and Pragmatic Concerns*. Oxford: Wiley-Blackwell

Carter, P. (2004). *Material Thinking*. Melbourne: Melbourne University Press

Coessens, K., Crispin, D. and Douglas, A. (2009). *The Artistic Turn: A Manifesto*. Ghent: The Orpheus Institute

Cook, T. (2009). 'The Purpose of Mess in Action Research: Building Rigour Through a Messy Turn'. *Educational Action Research* 17(2): 277–92

Daniel, J. and Moylan, T. (eds) (1997). *Not Yet: Reconsidering Ernst Bloch*. London: Verso

Duranti, A. and Goodwin, C. (1992). *Re-Thinking Context: Language as an Interactive Phenomenon*. Cambridge: Cambridge University Press

Edwards, A. and Kinti, I. (2009). 'Working Relationally at Organisational Boundaries: Negotiating Expertise and Identity'. In Daniels, H., Edwards, A., Engeström, Y. and Ludvigsen, S. (eds.), *Activity Theory in Practice: Promoting Learning Across Boundaries and Agencies*. London: Routledge, 126–39

Facer, K. and Enright, B. (2016). *Creating Living Knowledge: Community University Partnerships and the Participatory Turn in the Production of Knowledge*. Bristol: University of Bristol/AHRC Connected Communities

Fine, M. (2013). 'Echoes of Bedford: A 20-year Social Psychology Memoir on Participatory Action Research Hatched Behind Bars'. *American Psychologist*, 68: 686–98

Gibson-Graham, J.K. (2008). 'Diverse Economies: Performative Practices for "Other Worlds"'. *Progress in Human Geography* 32(5): 1–20

Hart, A., Davies, C. Aumann, K. Wenger, E. Aranda, K. Heaver, B. and Wolff, D. (2013). 'Mobilising Knowledge in Community-University Partnerships: What Does a Community of Practice Approach Contribute?' *Contemporary Social Science: Journal of the Academy of Social Sciences* 278–291

Hurdley, R. (2006). 'Dismantling Mantelpieces'. *Sociology* 40(4): 717–33

Hymes, D. (ed) (1996). *Ethnography, Linguistics, Narrative Inequality: Towards an Understanding of Voice*. London: Routledge

Ingold, T. (2011). *Being Alive: Essays on Movement, Knowledge and Description*. Abingdon: Routledge

Ingold, T. (2013). *Making: Anthropology, Archaeology, Art and Architecture*. London: Routledge

Kindon, S., Pain, R. and Kesby, M. (2007). *Participatory Action Research Approaches and Methods: Connecting People, Participation and Place*. London: Routledge

Langellier, K.M. and Peterson, E.E. (2004). *Storytelling in Daily Life: Performing Narrative*. Philadelphia, PA: Temple University Press

Latour, B. (2005). *Re-assembling the Social: An Introduction to Actor Network Theory*. Oxford: Oxford University Press

Law, J. (2004). *After Method: Mess in Social Science Research*. London: Taylor and Francis

McFarlane, C. (2011). 'The City as Assemblage, Dwelling and Urban Space', Environment and Planning D: *Society and Space* 29: 649–71

Miller, D. (1987). *Material Culture and Mass Consumption*. Oxford: Blackwell.

Mouffe, C. (2007). In: Markus Miessen, M. *Articulated Power Relations* – Markus Miessen in conversation with Chantal Mouffe. Markus Miessen, 2007-02-01 Original source: http://studiereis.fondsbkvb.nl/wp-content/uploads/2010/06/Miesse-Markus-Articulated-Power-Relations-Markus-Miessen-in-conversation-with-Chantal-Mouffe.pdf

Naqvi, R. (2014). 'Post-colonial Approaches to Literacy: Understanding the "Other"'. In: Rowsell, J. and Pahl, K. (eds), *The Routledge Handbook of Literacy Studies*. London: Routledge, 49–61

Nowotny, H. (2003). 'Mode 2 Revisited'. *Minerva* 41: 179–94

Ochs, E. and Capps, L. (2001). *Living Narrative: Creating Lives in Everyday Storytelling*. Cambridge, MA/London: Harvard University Press

Osberg, D.C. (2010). 'Taking Care of the Future? The Complex Responsibility of Education and Politics'. In Osberg, D. and Biesta, G. (eds), *Complexity Theory and the Politics of Education*. Rotterdam: Sense Publishers, 157–70

Pink, S. (2009). *Doing Sensory Ethnography*. London: SAGE

Ragin, C. and Becker, H. (eds) (1992). *What Is a Case: Exploring the Foundations of Social Inquiry*. Cambridge: Cambridge University Press

Tuck, E. and Yang, W. (2014). 'Unbecoming Claims: Pedagogies of Refusal'. *Qualitative Inquiry* 20(6): 811–18

Tuhiwai Smith, L. (1999). *Decolonizing Methodologies: Research and Indigenous Peoples*. London: Zed Books

Vasudevan, L. (2011). 'An Invitation to Unknowing'. *Teachers College Record* 113(6): 1154–74

Williams, R. (1985). *Towards 2000*. London: Pelican

SECTION 3

Future directions

Keri Facer and Kate Pahl

A changing context

In writing this book, we have had several audiences in mind. We have been writing for those participants in collaborative research who are looking for tools to ask hard questions of themselves about what they are doing as well as needing to narrate its legacy to funders, peers and partners. We have been writing for those institutional supporters of research who are seeking to understand what constitutes the value of this sort of activity, and how this might be judged both before and on completion of projects. We have been writing for that growing band of academics and consultants who are being asked to evaluate and make sense of these complex projects. And we have been writing for the students of collaborative research – in universities and communities – who are just getting started and for whom tools to reflect on the legacies they may wish to leave at the end of the process may be useful.

The process of assessing the value of research, of course, is never neutral. Research is conducted in social, political and economic contexts and attempts to define what counts as high-quality research are implicated in struggles for resources, symbolic power and positional advantage. Today, in particular, debates over the value of research are being conducted in the wider context of the contemporary battle over the idea, purpose and future of 'the university'. The UK, in particular, is at an 'interesting' moment of transformation (some might say crisis) in which the university's identity as an organisation that serves the public good is being increasingly challenged by ideas of the university as an organisation that should serve, primarily, the private and positional interests of fee-paying students and its governmental and commercial partners/funders (Holmwood, 2011; McGettigan, 2016).

At the same time, the technologies and tools available for research are changing significantly. The impact of massive computer processing power combined with large-scale datasets is encouraging the creation of large research teams, working with highly specialised statistical packages, and interrogating information drawn from populations and phenomena around the globe. 'Big data' is entering the Social Sciences, promising the capacity to model the social and produce new insights by identifying patterns of causation and relation only perceptible from massive quantities of data. Smart cities, highly instrumented and capturing information through ambient technologies as well as administrative systems, are belching out reams of data on human behaviour – from purchasing decisions to transport patterns, from attendance at schools to health outcomes. Understanding the social and interrogating what it means to be human – conventionally the terrain of Social Sciences, Arts and Humanities – is increasingly, in these contexts, seen as the property of the algorithm and the dataset, of the computer scientist and the city mayor, with all the loss of attention to the complex, embodied, material practices involved in living and learning in everyday life that such a standardisation and hierarchisation implies (McFarlane, 2011; Amin, 2015) These new technologies are creating a new landscape for research, reframing conceptions of the sorts of accounts of reality that could and should be generated from research practice.

In these contexts – the changing political economy of the university and the new socio-technical systems of research – it is very possible that the rich and complex processes of building embodied and embedded research partnerships between universities and communities will either be understood as offering something particularly distinctive – a powerful route to new knowledge and social change – or struggle to achieve any purchase. Understanding and narrating the legacies of these long-term, collaborative research partnerships between universities and communities beyond their walls, therefore, is an increasingly urgent necessity. It is no longer enough (if it ever was) to make the case that the process is intrinsically valuable; the questions of why it is valuable, what it distinctively offers and how this is distinguished from other methods need to be answered.

Addressing these questions requires research teams to enter the fraught arena of the assessment of 'research impact' with its language of 'auditable occasions of influence from academic research on another actor or organisation' (LSE Public Policy Group (no date)) and its framing of social and economic impact as something that can be monetised. It requires teams to enter a landscape in which new industries to demonstrate 'impact' are emerging, new skills in writing 'impact case studies' are developing, and new infrastructures to promote and disseminate what counts as impact are being established in universities across the country.

We have observed elsewhere the way in which the tools that are being used to support the process of 'accounting' for impact struggle to capture the multifaceted and rich legacies left by collaborative research – the friendships, relationships, networks, personal knowledge, practices, organisational change, capacity building and fieldshifting consequences that are evidenced in all of our examples in this book (Facer and Enright, 2016). Other analyses are also making similar arguments. Rachel Pain and colleagues, for example, neatly highlight the limitations of this model of linear research 'impact' for collaborative research: 'the attempt to measure "impact" as a concrete, visible phenomenon ... that is fixed in time and space, that one party does to another party ... whereas deep co-production is a process often involving a gradual, porous and diffuse series of changes undertaken collaboratively' (Pain et al, 2016: 4).

Indeed, all of the examples in this book point to the 'relational, contextual and performative' nature of the legacies being generated by this sort of work (Kelemen et al, Chapter Five). And yet, to respond to the contemporary demand to 'account for' the value of such research with a principled statement of the impossibility of narrating such diffuse legacies, risks leaving this research vulnerable in contemporary audit culture – as well as undervaluing the rich and sustained benefits of much of this research.

How, then, might we develop an approach to talking about the legacy of these collaborative projects that both recognises the complexity of such processes and finds a voice that can be heard in a landscape of research commercialisation, big data and monetised impact metrics? Indeed, how can we develop an approach to understanding legacy that helps us to understand what we think is going on in these projects, to ask ourselves hard questions and to continually strengthen and develop what we are doing?

Working productively with the dialectic of projects and processes

Our argument is that accounting for the legacy of these projects requires an approach that begins from the necessary dialectic of collaborative research – one that understands that such research is *both* an intentional practice in which research teams set goals through which they seek to produce particular forms of knowledge and social change *and* a mode of working that requires teams to remain open to the serendipity, disruption and messiness that necessarily emerges when different ways of knowing are combined. It is about keeping in mind the discipline required for a project team to work coherently together (for example setting research questions, developing clarity over the intended action) together with an awareness of the importance of enabling a disruption, disorientation and dislocation of the research focus in order to allow for unexpected and emergent outcomes.

This dynamic – in which the intentional and the serendipitous, the linear and the non-linear, the instrumental and the intrinsic are constantly in dialogue – is the distinctive characteristic of this form of research. It combines what Smyth et al (Chapter Nine) describe as the different imperatives of the 'anthologising' and 'miscellany' approaches to organising knowledge, and what Pool and Pahl (2015) describe as the holding together of the 'through line' of the project combined with a period of 'working through' of synchronous and emergent exploration. These two modes of working are distinguished elsewhere by Cook, who talks about 'single lens viewing' and 'kaleidoscopic viewing' (Cook, 2009). Ylijoki (2014) associates these two modes of working with two distinct temporalities – project time and process time: 'the tightly scheduled, linear, decontextualized, predictable and compressed project time and the unbounded, multi-directional, context-dependent, emergent and timeless process time embody opposite temporal logics' (2014: 94).

Both elements in this double dynamic are important in the creation of these projects. An over-emphasis on the delivery of intended outcomes (project time) at the expense of staying open to emergent possibilities leaves a project sterile and may impede the potential to exploit potential and unexpected project legacies, incapable of making the most of changing conditions. An over-emphasis on emergence, messiness, the play of difference (process time) leaves projects unable to focus and ask difficult questions, take action, demonstrate accountability, and understand whether intentions and aspirations have been achieved. Narrating the legacy of these projects only in one mode or another will be equally unsatisfactory – an account of project impact that simply reports against the goals defined at the outset will necessarily ignore the much richer and complex consequences of these activities; an account of project impact that simply traces all the multiple and complex routes that a project has followed without reflecting back on initial aims and intentions, risks obscuring important questions of accountability for both project team participants, their beneficiaries and their funders.

How, then, might we understand the legacy of collaborative research as a product of this double dynamic, of this productive tension between the intentional and the emergent, between the drive for specific changes and developments and the drive to keep things open?

Clearly, understanding legacy needs to work with a form of double vision. Judgements need to engage, on the one hand, with questions of purpose, intentionality, cause and effect, benefits and dis-benefits for participants and partners: to what extent are the legacies that are intended and desired being achieved? And on the other, questions of mess, provisionality, emergence, possibilities and new disruptive directions need to be explored: to what extent are unexpected legacies being imagined and created? Methodologies for evaluation therefore need to be able to both surface implicit and complex views across a range of perspectives in order to develop more nuanced accounts of what went in on order to inform further practice[1] and to provide rigorous and clear accounts of what went on for funders to be able to make sense of what happened.

Project teams and evaluators therefore need to work with project time – to draw on the wide range of tools and techniques that enable project teams to make explicit their assumptions, their intended goals and the way in which their processes will achieve (or have achieved) these. Here, the growing literature on 'theories of change' that we explored in the introduction, including the panoply of tools ranging from logic modelling to systems mapping, offers powerful resources to project teams (Weiss, 1997; James, 2011). Such approaches encourage groups to surface responses to a set of core assumptions (Reed, 2016): what is the intended aim of the research? How are these processes intended to support it? What is the context in which the research will be being conducted? Here, project teams might reflect on the mode of collaborative working they are operating within, the different traditions and assumptions about social change they are employing and the relation between these assumptions and their goals and methods.

Project teams and evaluators also, however, need to work with process time – and here, the lexicon we have outlined in the previous chapter is intended to make a contribution. It encourages project teams to pay attention to the ways in which research operates within and through complex, socio-material conditions that bring together different ways of knowing and that shape the production and, importantly, movement of research knowledge through different bodies, institutions, languages, places and material artefacts in unexpected and unpredictable ways. It encourages attention to processes of emergence, to unexpected tipping points, to the way that project knowledge and practice is translated by different groups and actors, to the way that materials, places and institutions appropriate and, in so doing, transform the knowledge into new materials, new practices.

Understanding legacy as a dynamic process

How might we translate these observations into the practices of research teams, their funders and their evaluators? As we have said before, we do not want to develop a new 'strong theory' of collaborative research, but to create a welcoming and exploratory environment in which we might ask questions that will deepen our accounts of the legacies being created by this work as it proceeds and as it concludes. To that end, we propose that we approach the question of understanding legacy from a spirit of abundance rather than scarcity. We start with the assumption that the processes of research are necessarily and always performative; they will necessarily change our understanding of the world and in so doing, change our realities. The research process is not an impoverished, narrow set of activities in which we struggle to find evidence of 'impact', but a highly complex, rich and human system in which ideas, relationships, partnerships necessarily emerge and cause change in many different ways.

To alert ourselves to this richness, then, we propose a fluid timeline of reflections on legacy that might be explored throughout a project's lifecycle and which flows into and out of the two sides of the double dynamic as the project develops. We conceptualise this as having three phases – the 'opening' phase, when projects are being designed, conceived and evaluated by funders and peers; the 'holding' phase when project teams are reflecting on and developing their work; and the 'reflecting' phase, when teams, evaluators and funders may want to learn from the project and explore its contribution to its relevant fields of action. Such phases may be repeated many times during long projects or sustained partnerships and will, in time, inform each other.

Opening a project

Many collaborative projects operate with a set of core assumptions about their aims and purposes, and about how these might best be achieved. It is at the opening phase of a project that clear articulation of these assumptions and about the theories of change that they imply is most helpful, as Duncan and Aumann (Chapter One) have made clear. Is the project hoping to influence policy or to create a new community, to develop embodied learning and skills, or to create new products and services? Here, the clearly focused articulation of desired legacies as well as a clear-eyed analysis of the methods that are being assumed to achieve them, is desirable. This is a navigational moment, a space in which the different partners can come together to clarify aspirations and trace potential trajectories towards them. Here, participants and reviewers of projects will be working to ascertain whether the methods proposed are likely to achieve the goals and desires presented. This is a moment of focusing and attention to linear relations of cause and effect. How do we get where we want to get from here? There are many tools that can support this process – from Brigstocke et al's approach to mapping intangible legacies (Chapter Three), to the processes of community evaluation outlined by Matthews et al (Chapter Two), to the range of tools to support theory of change analysis outlined elsewhere (James, 2011).

To conceptualise the opening stage of a project as a moment of 'project time' alone, however, would be a mistake. Even at the outset, projects need to understand how they will work with and acknowledge process time, to explore how they will create space for divergence, how they will handle difference, how they will stay open to new and unexpected opportunities, and how will they recognise this within shared outputs while acknowledging difference and diversity.

This opening phase, therefore, is a time for thinking not only about the basis on which the teams might want to be judged when they finish (what will success look like if our project works out as planned? What legacies do we want to be judged by?) but also a space for exploring how projects will create and proliferate legacies, how the project will open up new directions that intentionally deepen and enrich this initial plan.

For project teams, peer reviewers, evaluators and funders wanting to understand how legacy is being framed and generated within a collaborative research project, seeing evidence of how these two practices are being conceptualised and framed at the beginning will be important.

Holding a project

The collaborative research process is, as is clear from our examples in this book, not a simple matter of a single moment of joint agreement, but involves the ongoing negotiation of difference and an openness to new possibilities within the project. In the process of conducting these projects, then, there needs to be an alertness to the new opportunities that are emerging, to the ways that original intentions might need to be altered, to the abundant trajectories that are only now becoming visible as the project is under way. Throughout the project, the project team needs to work productively with difference, emergence, complexity; to pay attention to the ways in which the value of the project is being understood differently in different places, to its translation and narration in different contexts, to the developing and changing understanding of participants. These phases are expansive, disruptive, challenging of the original 'plan'.

In terms of accounting for the legacy of a project, the critical challenge at this stage is to explore how these disruptions encounter and transform (or not) the original project plan. This is a case of making clearly visible the way in which new opportunities and unexpected developments are, first, made apparent to the project team and, second, woven into the fabric (see Bashforth et al, Chapter Four) of the project. Accounting for the legacy of the project at this stage is specifically processual, understanding the way that practice time and process time are being negotiated.

Reflecting on a project

The final stages of a project offer the opportunity to weave together these two trajectories – the challenge is to narrate how the theory of change (Weiss, 1997) that underpinned the project was both enabled, disrupted and extended in practice; the way that original intentions encountered the situated and contextual nature of research practice. This final stage requires attention to both the formalised questions of accountability – how did we do against our original aims? – and to the creative and generative nature of collaborative research – what new possibilities flourished in our processes?

We might visualise the relationship between these dynamics as something like an increasingly interlocking spiral in which intentionality and emergence are related to each other and come to create a new collective object. Rather than having to choose between the kaleidoscopic and the single lens view, as Cook suggests (2009), we argue that project teams will necessarily work iteratively between these two perspectives, between the moments of intentionality and the moments of emergence, between the laser focus on goals and the expansiveness of exploring rich connections and developments.

This alertness to the double dynamic of collaborative research throughout the process will begin to lay the foundation for this distinctive form of research to stake its claim to a distinctive contribution to both knowledge production and social change in the contemporary research landscape. By working with this dynamic throughout the research process, project teams will be able to account to themselves, to their funders and to the wider public both for their success (or otherwise) in achieving their original goals and for the much richer and more complicated legacies that this research will necessarily generate.

What does this mean practically?

The conception of legacy as produced through the dynamic inter-relationship between intentionality and emergence has a number of implications for the current systems of research evaluation both at peer review stage and at the end of the process. It implies that at proposal stage, projects should be able to be clear about the assumed relationship between their methods and the sorts of legacies that they might want to achieve, but also clear about the methods that they will use to respond to and adapt to change, to explore new possibilities and to respect the unexpected developments that necessarily emerge from combining different forms of knowledge. It also implies that on completion, such projects should not be held strictly to account for the success or failure of their projects against the initial specified aims, but against the ways in which their aims and the possibilities that have emerged throughout the project have been held together.

Only in understanding that the distinctive feature of collaborative research is that its legacy is a product of interaction between what is expected and what emerges, between common goals and the necessary disruptions caused by bringing different perspectives into encounter, can the true value of collaborative research be understood. A project that simply achieves what it set out to achieve might, in usual circumstances, be understood as a success. For the collaborative research field, however, such an account might reasonably be taken to imply that the productive tensions and new openings arising from combining different sets of expertise had failed to be noticed and explored.

Conclusion

As we have seen from Connolly et al's chapter in this book, without the collaborative conduct of research, without the rich human relationships that emerge when people come to learn each other's language, all the high-quality research in the world is likely to struggle to leave a legacy as the gulf between researchers and publics widens. Even as large data sets and supercomputers become more able to ask more specialised questions of universal populations, so they struggle to speak the language and understand the concerns of the people, policy makers and practitioners who most need to make sense of it. And in place of the powerful dialogues we might expect between universities and societies, we will then be left with impoverished remedial action that seeks to hold universities to account for their 'impact' after the completion of the research. This is despite the fact that we have known since the idea of 'mode 2 knowledge' began to circulate over 40 years ago (indeed, since any socio-cultural theories of learning began to be formulated in the early years of the last century) that learning, much less the sort of social learning required for developing new practices, structures and ways of working, does not proceed by means of disembodied 'knowledge transfer'. Rather, it requires humans to make sense of knowledge in ways and for purposes that are important to them; they need to encounter ideas in relation to their practice; and they need to tell stories, to each other and to themselves, of what these ideas mean to them. They need not only to encounter other knowledge, but to change it and themselves in the process. They need, in other words, to work with and learn with others as knowledge is produced, to develop what Hart et al have called 'mode 5 knowledge' (Hart et al, 2013).

The complicated, situated, embodied business of collaborative research between academics and partners outside the university walls, then, is an essential component of any research community that seeks to do more than speak narcissistically to itself; and funding the time and relationships required to make it work is essential to any government, politician or civil servant seeking to ensure that research 'impacts' on society.

In a context of increasing competition for scarce resources it is not enough, however, for the proponents of collaborative research to simply state these evident realities or to claim that this research is intrinsically valuable. In a context in which both academics and community partners are having to assess how they spend their time and determine what constitutes 'good value' for the groups to whom they are accountable, it is important that project teams can articulate what constitutes the legacies from this sort of work, how participants and publics might value them, and the conditions that are necessary to strengthen such legacies. In a context in which universities are increasingly being challenged to make the case for their continued existence as a public good rather than a private investment, it is essential that collaborative research practices are able to articulate why they are important for both knowledge and for social change (Pahl, in press) We hope, in this book, that we have provided some of the questions that might support the reflection necessary to begin to answer these questions.

References

Amin, A. (2015). 'Animated Space'. *Public Culture* 21(2): 239–58

Cook, T. (2009). 'The Purpose of Mess in Action Research: Building Rigour Through a Messy Turn'. *Educational Action Research* 17(2): 277–92

Facer, K. and Enright, B. (2016 *Creating Living Knowledge: Community University Partnerships and the Participatory Turn in the Production of Knowledge*. Bristol: University of Bristol/AHRC Connected Communities

Hart, A., Davies, C., Aumann, K., Wenger, E., Aranda, K., Heaver, B. and Wolff, D. (2013). 'Mobilising Knowledge in Community-university Partnerships: What Does a Community of Practice Approach Contribute?' *Contemporary Social Science: Journal of the Academy of Social Sciences*, DOI:10.1080/21582041.2013.767470

Holmwood, J. (2011). *A Manifesto for the Public University*. London: Bloomsbury Academic

James, C. (2011). *Theory of Change Review: Report Commissioned by Comic Relief*. London: Comic Relief. http://mande.co.uk/blog/wp-content/uploads/2012/03/2012-Comic-Relief-Theory-of-Change-Review-FINAL.pdf

LSE Public Policy Group (no date). *Maximising the Impacts of Your Research: A Handbook for Social Scientists*, Consultation Draft 3. http://blogs.lse.ac.uk/impactofsocialsciences/introduction/

McFarlane, C. (2011). 'The City as Assemblage, Dwelling and Urban Space'. *Environment and Planning D: Society and Space* 29: 649–71

McGettigan, A. (2016). *The Great University Gamble: Money, Markets and the Future of Higher Education*. London: Pluto

Pahl, K (in press). *The University as the Imagined Other. Collaborative Anthropologies*

Pain, R. et al (2016). *Mapping Alternative Impact: Alternative Approaches to Impact from Co-Produced Research*. Centre for Social Justice and Community Action, Durham University. https://www.dur.ac.uk/resources/beacon/MappingAlternativeImpactFinalReport.pdf

Pool, S. and Pahl, K. (2015). 'The Work of Art in the Age of Mechanical Co-production'. In O'Brien, D. and Mathews, P. (eds), *After Urban Regeneration: Communities Policy and Place*. Bristol: Policy Press, 79–94

Reed, M. (2016). *The Research Impact Handbook*. Huntly: Fast Track Impact

Weiss, C. (1997). 'Theory-Based Evaluation: Past, Present and Future'. *New Directions for Evaluation* 76 (Winter)

Ylijoki, O-H. (2014). 'Conquered by Project Time? Conflicting Temporalities in University Research'. In Gibbs, P., Ylijoki, O.-H., Guzmán-Valenzuela, C. and Barnett, R. (eds), *Universities in the Flux of Time: An Exploration of Time and Temporality in University Life*. London: Routledge

Note

[1] See the 'Understanding the Value of Arts and Culture' AHRC Cultural Value project report by Geoffrey Crossick and Patrycja Kaszynska (2016) on mapping alternative frameworks for evaluation.

Index

Note: Page numbers in *italics* indicate figures, images and tables.